Love, War, and the
96th Engineers (Colored)

Love, War, and the
96th Engineers (Colored)

THE WORLD WAR II NEW GUINEA DIARIES
OF CAPTAIN HYMAN SAMUELSON

EDITED BY

Gwendolyn Midlo Hall

University of Illinois Press   *Urbana and Chicago*

Library of Congress Cataloging-in-Publication Data

Love, war, and the 96th Engineers (Colored) : the World War II New
  Guinea diaries of Captain Hyman Samuelson / edited Gwendolyn Midlo
  Hall.
      p.   cm.
    Includes bibliographical references and index.
    ISBN 0-252-02179-7
    1. Samuelson, Hyman—Diaries.   2. World War, 1939–1945—Campaigns—
New Guinea.   3. World War, 1914–1918—Personal narratives,
America.   4. United States. Army—Biography.   5. Soldiers—United
States—Diaries.   6. United States. Army. Corps of Engineers
(Colored). Battalion, 96th—History.   7. World War, 1939–1945—
Participation, Afro-American.   I. Samuelson, Hyman.   II. Hall,
Gwendolyn Midlo.   III. Title: Love, war; and the Ninety-sixth
Engineers (Colored)
D767.95.L68   1995
940.54'26–dc20   5-5729
                                                                                  CIP

To the men of the 96th Engineers,
wherever you happen to be

Contents

Editor's Preface

Let me begin by explaining how this book came about. As a working historian, every day I seek out and study written materials that throw light upon a great human heritage: our experience in the past, which can teach us, guide us, and lead us to the wisdom we crave. The books I have written are about slavery and race relations in the Americas. My research has turned me into a detective, hunting materials by and about ordinary people who usually leave no written trace.

The generation that lived through World War II, both at home and abroad, is getting old. I knew that my uncle, Hyman Samuelson, had served throughout most of the war in New Guinea as an officer in an engineering battalion whose enlisted men and noncommissioned officers were all African Americans in those days when racial segregation prevailed in the Armed Forces of the United States. He was one of the first American officers to arrive in New Guinea and spent two and a half years there. I also knew that he writes well and has always kept diaries. Diaries and letters actually written at the time of the events are documents of great historic value, far superior to memoirs. Memoirs are more common but less reliable.

There are probably few interesting diaries from World War II, and letters sent home from the battlefront are severely flawed. There was censorship and also self-censorship to avoid having letters cut to ribbons by the censor. There was a certain amount of embarrassment about writing intimate feelings, things that would be read by a censor whom the men knew. Nor did soldiers want to worry their loved ones at home, and they often concealed the true situation they were in. Diaries were, in fact, outlawed as a potential security risk in case they fell into enemy hands. Nevertheless, soldiers kept diaries, mainly fragmentary in nature. Few soldiers were in the same theater of war for long periods. Battle sites shifted. But in the Pacific, soldiers partially acclimated to tropical diseases, especially engineering troops, were kept on for extended periods.

Knowing that my uncle had health problems, I wanted to try to make sure that his diaries would not perish along with him, so I asked him about them. He said that they were stored in his attic; no one had ever read them since he had written them nearly fifty years earlier. I urged him to look at them and told him that they could be of interest to an archive that collected and preserved materials about World War II. He called a few days later and thanked me for making the suggestion. He had found the diaries more interesting than he remembered. He added that he also had the letters he had written to his late wife, Dora. I asked to see everything and that he not edit or hold anything back. I had no intention of devoting more than a few hours to the letters, diaries, and, as it turned out, brief essays, nor did I expect to look at them right away. My purpose was to suggest an archive where they could be placed and preserved.

That is not what happened. My uncle lives in Austin, Texas. I was living in New Orleans, directing a research project. I was visiting my children in Albuquerque when my uncle drove up with a box of letters and several diaries. It was an unusual moment because I was away from my computer and research and had time to read the documents. The material thrilled and moved me, and, knowing that no one else would edit them for publication during my uncle's lifetime, I decided to do so myself. If he was willing, I told my uncle, I would prepare the documents for publication and seek out a publisher. The project escalated. My uncle hunted further in his attic and came up with much more material, photographs and more diaries and letters, some from Dora. These came to me in several separate mailings and greatly enriched the book.

This book contains excerpts from the diaries and letters and comprises only a fraction of the materials he sent. The documents are informative about the inner workings of the military bureaucracy and the unsung role of the engineers, especially of the African-American troops who made logistics possible at a decisive time and place. The diaries describe the situation and attitudes of men in a segregated labor battalion. They reveal the morale problems of officers, noncommissioned officers, and troops faced with bombings and strafings, the imminent threat of invasion, tropical diseases, and psychiatric problems. The documents also reveal courage in the face of overwork and adversity. Some of the many themes that can be developed concern attitudes toward women, relationships between male officers and nurses, drinking and sexual deprivation, and the situation on the home front. There are copies of the records of Company A during his command.

The process of editing involves selecting what is most urgent and then making the material as accessible as possible. My uncle's voluminous documents have been greatly condensed. Much information has been omitted about the books he read, the music to which he listened, and the movies he saw. He was an avid reader and deeply appreciated classical music as well as the spirituals sung by his troops.

In order to avoid violating my uncle's writing style, few sentences have been changed. Instead, entire letters, diary entries, and sections thereof were omitted. Occasionally, the order of sentences has been changed and parts of sentences and some entire sentences omitted. In order to avoid interrupting the flow of the narrative, there are no ellipse marks to indicate omissions. The letters from which Captain Samuelson quotes or those he copied into his diary are set off from the surrounding text. The original documents have been returned to my uncle, who will make the final decision about which depository will receive them. They will eventually be made available to researchers and will surely become an important historical source for more specialized studies of World War II.

Captain Samuelson was one of the two officers in command of the first African-American troops who came under enemy fire during World War II. They were also the first American troop unit that landed in New Guinea. The 96th Battalion, U.S. Army Corps of Engineers (Colored) arrived in Port Moresby on April 23, 1942, to find it in ruins from repeated, extensive Japanese bombing. With inadequate equipment they quickly built airstrips, docks, and roads from which the Allied air forces could operate. Although the 96th Battalion started out as a labor battalion rather than a group of skilled workers, it was converted into a general service regiment, eventually becoming the best trained and equipped unit in the Southwest Pacific Area.[1]

As the African-American troops landed at Port Moresby, they were greeted enthusiastically by the Australians there, and with good reason. Although the ill-equipped town had no fighter planes, a small airfield, and a grossly inadequate dock, Port Moresby was Australia's last line of defense against Japan. Within three months, the Japanese had sunk the U.S. Pacific Fleet at Pearl Harbor and conquered the Philippines, Singapore, Guam, and Rabaul in the Solomon Islands, where they created a huge naval and air force base from which they bombed Port Morseby. Japan's next major objective was the conquest of Australia, thereby cutting off its use by Allied forces in the Pacific.

The successful defense of Australia was doubtful in April 1942. Her entire population was only seven million, her coastline was long and exposed, and her military forces had been dispersed throughout

the world to support Britain's war effort long before war broke out in
the Pacific. When Rabaul fell, the fleeing Australian troops were
caught and massacred. When Singapore fell, sixty-four thousand
Allied troops, including 15,365 Australians, surrendered with their
guns, transport, and equipment. Only a few militiamen, largely
untrained and ill-equipped, remained to defend Australia.

When General Douglas MacArthur arrived in Australia from Cor-
regidor in the Philippines on March 17, 1942, to take command of
the land forces of the Southwest Pacific Area, the Australian chiefs
of staff had already decided that Port Morseby was indefensible.
MacArthur, however, concluded that New Guinea was the key to the
defense of Australia because it protected the Brisbane-Melbourne
coastal belt, and the possibilities of taking the offensive against the
Japanese hinged upon keeping Australia in the hands of the Allies.[2]
His defense strategy was handicapped by the priorities of the Allied
High Command. The European Theater came first, and extensive
resources were not to be sent to the Pacific Theater until after the
Allied victory in Europe. "The immediate aim of the [U.S] Joint
Chiefs was not to defeat the Japanese nation, but to protect Australia
and New Zealand by halting the Japanese southward advance from
Rabaul toward the air and sea lines of communication that joined the
United States and Hawaii to Australia and New Zealand."[3]

Shortly after the 96th Battalion arrived in bombed-out Port Morseby,
a Japanese invading force approached the town by sea but was
stopped during the Battle of the Coral Sea (May 5–8, 1942). Although
both sides sustained substantial losses, the capture of Port Morseby
was prevented. On May 18, 1942, Admiral Yamamoto was ordered
to seize Midway quickly, along with the Aleutians, New Caledonia,
Fiji, Samoa, and Port Moresby, in order to cut off communications
between the United States and Australia. Japan's decisive defeat at
Midway on June 4, 1942, severely damaged its fleet and greatly
reduced the risk of a renewed attempt to take Port Moresby by sea.
Instead, the Japanese decided upon a land strategy, establishing beachheads on the north coast of New Guinea (July 21–22, 1942) and pushing overland across the Owen Stanley Mountains beyond Kokoda
to threaten Port Moresby.[4]

The 96th Battalion was thrown into this cauldron with inadequate
support, training, and equipment, shouldering the responsibility of
creating facilities that could receive and support desperately needed
air cover. The labor battalion was expected to defend its position if
the Japanese invaded—an extremely likely prospect during most of
the 96th's first year in New Guinea. Although in theory African-

American soldiers were supposed to be as well equipped and trained as white soldiers, the men of the 96th had old Springfield rifles. Some had never fired a gun.

Captain Samuelson's diary documents the men's contribution, which has hardly been acknowledged. Almost all of the sixty-three illustrations published in the official history of the New Guinea campaign, for example, are photographs, and none show African-American soldiers. The fact that African-American soldiers built the Tatana Island docks and causeway, which greatly extended the facilities of Port Moresby, is also unacknowledged.[5] However, in his general history of African-American troops during World War II, Ulysses Lee, an African-American historian, does discuss the role of the 96th in some detail and cites official recognition of the importance of its work:

> 1. Every officer and man of the Ninety Sixth Engineers looks back with pride on the early days at Port Moresby. In those days, plain for all to see, on their work in maintaining and improving airdromes under fire and pushing through the Tatana Island project depended our success in stopping the Japs. In those days the issue trembled in the balance, and every man could see his weight throwing the scales our way.
> 2. With a handful of worn equipment, without experience, but with no end of guts you threw yourselves into the scales. The regiment was weighed and was not found wanting.[6]

The 96th moved forward to Sansapor in Dutch New Guinea in August 1944. In February 1945, Companies A and B took over the defense at Table River for two days while the infantry regiment to which they were attached searched for attackers. In April 1945, they moved on to the Philippines, maintaining roads and bridges on the supply routes in the Mindanao campaign.[7]

Captain Samuelson was born in Donaldsonville, Louisiana, in 1919 and was raised in New Orleans. Before he was drafted into the army and assigned to the 96th Engineer Battalion (Colored) as a second lieutenant, his experience with African Americans was limited largely to the women his family employed as domestic servants, mainly child-care workers. He entered the army thinking in stereotypes and was woefully ignorant of the conditions under which African Americans were forced to live. But he learned rapidly as he began to perceive his men, to identify with them, and to learn something of what they were up against. He began to be proud of them, to defend them and teach them, and, as he wrote to his wife near the end

of his stay in New Guinea, to love them. He was well aware that his
men hated their officers for being white. On October 11, 1943, he
wrote in his diary:

> Before I die I must help stamp out this crazy idea that the white man
> has about his superiority over the colored man. In no concrete way has
> he ever demonstrated it. Here we fight the Germans because they
> declare themselves a superior race. Individually they have demon-
> strated their boast. Their medicine, science, manufactures are, or at
> least were, superior to that of any other nation. Yet this did not give
> them the right to declare that they were superior to all other men and to
> be able to dictate to others. Yet we Americans, the ones who are trying
> to thrash out Germany's idiotic ideas, feel the same way about the
> negroes.[8] It's wrong—damn wrong! The negro is our equal physically.
> He is superior to us spiritually. He has the same intelligence as a white
> man. What he lacks is opportunity, opportunity to get an education, a
> decent job, decent living conditions. And these are the things which we
> white men deprive him of. And they are smart enough to know that we
> are wrong, but being in the minority they can do nothing about it.

But he did not begin to fathom the depths of discrimination and
oppression that African Americans suffered. Between 1920 and 1940,
Benjamin O. Davis, Jr., who became a brigadier general during the
war, was the only African-American officer in the regular army and
the only African-American graduate of West Point. The only other
African-American officers in the history of the regular U.S. Army
were three men commissioned during the late-nineteenth century.
When the United States entered World War II, there were, among the
five African-American regular army officers, three chaplains, who
were more readily accepted for their role as mediators between the
officers and the men. The army was not only segregated by race.
During the Great Depression, only white recruits were allowed, and
African Americans were sharply underrepresented in proportion to
their numbers in the population.

After the United States entered the war, governments throughout
the world importuned the U.S. government not to send African-
American troops to their countries. Captain Samuelson was obviously not aware that the reason his troops could not go to Australia
on leave had to do with U.S. acceptance of Australia's nonwhite
exclusion policy. On March 29, 1942, General MacArthur supported
the Australian government's proposal that no more African-American
soldiers be sent there and that those already there be returned to the
United States or shipped to New Caledonia or India. MacArthur
wrote: "I will do everything possible to prevent friction or resentment

on the part of the Australian government and people at the presence of American colored troops. . . . Their policy of exclusion against everyone except the white race known locally as the 'White Australia' plan is universally supported here."[9]

Getting able white officers to command African-American troops entailed special difficulties that had as much to do with the officers' attitudes as their abilities. White officers serving in African-American units were looked down upon. Many pushed hard for transfer to white units.[10]

It is clear from these letters and diaries that Captain Samuelson had an open mind toward "the other," which allowed him to perceive and respect properly those of a culture and color different than his own. His appreciation for the people, the culture, the language, and the technology of Papua-New Guineans is clear, even when he at times echoes the attitudes of the more "informed" Australian colonists and administrators. His attitude toward the Japanese was consistently respectful. His open-mindedness probably stemmed from the fact that he was a southern Jew, a reality that made him aware of group oppression and also gave him the perspective of the perpetual outsider.

Captain Samuelson graduated summa cum laude in June 1940 from Louisiana State University with a degree in civil engineering. He had joined the Reserve Officer Training Corps (ROTC) at Louisiana State and was an officer in the U.S. Army Reserve.[11] Unable to get a job with an engineering company, he attended a summer camp in Alabama for two weeks, earning $6 a day as an officer, and then served for a month with the 20th Engineers on maneuvers in Louisiana. Both experiences convinced him that he was not cut out to be an army officer. That fall he entered Tulane graduate school with a teaching fellowship that paid $100 a month and started work on his master's of science degree in civil engineering. Colonel Fox, who directed the classes in surveying, went on active duty and Dean Derickson let Samuelson take over Fox's job. He loved it. He had found his niche in life: as a university teacher. During the summer of 1941, he went to work for the navy, doing engineering work on the construction of a naval base in Burrwood, Louisiana, close to the mouth of the Mississippi River. In September 1941, he was called to active duty and reported to the 96th Engineers, then on maneuvers around Fort Bragg, North Carolina. From that point the story can be followed in the text.

These diaries and letters are more than valuable sources that illuminate the history of the times. This is a profoundly human story. As Steven Ambrose has written, it is "a vivid, heart-breaking account of a man at war. Any war. Any place. Any time."[12]

Love, War, and the
96th Engineers (Colored)

ONE

Leaving Home

September 17, 1941–March 5, 1942

September 17, 1941, Burrwood, Louisiana

Back on the job again and hard at work. The ride down river today was very enjoyable; the water rough and little *Plaquemine* bounced plenty. No word about deferment. Feel confident it will come through all OK after seeing today a copy of the letter Captain Burrell has sent to the Commanding Officer of the Third Military Area. I really hope it comes through. I am first learning to like my work a lot and want to see the job through to the finish.

September 18, 1941

No deferment. Tomorrow I return to New Orleans and Saturday to active duty. Not happy over set-up but feel that it is for the best. One thing definitely good. If I am in the army for only one year when I do get out, I'll be able to return to Tulane. If I received a deferment until November 30th and then had to go into the army, I would get out in the middle of the school term. This way might be the best after all.

Bruns worked me to death today. Says he wants to get all possible out of me before I leave. To bed, for my last night in Burrwood. It was a pretty good place after all. Another hurricane is brewing 180 miles south of here. The winds are 15 to 20 miles an hour now and will probably be higher in the morning.

September 19, 1941, New Orleans

This will be the last time I shall sit at this desk for another year. I left Burrwood this morning at 10 o'clock carrying my own suitcase

Hyman Samuelson at Bur-
wood, Louisiana, shortly
before being inducted into the
Army.

and radio and some papers for the Eighth Naval District. The ride up
the Mississippi in the *Samuel* was fun. The rough waters gave us an
awful beating, and at the Head of Passes we looked more like a
submarine than a surface ship. I delivered dispatches to the Federal
Building in New Orleans. The officers at the Eighth Naval District
treated me swell. All of them seemed to know about me. Dora's voice
was sad when I called her. She knew why I had come in.

We rode all around, talking loosely—sad but happy talk. We
stopped for sandwiches and sundaes and parked on the lakefront and
loved. The waves were dashing over the top of the seawall and made a
pretty sight. Dora didn't cry all evening—not even when, just a few
minutes ago, I told her goodbye. I am proud of her for not crying. I
hate crying.

September 21, 1941

Still home. Spent the weekend with the folks and Dotsy [his sister]
at Henderson's Point.[1] Herman [Herman L. Midlo, his sister Ethel's
husband], Papa, and I went fishing this morning. The storm is moving
north and should strike the coast within the next 24 hours.

Dora's and my last evening together in a long time. No tears from
her. Not a lot of emotion on my part when we parted. Must have been
tired. All packed now, ready to leave at 8 A.M.

September 25, 1941, somewhere in the woods around Ellerbe,
North Carolina

As the *Southerner* pulled out from the station, Papa looked good,
Dotsy looked sweet, and Aunt Shanie, with her reddened eyes, looked
disgusting. I had a sinking feeling as we rode along and it didn't leave
me for a couple of hours. The ride between New Orleans and Atlanta
on the streamlined aluminum *Southerner* was very enjoyable. First
time ever on a streamlined train. The lady behind me and some
yankee got into an argument about the intelligence of the southerner
and the northerner. When he started telling her that Georgia—she
was from Georgia—should have never been included in the Louisiana
Purchase, I couldn't resist giving him hell. He finally agreed the
southerner had normal intelligence. More discussions followed. The
one about who appreciated the other more, the husband the wife or
the wife the husband, involved nearly the whole coach. I took out the
box of candy Dora had sent me before leaving home, and we all
enjoyed the top layer of chocolates.

Arrived in Fayetteville around noon and took a taxi to Ft. Bragg.
An awful feeling seized me as I drove past the M.P. [military police-
man] and beheld the post. Soldiers and dust! Lines of men! Men or
animals? I hated Fort Bragg on first sight. No one was at Post
Headquarters, so I reported directly to headquarters, 96th Engineers.
Lt. Colonel Pohl arrived. He is the battalion commander. He impressed
me as the ideal commander. Well built, manly features, friendly and
stern. I liked him from the start. I hoped the other officers of the
battalion would be like Divers and Pohl. We picked up my trunk in
Fayetteville and then drove out about 60 miles to these woods,
arriving in time for supper. Lucky I was plenty hungry. Army food
isn't the best in the world. I met most of the officers, about 20. I have
been assigned to Company C with 1st Lt. Schwalbert as company
commander. Last night we had a little party on the ground by lamp
light. Colonel Pohl and Major Martin, executive officer, joined us just
as if they were shave tails [second lieutenants]. They are great guys. I
brought out the rest of my box of candy. One fellow brought out a
cake he had just received from home. Another brought out some
limburger cheese and crackers, and one bought some beer. It was
really great fun. Everybody talked, one at a time. The conversation
was about everything except women and the war, the only two things
ever discussed in Burrwood. These fellows are real gentlemen. I have

New Orleans, 1939, left to right in rear: Sam (Papa), Beryl (brother), and Jake (cousin); in center: Sally (cousin); in front: Aunt Shanie (stepmother), Hymie, and Dotsy (sister).

never seen 15 people take part in a conversation so smoothly before in my life. All college graduates and intelligent. The enlisted men of our separate battalion consists of over 1,000 negroes. It seems to me that negroes make good soldiers.

Last night's sleeping was delicious out in the open. Up this morning at six o'clock. It is cold and dark. Reveille march a few minutes later, then assembly. Still dark! Back to the tent for a painful shave. Just getting light! Breakfast. Poor food. Schwalbert took me over the place, showing me the organization of the company. I asked to do some work but he told me to take it easy for awhile. I believe I'll be administrative officer. It ought to be good experience. Still have the whole day ahead of me. Will go back to Bragg tomorrow. I wish I was already settled. Everybody treats me kindly. I am in a good outfit, and ought to like it.

6:30 P.M.: I wish I knew more about my duties. In fact I don't know where I am around here or just where I fit into the picture. I like Roberson, and enjoyed the afternoon with him watching him supervise the construction of a spar bridge made of logs lashed together with rope. He was cadet colonel at Tennessee last year and impresses me as having been a good one. The negroes like him. They gave me a loud welcome when Roberson introduced me to them. I think working with negroes is going to be all right. Wish we had lights so that there would be something to do at night besides talk and sleep.

September 26, 1941

Dusk! Raining! Writing by light from weak flash light. This is the kind of life I shall have to lead during the next year. I shall work hard, study and read and avoid even the simplest of comforts. I have a lot of equipment and clothing now and shouldn't need anything expensive for some time to come. This year won't be a particularly happy one. That much I can foresee. But I should be able to make it a profitable one, physically, financially, morally, and mentally. I must see to it that no time is wasted. I must make my pennies count, too and discipline myself the same as I discipline the men under me.

September 27, 1941, Ft. Bragg, North Carolina

Did my first day's work today. It wasn't much of an assignment. All I had to do was lay a cover of dirt six inches thick and 12 feet wide across U.S. Highway 15 at its intersection with a dirt road over which the 79th Field Artillery were coming to the maneuver area. The work was of the simplest type, my sergeant was efficient, and the men good workers. The job was easy. I enjoyed seeing the tractor-drawn 240mm guns thundering by. They are, I believe, the heaviest field guns in our army and look mighty mean. The horse drawn artillery is a pretty sight too. Have seen more of such troops so far than I thought in existence in our army. Believe they are out of date. Whenever you reach the place where the going is too rough for a tank, it is too rough for horses also. Am taking the men to the show this evening. It will break the monotony of this early to bed, early to rise business.

September 28, 1941

Have Dora's picture in my trunk and the fellows thought her very pretty. Tallied up the company's collection sheet today. Read the Sunday paper through and through. Germany still making fantastic gains in Russia. I wonder how long it will be before she collapses from within. Germany has a pretty good chance of reaching the Caucasus and the oil she needs so much. Here in the army there is very little talk of the war. Most of the men—I am talking about the officers now— believe that we will get into it all right but not for at least another year. Public sentiment, they claim, is too strong against it. Who knows?

September 29, 1941

Routine work with the company today. I am afraid that my mind is going to get rusty in the army. There is little opportunity for original thinking. Even the ink I use in my pen has to be "regulation" stuff. A letter at last from home. It was short. No word yet from Dora, and I miss her.

September 30, 1941

The officers have put up a tent which they call the U.P. Club. It is for the purpose of eating and drinking—about the only recreation a fellow can find out here. These men drink so differently from those at Burrwood who drank for the sole purpose of getting drunk, to make

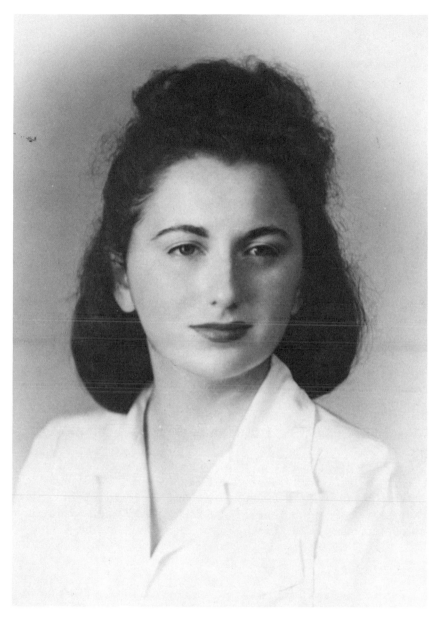

Dora Reiner in 1941.

their mind numb so that their life was blotted out, at least until they sobered up. They were half wrecked, drifting along from day to day. Drinking for them broke the monotony of living. Now these officers are different. They drink to be sociable. They try *not* to get drunk. So far I haven't touched a drop of the stuff here, and I don't intend to. I am willing to put in to buy food but not liquor.

Still no word from Dora. I have been dreaming about her every night, and I miss her very much. The letter I wrote her this evening was more than sentimental and didn't look like my writing at all. I expect to hear from her tomorrow. Gee, but I hope so.

Read a field manual on explosives and demolitions. In my spare time if I read these various field manuals I should be able to learn a lot of stuff from being in the army. I have been going around with Roberson, training officer, whenever he takes out the men. Been getting back into the swing of marching soldiers, calisthenics and the like. I am afraid, however, that unless there are some changes soon, my year in the army will not be the most enjoyable thing.

October 1, 1941

Today was a little better. I was kept fairly busy. Finished making up the payroll, and it checked to the penny. Schwalbert, surprised and pleased, says it seldom happens that way — at least with so little effort. Spent a lot of time with the company, inspecting sanitation conditions, supervising the putting up of some new tents for 29 men who are coming in this evening. Tomorrow morning I take out the company on a ten mile hike. Since it will be pay day, we want to be in for 12 o'clock. That means plenty of fast stepping, under full pack, too. I guess I'll be able to take it all right. I like Roberson more and more.

And still no word from Dora. And nothing from the folks. Never before did I realize how much I would miss Dora. Her picture makes me feel blue as the dickens. I have made up my mind to stay here straight on through for the whole year, not a single furlough.

October 2, 1941

The hike went off in fine shape. We covered the ten miles in three hours and fifteen minutes, including three ten minute rest periods. I stood up under it better than I thought. Hardly got tired.

An example of how these poor negroes can be cheated. Today was pay day. Each negro is given an envelope which contains his money. On the outside of the envelope are written (1) his gross salary, (2) his debts as indicated by the collection sheet, and (3) his net pay. At the end of the pay-off, the men are given the opportunity to come up and check their envelopes. Many do. Usually we can show them their mistake, or rather point out where their envelope is correct. However, there were two who complained about being charged $2.75 *three* months in a row for a picture (or rather a set of pictures) which cost only $5.50. At first we thought it was only their imagination that made them think they had paid three times and we checked the records to show them they had paid only twice. Much to our surprise, we found that they were right, that they had actually paid $2.75 too much. Upon examining the books further we found that nearly 50 other men who had not contested our records had been overcharged. We refunded the money, of course.

A letter at last from Dora. It was sent by airmail, and apparently she answered me just as soon as she received my first letter. I guess I was extra impatient. The letter didn't say much in all of its 12 pages, but I enjoyed every word of it.

Courts martial tonight. I was the assistant defense counsel. There were five cases. Three entered pleas of guilty. One pleaded not guilty but had so much evidence piled against him that it was a hopeless case—for the defense, anyway. The fifth case was not completed. The prosecution's chief witness was not present. This happened because the accused had told Willie Hering, the defense counsel, that he would plead guilty at the trial. It made me happy to see at least one of these negroes who could stand up for his rights. I don't like this railroading. I think we might get him released. I am going to plan a real defense for the rest of the trial and try to free him. See what kind of lawyer I'd make. In spite of losing the case tonight, I think I did pretty fair. Poor fellow was lying and there wasn't much for me to do.

October 3, 1941

Most of the officers and several of the non-coms went on critique today.[2] I being the junior officer of the company remained with Company C. It was an enjoyable day. First I gave the men mass calisthenics. It was the first time they had ever done it, and it went over big. I know I liked mass commands when I was in the ranks. I think it is excellent all-around training. After an hour of calisthenics there was a half hour's rest. Then followed a two hour period of map reading. I taught the men how to scale distances on the map, how to get distances between towns or road junctions along curved as well as straight roads. They paid close attention and at least three out of four learned what I was trying to put over. Then I had the men assemble and dismissed all of those except the ones who wanted further individual instruction. There were 14 who remained. Poor devils didn't know how to read. Several couldn't even read numbers. It is a hopeless task trying to teach them some things. It seems to me that the army ought to try to send these men to school, to teach them reading, writing, and a little arithmetic. For this afternoon's work I gave them a problem in scouting and patrolling. I sent the first platoon, under Sergeant Jeeter, one mile down the road. At this point he was supposed to give instructions to his platoon for its advance through a certain area which I pointed out to him. As soon as he had given the instructions to his men, he could advance. The second platoon, under Sergeant Horton, was instructed to defend the area. I was to serve as umpire. If the scouts of the attackers were able to find the defenders and tell me how many men there were and then meet these with stronger numbers, I would consider that they had won a victory at the point and could advance. Now, on the other hand, if the scouts of the attackers came within effective fire of the defenders or if any other men of the attackers advanced within effective range of the defenders or if the attackers advanced on the defenders with insufficient troops, I considered these as being destroyed. The battle raged for a couple of hours. Neither side won. Both sides did an excellent job. They concealed themselves so well that at the time I called a halt to the fight some men were within 100 feet of an enemy without seeing him. When I made all the troops stand up and show themselves, both sides were surprised to see that many of the enemy's forces could have shot them. The men seemed to like this exercise a lot. So did I. I went on as Officer of the Day at noon and inspected and mounted the guard this evening. I'll have to get up some time between midnight and reveille and inspect the guard.

Was greatly disappointed that Floyd, the accused in the unfinished courts martial case is A.W.O.L. [absent without leave] and couldn't appear in the completion of the trial which was supposed to have been tonight.

"Poor nigger," I said, "He could have beat his case, too." I was laughed at.

"That's what you think," said Captain Barco, president of the Board, "You haven't been around much."

I left and went for a walk.

October 4, 1941

Roberson went to the Tennessee—Duke football game, and Schwalbert and Miller both went home, so that left me in charge of the company again. Shortly after supper, Sgt. Bowie, our 1st Sergeant, reported to me that we had a number of men in jail in Hamlet and he wanted permission to go to get them out. He said it was customary, but I told him no, that if they were in jail, they deserved being there and there is where they should stay. Then I went to see Capt. Jago and he said that he thought it advisable for *me* to go to Hamlet to investigate.[3] The ride to Hamlet was beautiful. A big full moon rose above the tree tops as we got on top of a hill and then sank out of sight as we drove down into a valley. Venus shone brightly in the fading rays of the sun. In Hamlet we found that only one man from the 96th was in jail, and he was being held by the civilian police; so we could not get him out. The driver got lost on the way back home. I had a map on my lap and could have got him straightened out, but instead I let him drive around trying to find his way back. I excused myself on the grounds that it was good training for the driver. Actually, I was enjoying the ride.

October 5, 1941

Thank God gnats and flies sleep at night. Otherwise I fear I would be driven insane. They were mercilessly annoying all day long. How I managed to read with the pesky insects fighting for possession of my ears, eyes, nose, and mouth. This evening I started reading Douglas Southall Freeman's biography of Robert E. Lee. Must have read about 50 pages. I brought two of the four volumes with me. They are Herman's books. When I finish reading them and the other books I brought I'll send these home and have them send me more. As long as I have plenty of good books and as long as my eyes remain healthy I can keep from being lonely.

Other three company officers still away. Having control of the company is pretty good experience but it is a tremendous amount of work and responsibility, and I'll be glad when the others are back. As officer-of-the-day, I expect some trouble tonight. About 80 men in the battalion are A.W.O.L. Many will be staggering in tonight. Corporal of the Guard just reported that a man was just brought in with his face all cut. Poor black devil is drunk, claims he hasn't been drinking, that six white soldiers attacked him for no reason at all as he walked alone down the streets of Hamlet. I guess this will be going on all night; just hope it is nothing more serious.

October 6, 1941

Very much depressed this evening. Tired of these poor negroes, tired of punishing them, trying to reason with them. Such a shame for people with education to let such ignorance exist. If they were ignorant but happy, I would say nothing, but they are miserable. Superstitious, emotional! I never knew what it was before to see a 25 year old man come crying to me because so-and-so stole his cigarettes. What goes on in a man's mind who can't tell a seven from a two? Men who can hardly understand English—how can they be good soldiers? And citizens? Is it fair that we treat them as our equal when we go inducting them into the army and treat them as a domestic animal when it comes to education. What horrid creatures we whites are!

I messed up the courts martial case against Floyd this evening. My evidence in his defense was either irrelevant or it was laughed at. Poor negro got six months of hard labor with forfeiture of 2/3rds of his pay during the time. When I close my eyes at night, I see the fear-marked faces of these darkies. Their tears when you scold them for being unable to execute "inspection arms" properly. Their dirty uniforms! Their scars. Their salutes—what a wild and nervous look in their eyes when they salute; fear that they will do it wrong. They salute horribly. I walk among them with a sick feeling. Hundreds of men sleeping on the ground. Most do not know the names of their tent mates. Some cannot write home; they don't know how. Some don't get mail; they couldn't read it anyway. Many don't know where they are. Some don't care where they are going. I wish there was something I could do. But I'm helpless. I saw that more than ever at tonight's courts martial.

No mail! I am unhappy this evening. Hardly feel like speaking, and writing is difficult with this frame of mind.

October 7, 1941

A letter from Dora today made me feel better, and my answer to her—pouring out all the things which were bothering me—made me feel still better. But I'm still pretty gloomy. Perhaps after awhile I'll get used to taking these negroes' problems as part of my work, but life is going to be pretty gloomy for me during the transition.

October 8, 1941

Other company officers away and me placed in charge of training as well as mess, supply and administration. A busy day. But I like it that way.

A smart nigger on trial tonight and the first to beat the prosecution. And I must admit that he did it without the help of Willie and me. Glad to see at least one blackie with enough sense to defend himself. However I think he is a bad egg and should have been punished. It's funny how the ignorant get such hard sentences and the more intelligent get off easily. I'm for more people being more intelligent.

October 9, 1941

Eight hours of training today has got me pretty well worn out. The hike itself was only about 10 miles which took three hours. But I put the men through some combat tactics under an assumed gas attack and this was most fatiguing.

The U.S.O. came around this evening and put on some movies. They were entertaining and the appreciation of the men was demonstrated by loud applause after the movie was over. It is too bad that we don't have more of this kind of entertainment for the men.

October 10, 1941

I feel very much like the Lord High Everything Else in *The Mikado*. Today I served in my official capacity of Supply Officer. Our supply records are in completely uninterpretable shape. I doubt that they will ever be correct and understandable.

October 12, 1941

This afternoon I went to a negro tea social in Hamlet. I enjoyed watching the negroes having a good time. They are surely advancing. I love to hear them sing spirituals, too.

October 13, 1941

Been tramping through woods all day—by compass—training the men—exhausting stuff—made excellent land falls—nose stuffed—head hurts—Schwalbert reprimanded me for quitting my post (issuing equipment) to go to town for a haircut. Felt plenty hurt cause I had been working hard all day. Tired, feel like getting flu. Moving out 6:15 tomorrow morning.

October 14, 1941, North Carolina countryside near Ft. Bragg

Right now we are in the "brains" of the army, the First Army of the United States. Of course our job is "fetch and carry" work, but it is good experience to see the point from which our army is controlled. It looks disgustingly inefficient to me—contradictory orders! Too many orders! Everybody looking for his own comfort. Lights in the colonel's tent is more important than getting the men fed. I was assigned "making camp" while Schwalbert and Miller took charge of more technical work. Roberson didn't come out with us. Making camp with thirsty and hungry men is no fun. To sleep now.

October 15, 1941

Sleeping on the ground tonight about 23 miles from last night's location. A million and one problems all day long—food, water, supply, fights among men. Lots of quick thinking. The officer who is in charge of making camp on a quick movement like this has got to give so many orders that a large percentage of them have to be changed or if not changed they turn out to be poor policy. Of the four officers of our company I rate Miller as the best, Roberson second, Schwalbert third, and myself last. I definitely feel my deficiencies when in the presence of these other men. Of course I am "newer" than they are, but that does not mean that I should be content to remain the weakest officer. I must work hard and succeed as an army officer the same as I have succeeded in those enterprises which I have tackled.

At supper tonight I mistook the head of the table for the foot and sat on the right of the Chief of Staff, who was sitting at the head of the 54 foot long table. I realized my mistake and wanted to excuse myself, but he insisted that I remain. He asked me from what outfit I was; and when I told him, he said he wanted to compliment the officers and men of the 96th for the splendid work they had done in setting up the camp for headquarters. He was particularly pleased with Miller's job of wiring the camp in so short a time. I never realized how well disciplined and courteous our men are until yesterday and today, when I came in contact with these white soldiers. They are horrible.

October 16, 1941

More than 500 men messing with us now; about 250 of our own men, 100 truck drivers from various provisional companies, and 150 men from Company D. These last men arrived today to help us in our previously almost impossible task of "moving" Army Headquarters. As mess officer, I have my hands full trying to draw rations for these men and seeing to it that they all get fed. I have driven all over the countryside getting enough food to feed them tomorrow. Colonel Pohl, 96th Engineers commander, informs us that we are liable to be attached to First Army Headquarters throughout the maneuvers. It doesn't matter very much to me what we do. I feel that I am just a molecule in a large wheel. Which molecule I am, I don't know. Nor does it matter. I feel that the wheel would still exist without me, that I am such a small part that it will be hard to find my purpose. My brain is numb. I am turning into a machine, just like the rest—or at least like most of the army officers.

October 17, 1941

We're going to move today. Looks as if Erdley will be the last officer to leave this time and see that camp is left in good shape.

6 P.M.: Finally got enough food for tomorrow. Men are loading truck now.

9:45 P.M.: Back in our bivouac area, ready for bed. They claim we might have to move out again tonight. Such a movement would be exhausting. Also claim possible gas attack tonight. Perhaps a parachute troop attack at dawn.

October 20, 1941

I am convinced that courts martials are good and that Captain Barco makes an excellent president of the board.

October 21, 1941

Short arm inspection [for venereal disease] this morning. These negroes would give most white men an inferiority complex, me included. Still working hard on supply records. Don't know whether I'm making much progress or not, but I am collecting all kind of piecemeal records into consolidated ones. No telling what the final result will be.

October 22, 1941

I am beginning to like working for and with our company. I am learning the names and faces of many of the men, who is good and bad, dependable and incapable. Along with this growing interest in my work I feel a diminishing state of loneliness and longing for home. I hardly miss anyone. My mind has grown insensible to thoughts of those who about two or three weeks ago caused me a lot of mental discomfort.

October 23, 1941

I did something in the courts martial case this evening which Captain Barco thought was wrong; something which the Courts Martial Manual states the defense counsel should not do, and something which by doing makes it impossible for me to face one Corporal Green of the medical detachment. The case started last night, but because all the witnesses were not available it was recessed and continued again tonight. I interviewed the accused yesterday before the trial, as is the custom with the defense counsel, and he told me his story. He admitted that he had added 1,000 tablets of sulfanilamide to an order blank signed by Dr. Carithers when he (Green) went to the medical supply house at Ft. Bragg to get some articles for our dispensary here which Carithers had placed on the order blank. Obviously he was guilty of forgery, stealing government property and carrying a dangerous drug. I told him that his case was nearly hopeless but explained his privilege of pleading "not guilty," that if he so pleaded, it would be the job of the prosecution to prove that he was guilty. He admitted to me that he was guilty but that he wished to plead "not guilty." The trial went on tonight. The evidence introduced by the prosecutor, Lt. Eddy was inadequate. The testimony of his witnesses was puzzling and conflicting. When, at length, he stated, "The prosecution rests," it was obvious that Green was absolutely safe if he didn't take the stand. I knew this but didn't say a word. Willie said what the defendant had told him to say before the trial: "The accused wishes to make a sworn statement."

Green took the oath and sat down. Willie questioned him, asking him to tell his story. Green was clever enough to say very little. Eddy cross-examined him, but for some reason he wasn't getting down to facts. Green was going to beat the rap. Then I asked one question, a question the answer to which I knew and which Green knew I knew.

"Did you add the words 'sulfanilamide 7.5 grains 1000 tablet' to that order blank *after* it had been signed by Lt. Carithers?"

He looked at me, just as if I had placed a noose around his neck. A lie at this point would acquit him. He answered, "Yes."

He wound up with the maximum punishment a special courts martial can give. The officers thought it a grave injustice that I should double cross the man I was defending and showed me in the courts martial manual where I should defend him regardless of what I know or how I feel. I answered them that if they wanted justice to be dealt out, that the truth in all cases should be brought forward. Trials should not be a battle between lawyers but a means of obtaining the truth and administering justice. I knew the man was guilty and thought he should be punished. I didn't think he should go free because the prosecution had failed to bring out the truth. Some agreed with me; others didn't.

October 27, 1941

I had my supply sergeant busted today and recommended to Schwalbert that Partlow replace him. Rivers is an intelligent boy but he was lazy and a supply sergeant like this is going to add work and responsibility to my already loaded routine. I am tired of seeing records kept on scrap paper or of seeing no records at all.

October 29, 1941

Still working on supply records. Horrible. Have just about complete physical inventory of supplies and equipment. A good army officer I will never be. I hate routine, and the army's very guts are based on such stuff. I believe I made a wise choice in Partlow. He is slow and doesn't have that "new broom" attitude, but he is deliberate and should make a competent supply sergeant.

October 30, 1941

Very depressed this evening, lonesome and blue. A letter from Dora makes me long to be near her. Feel as if I ought to go home around Christmas and get married and take Dora back with me—wild dream, stupid idea! Just can't get into the swing of this army life. I hope I can get out of it in a year's time. Last five weeks have been unhappy ones. Restless this evening. Don't know what I want. We move out tomorrow.

October 31, 1941

Camped on the crest of a pine-studded hill about a mile from First Army Headquarters with a moon that is nearly full dashing through wind-swept clouds. I feel content as I lay on my bedding roll. The darkies are still singing around the fire which remains as a symbol of the wiener roast we had this evening. There is a happy feeling in sleeping on the ground. The ground always looks friendly and familiar, something like the stars.

November 1, 1941

We took up a new position today, about four miles east of Marston. We are the Blues, an invading force which has landed successfully on the Atlantic Coast and is now pushing inland against the defending Red Army. Our location is supposed to be a strictly guarded secret, for no doubt the Reds would attack us with bombers and parachute troops if they knew where we were located. Not that they are interested in wiping out 250 negroes. But we are to the First Army Headquarters what the skull is to the brain. We keep Headquarters concealed from enemy observation, move it quickly and silently to a safer location when its position has been found, and fight with all our strength if it is attacked by parachute troops. Naturally we are helpless with our rifles and revolvers against aircraft, especially bombers; and we feel certain that these are going to be used against us if and when the enemy finds our position.

November 2, 1941, Ft. Bragg, North Carolina

Tonight is the first time since I left home that I am about to sleep in a room with wooden walls around me and a wooden floor beneath me. I am in the Officers Barracks on the Post, enjoying the radio. If there were heat and running water in this deserted building, I would be very content. The reason I am enjoying these comparative comforts is that today was pay day, and Schwalbert and I have been traveling all over the maneuver area distributing the $10,000 payroll. Tonight we wind up at Fort Bragg. This is convenient for Schwalbert for his wife and boy live in Fayetteville, and he has gone out to spend the night with them. He will pick me up in the morning.

November 3, 1941

Always when I'm around Schwalbert I feel mentally inferior. He has a vast storage of engineering knowledge which makes me feel definitely his subordinate. But after being with him and working with him, I see that he is not only full of personality and brains, but he is a good officer as well. Miller's success in our company can be attributed to Schwalbert's allowing him the opportunity to show his stuff more than anything else. Now that Miller is gone, Roberson is second in command and is shining like a star. It's Schwalbert's giving him enough rope to work with (or hang himself) that permits Roberson to show what he can do.

While in Fayetteville I visited Schwalbert's wife and little boy Greg. She is going to have another baby. Seeing them made me feel very empty, wanting to be married. If I were sure that I had to stay in the army more than a year and if I were sure we were not going to war, I'd marry Dora next time I go home. But as it is, I think I had better mark time. She is relatively happy at home. There is no sense in dragging her away—somewhere where she would have to sleep alone and be alone except over those weekends when I could get off to go see her. It wouldn't be fair to her to ask her to marry me now. Her schooling is more important.

November 6, 1941

I was surprised today at dinner to see the way I stood up for our troops. There was a doctor at the table talking to someone else saying he was worrying about leaving his two negro first-aid men with the 96th.

"They'll surely catch syphilis if they eat their food, and it's no fun in catching it that way."

I jumped all over him: "I eat their cooking and it's damn good. We have first-aid boys of our own and don't need yours."

He made me mad belittling our men. I was sorry though that I had lost my temper. But it only resulted from the squabble I had yesterday at the motor pool. I sent the trucks to be gassed and they came back empty. So I went down myself with them. The lieutenant in charge said that he was running the First Army Motor Pool and my trucks were 96th Engineer trucks.

"But we are *attached* to the First Army."

"Well, you ought to have your own motor pool."

"Look, we have *three* trucks—only three trucks! And there are about 300 of us working night and day for the First Army. Our men don't mind being pushed around, but our trucks insist on getting gas; otherwise they won't run. We need gas. And *here* is where I think we ought to be able to get it. If you refuse to give it to me, I think you might hear a big stink from First Army."

I got the gas. And since then a sergeant can get it, too.

November 10, 1941

As I think about it, it all seems like foolishness, but last night I promised myself to get married as soon as possible. Even if it meant no honeymoon or car, not a furnished home, not a big ring for Dora—all of that gone. I was going to ask Dora to marry me anyway. If I had had pencil and paper with me, I would have written her right then and there. We would be married over the Christmas holidays.

November 13, 1941

I made an important decision this evening. I am going to ask Dora to be engaged to me over the Christmas holidays, and we will be married at the earliest practical date, which will be some time after her school year is over. I might be plunging, but I feel happy over my decision.

November 14, 1941

I must be getting hard. I am having two men courts martialed, one for direct disobedience, the other for not fulfilling some punishment I gave him earlier. I'll write the letter to Dora tomorrow morning. I must think long and deep tonight.

November 15, 1941

The first thing I did this morning was to write to Dora. Slowly and deliberately I wrote down why we should be married sooner than we planned. But I enumerated the sacrifices that she will have to make—a smaller ring, no long honeymoon, no car, not even our own furniture. And I went on to say that if she thought it best that we wait until the time we had previously planned, I would understand. But I am sure of her reaction. She will say, "Everything will work out wonderfully."

The letter still lies on the table with a pack of outgoing letters.

Oddly enough King, not knowing what I was writing, wrote a similar proposal to his girl. His too is in the pile of letters.

November 18, 1941

This is a copy of the letter I received from Dora today:

Dearest little Angelpuss,

I just got your letter. I never thought about your having to be on duty while I was there. I had visions of us running all over everywhere, seeing everything, being together all the time. I guess I forgot you weren't in L.S.U. anymore—but really in the army. I miss you so much, little boy, that your letter sort of made me want to cry. I didn't though. But I feel right on the verge of it. If you'd just say the word, I'll come up there and marry you. There's nothing in the world I'd rather do right now. We won't need much—as long as we'll be together—even if it's for a little while—even if you have to go to somewhere far away—you'd be back soon, and I'd be there waiting for you—always. Honest, little boy, I'm willing to live anywhere with you—any old tent or anything would be heaven if you were in it too. I feel more and more every day as if I'm dying—as if something inside me is growing number and number. Please wouldn't you like to marry me? Today? Real, real soon?

It's amazing how we both "cracked" at the same time. Both of us broke our plans of a "sensible" marriage on nearly the same day—independently of each other—and wrote the other that we wanted to get married sooner. Our letters probably crossed in the mail.

November 19, 1941

It seems that the Reds are making a last attempt to take this place. Several hundred parachute troops have landed around here, within 25 miles anyway. And all haven't been "eliminated" up to now. The men are sleeping with all clothes on, rifles and gas masks near at hand. Even Schwalbert, King, and Rube are sleeping with their clothes. I think I'll take mine off. I can dress quickly and my function in case of an attack is very simple, merely issuing ammunition, answering phone calls, and sending messengers. Anyway, I'm sure this will be a false alarm like the other "attacks" we have had.

November 20, 1941

False alarms again today. Some fellows in Ledbetter celebrating Thanksgiving Day with fire crackers aroused the whole headquarters about an hour ago. Today makes two months that I have been in the Service. I still haven't "adjusted" myself to the life, but I am reasonably happy. I guess the principal contributing factor is that there are all kind of things to fit into all my moods. If I want to argue, I have Roberson. He is anti-everything, and he will give a fair argument on any subject. If I want to work, I have no trouble finding it. Finding Schwalbert is usually sufficient. King furnishes the fun and foolishness for us all. His keen mind and wit keeps us laughing all the time. If I feel grouchy I just step outside — and behold — 300 men! All of them subject to any of my cranky ideas. How wonderful! If I want to read, I read. If I want to write, I write. If I want to listen to the radio I do so. Plenty of good food, sleep, and rest, spiced with a moderate amount of exercise all make a pretty good diet. One of the pleasantest things to think about, to dream about, is the coming Christmas holidays, now only one month away.

November 22, 1941

The day started off on the wrong foot. Schwalbert bawled me out because there was no garbage pit and hot water for mess kits in the kitchen.

"If I take the men off their cooking," I argued, "the guard won't be fed soon enough to report at seven."

"If they aren't, it will be because you have fallen down on the job. You're getting bad as Bowie — reading instead of being on your job."

That cut. I felt so hurt that I don't believe I spoke to anyone for fully an hour. My job with the company, as supply officer, mess officer, and assistant administrative officer, is the nastiest of any of the officers; but I haven't complained. But as the day went on, I saw that Bill was right. Damn it! I could do a hell of a lot of a better job. By supper this evening, the kitchen looked better than at any other time since I have been here. Perhaps a little bawling out does us all some good. I'll try not to slip again. This is the second time Schwalbert has had to "crawl" me. Of course it doesn't mean a lot — especially in the army — but I hate to admit that it doesn't bother me. In fact I can't say that, for I would be lying.

Lt. Little says that I won't get 15 days leave. He is the battalion personnel adjutant and says I am entitled to 2½ days per month. But he is generally wrong about most things; maybe he will be wrong in this case, too. At any rate, I'm not going to let this mess up my plans to go home for Christmas and have the most wonderful time of my life.

November 24, 1941

I like army life more and more. Rube, Bill, and King are absolutely tops. And the enlisted men are swell. I know many of them now, their troubles and fortunes. I like them more than I thought it possible for me to like negroes.

November 25, 1941

I am becoming a better officer. There was a time when, after bawling out a man, I felt my knees shaking and my heart beating harder. And most of the time I felt sorry and wanted to apologize. But now it's different. I can scold a man and look as mean as hell and feel no worse than if I had told him "right face." In other words, it is more like a military duty than an attempt to help the individual. As a result, I find the kitchen and supply in a lot better shape than it has ever been before. I always advanced the theory that you could always reason with people and by calling to their attention their faults and mistakes cause them to become better and more efficient. But in the army it is different. With 80% — perhaps 90% — this sensible treatment still works, but with many of the soldiers you have to *order* them to do so and so; otherwise you get nowhere.

November 27, 1941

Schwalbert, Rube and I took in *Sergeant York* in Troy this evening. I enjoyed it a lot, in spite of the capture which was ridiculously performed on the screen. It was chock full of that kind of propaganda which America needs right now: that we should go kill the Germans to preserve our heritage, our freedom, that in killing them we would be defending ourselves, not committing any sin. I do believe it might be necessary to fight for these things which we Americans love so dearly, but it is a shame that diplomats let the world get into this sad shape.

December 1, 1941

The way Schwalbert tells the story, Colonel Pohl told Miller he could select any officer in the Battalion, aside from company commanders, to be his assistant. Miller chose me. I think that this is truly a honor. It should widen my experience. Over two months in a "lettered" company is enough for me. I'm going to miss Schwalbert,

Rube, and King; but I'll enjoy working for Miller. I must do a good job for him. I have had charge of the company all day, handling the "shakedown" inspection of the whole company for clothing and equipment. I am pretty well worn out tonight.

December 2, 1941

Today was a busy day. I spent the morning completing my shake down inspection of clothing and equipment and the afternoon in turning over my records to King. I must admit my records were not in the best of shape, but they are at least orderly. Colonel Pohl threw out my charge against Joseph Taylor. I was having him courts martialed because he failed to tell me his name when I asked him three times.

"How did you order Taylor to give you his name?" the colonel asked me.

"'What's your name?' "'

"That's a question, not an order."

"I asked him the same question three times and told him I wasn't interested in his argument."

"That was wrong!" the colonel said with a frown on his face, "With these men when they are excited, let them argue. They are emotional and become angry and have to get it off their chest. Let them say what they want. Never clamp down on them while they are excited."

"Yes, sir."

I felt very much like a criminal myself. The charge was withdrawn. The funny part is that tonight at the courts martial of another individual a man was accused of disobeying a non-commissioned officer who had said to him, "Will you get out the kitchen!" As defense counsel for the accused, I used the argument that this was a question, not an order, the same argument Pohl had used on my case against Taylor. It was no good. The man was found guilty. The men of this battalion will really get a lucky break if I should be appointed Trial Judge Advocate, prosecutor of a Court.

December 3, 1941

Two top kick N.C.O.s [noncommissioned officers] are A.W.O.L. with 10 or 20% of the company. Sgt. Farmer, General Drum's personal orderly is drunk, attacked guard with knife—a horrible mess. The men want a "break" from this confinement they have suffered for nearly three months, and with nobody knowing when we are going back to the Post, the morale is bound to hit rock bottom.

December 7, 1941

After dinner I lay down to read some of Lee's biography. I was on the part where in the Mexican War, he was lying hidden under a log by the enemy's water hole when I heard a flash on the radio outside: Hawaii had been bombed by Japan! Another flash! Manila had been bombed! Most of the officers took the flashes in a most unconcerned manner. Most went on reading the Sunday papers. I cursed when they kept interrupting Arthur Rubenstein's playing of Brahms Piano concerto. Talton, Miller, Eddy, King and I went to Rockingham this evening to take in a movie and a T-bone. To look at and hear the men around here, one would never believe that tomorrow we are going to declare war on Japan. That is bound to happen.

December 8, 1941

I looked around at the faces of the officers in a ring around the fire this afternoon as President Roosevelt asked Congress to declare that a state of war exists between the United States and Japan. The faces were stern and showed more interest than yesterday. In the mind of each officer were many problems. You could see them at work. When the speech was over, the officers started joking again. Their outward apathy hid the torturesome worries that clouded their brains. I have a problem. It is a mutual problem with Dora. For the last month I have been asking myself this question, "If war comes, will you ask Dora to marry you or will you tell her that she and you will have to wait until the war is over?"

As yet I have been unable to answer the question. Tonight I had to write Dora a letter which was very serious. I tried to get her to look at the present situation from a viewpoint free from emotion and sentimentality. I told her I loved her and wanted to marry her, war or not. Then I explained to her how I looked at the present situation. We are in a long war, perhaps for another five years. But we are on the stronger side and, God willing, should eventually come out on top. My battalion will probably remain in the U.S. for at least another year, and that year of married life should be heaven. We could possibly have a child during the time. Then I'd have to go abroad. If I'd return, we would be very happy again. If I were killed, she would be secure monetarily for I shall have $15,000 insurance by then; and, in addition, she will receive a lifelong pension. She will still be young; and if she so decides, she could carry on with someone else. However, if we were married, she would have to leave everyone she loved—

except me, not much compensation. And then when I did leave, she'd feel pretty empty. And if I should be crippled in the war—well, I don't know of anything worse a man can bring back to his wife than a disfigured body. So I put the question to her. I said I had to think about it longer myself, but I wanted to know how she felt.

December 10, 1941

I like H & S Company work.[4] Miller allows me to stick out my neck as far as I desire. I like that, although I know it's the way to get hurt.

December 11, 1941

Two letters today which prove—well, I don't know what they prove. From Dora came this: "I just heard the President's speech—we're really at war now, huh little boy? I was so stunned yesterday that I couldn't quite think straight—but if it had to happen I guess it's best it happened like it did—now we're more united—all united in fact and maybe now this awful struggle will be over sooner and we can have peace at last and always."

From Dotsy, who always writes the very lightest stuff, came this: "It struck so suddenly, so powerfully, that it seemed like a dream that would pass over with the night. But it didn't pass over. We are at war! Our brothers, cousins, closest friends, and perhaps even some fathers will soon be there fighting for what they believe. Is this war? Is the crying of mothers, the weeping of sisters, and the wishful hoping of sweethearts what the congress of the United States voted for, almost unanimously? I hate it!"

December 12, 1941

A letter from Phil Shein was interesting. I thought that this frank admission of his was particularly good: "I'm scared stiff. The thought of fighting, the pain I may go through, or possibility of losing a leg, arm, eye, or being disfigured."

That may not be a very heroic thing to say, but any sensible American must have such thoughts in the back of his mind regardless of what his outward comments might be.

December 14, 1941

Stockade turned to me and asked, "Do you think you'll pull through it alive?"

I lifted my eyes from the book I was reading and simply replied: "I have a notoriously famous record for having lived through everything up to now. It has sort of become a habit with me—living through things."

December 15, 1941

Wonderful news! I am to get a leave for ten days starting next Sunday. It is almost too good to be true. Just think, one week from now—just a mere 168 hours—I'll be home! It will then be nearly a hundred days that I have been away—the longest I have been gone from home in my life. I wrote Dora the good news this evening. I asked her did she want to get married then. I told her I had only enough money to buy a ring and a second hand car—the darn truth—but it would be wonderful. Gosh, just think, I'll be a married man in less than a month. A wife to look after, to support! How wonderful. I know that we shall be extremely happy.

February 13, 1942, Raeford, North Carolina

Next Sunday I shall have been married seven weeks. I guess it isn't exactly complementary to one's wife to say that seven weeks of married life seems like a long time. But to me it does. Dora and I had our first date nearly six years before, and we had gone steady more or less ever since. We had talked about marriage a long time ago. I remember that the first date we set was in June, 1944. It was to be a perfect match. We would have everything by then. I would be a prosperous young engineer with a couple college degrees. Dora would have her B.S. in medical technology. There would be a lot of money in the bank, a car, a furnished home, a $500 three month honeymoon. Yes, those were our original plans. Not so long ago, although it does seem pretty long ago at that, we decided to cut a year off and get married in June, 1943. We decided this when I was called to active duty. We felt that I would have to serve a year in the armed forces, and then I could return to Tulane and finish my graduate work.

I left New Orleans in September of last year and came to Ft. Bragg, North Carolina. Three months of hard maneuvers followed. Somewhere toward the end of November Dora and I, through correspondence, decided to get engaged the forthcoming Christmas and married the following June. Well, not so very long after we decided to get engaged, war was declared. I remember the torture my brain experienced at this time. To write about it now after it is all over wouldn't do it justice. We decided to get married over the Christmas holidays instead of getting engaged. It is a funny thing how we always planned on getting married in June and finally wound up being married in December.

We were married at noon on December 28, 1941. We had planned it to be just like an ordinary wedding, but the day before we were to be married, the left side of my face became swollen and Dr. Jacobs diagnosed the case to be no less than mumps. But Dora and I were going to get married regardless. The rabbi had to come to my house, and the only guests who were present at the ceremony were those who had had the mumps or who weren't afraid of catching them. This meant we had a house full. At 1 P.M., just an hour after the marriage ceremony, I entered La Garde General Hospital. Here I was confined for two full weeks while the doctors decided that they didn't know what was wrong with my neck. I must have lost a quart of blood in tests and if I had been troubled by cancer, I believe I would have been cured by so many x-rays. But the next two weeks at the hospital were very pleasant. I received passes daily, and Dora and I enjoyed a delicious honeymoon in New Orleans. Three weeks ago tonight Dora and I slept together at her house. It was wonderful.

The next morning we were to leave for North Carolina. Our car loaded to capacity, we hit the road. The trip was wonderful too. We took our time, and enjoyed the scenery and the food along the way. Dora is the kind of person who believes that tomorrow will take care of itself. Her pure optimism is her most divine characteristic. With the 80,000 men at Fort Bragg, I didn't see how we would be able to find a place. She *knew* that we would find a nice furnished apartment after we arrived. And we did. We live in Raeford. We have a bedroom, a living room, a kitchen, and although we have to share the bathroom with Nick and his wife, it is a big bathroom and we never have any conflicts. Our car, a second-hand Plymouth, behaves pretty well. Sometimes it decides to be hardheaded and doesn't want to start, but up until now it has never failed when we really need it. There are six other 96th Engineer officers and their wives living in Raeford so we have a lot of company, and by taking turns with our automobiles, we cut the cost of commuting to a fairly reasonable figure. Dora and I have a budget. It is, I believe, a very good budget, and although it doesn't have any "savings department," we do allow ourselves enough

)AY, DECEMBER 29, 1941   Matter Under Act

All's Well; Yea, 'Tis Even Swell

—Photo by The Times-Picayune.

LIEUTENANT AND MRS. HYMAN SAMUELSON

Refuses to Let Din of War and Case of Mumps Block His Pathway to Altar Here

Lieutenant Weds and Goes to Hospital Under Quarantine; Honeymoon Trip to North Carolina Off

If the outbreak of the war could not disrupt his wedding plans, First Lieutenant Hyman Samuelson was not going to let a case of the mumps do it, so he was married to Miss Dora Reiner at noon Sunday in a quiet cere-

mony in the bedroom of his home, 3938 Delachaise street.

Lieutenant Samuelson obtained a Christmas furlough from his station at Fort Bragg, N. C., and had planned, with Miss Reiner, a large wedding at the Beth Israel Synagogue today.

Two days ago he became ill, and his jaws began to swell Saturday night. The case was diagnosed definitely as mumps Sunday morning. Miss Reiner, who has had the mumps, and Lieutenant Samuelson got in touch with Rabbi Uri Miller of the synagogue, who agreed to marry them at home.

Not only were the wedding plans altered, but a planned honeymoon in the North Carolina mountains was also called off. After the ceremony, Lieutenant Samuelson was dispatched to La-Garde General hospital where he will remain under quarantine.

Lieutenant and Mrs. Samuelson will go to Fort Bragg to make their home when he is dismissed from the hospital.

The bridegroom was valedictorian of his graduating class at Louisiana State university in 1940, where he received a civil engineering degree. He continued his engineering studies on a fellowship at Tulane university until he went into active service four months ago. He is the son of Mr. and Mrs. S. J. Samuelson.

Mrs. Samuelson, the daughter of Mr. and Mrs. Jacob Reiner, 2632 Milan street, attended Loyola university. She wore a light blue suit at the wedding with a matching hat.

The bridegroom's best man was his brother, Beryl Samuelson, and the bridesmaids were Misses Dorothy Samuelson, Razele Midlo and Gwendolyn Midlo. They had all had the mumps.

Clipping from the *New Orleans Times Picayune,* December 29, 1941.

to live on comfortably. I really shouldn't say that there is no "savings department" for it does allow for the purchase of an $18.75 defense bond every month. These will be worth $25 ten years from now.

Married life agrees with me. I seem to be happy always. I don't get all the sleep that I should, but for some strange reason I am bounding with energy. My work in H & S Company is excellent. Miller has given me nearly a free hand in supply, and I am doing a good job. I am becoming a much better officer, too. We get plenty of mail. Dora's folks write at least once a day, and they send us so many packages that we don't know what to do with all the stuff. Dora and I want to have a baby. We tried the first time we went to bed together and have tried ever since. I am afraid she feels too well to be pregnant, but Dora is the kind of girl who could have a baby as easy as most people can blow their nose. So she might be pregnant after all. We don't think about the war. We know that the Allies are taking an awful beating right now, but we also know that they are going to come through in the end. So far, everything with Dora and me has worked out wonderfully well. We know that some day I am going to leave Ft. Bragg and that the chances are that it will be to go to some place where Dora won't be able to come. But we will worry about that when the time comes, just like the rest of the problems that have confronted us. The best thing about being married is being in love. Love is pretty good stuff before you're married, but if a man gets the right girl for himself, he doesn't know what love is until after he is married.

February 23, 1942, Indiantown Gap, Pennsylvania

Dearest Dora,

It isn't quite midnight; and if I wanted to, I could go to sleep right now; so you see I am really leading an easy life again. If you hadn't left Saturday afternoon, we would have had Saturday night and most of Sunday together, for at the last minute Miller, an enlisted man, and I were designated as a rear detachment to finish up some paper work. This was completed around 6 P.M., and we took off the next 24 hours recuperating from our hellish nightmare.

We left Fayetteville Sunday around 6 P.M. and had a very uncomfortable trip up here. The five hour wait in the Pennsylvania Station in Washington reminded me of my trip to New Orleans recently. Indiantown Gap is a beautiful place. It is cold—the coldest weather I have ever experienced—but it feels good. The rivers and mountain streams are frozen over, something very pretty to see. It's a shame to think how man wants to fight and kill when everything looks so clean and peaceful. We do not know how long we will be here. At first I had hoped that it would be a month or two, but apparently a day or two would have been a more accurate estimate. From here we go to New York. From there nothing is definite. It seems that we are part of a fairly large force sailing away on a construction job. Although there will be some infantry with us, they will serve as protectors. In other words, we are not going to make any kind of invasion or seek any trouble.

How was your trip home? I hope that it wasn't too tiresome. I bet you were glad to see your folks again, and I know that they almost ate you up. Are they happy to know you are going to have a baby? Gee, isn't that wonderful? I hope that it won't be too old before I get home. I guess we will all add a few gray hairs to our heads before this thing is over. Did the car and packages arrive safely? You did a wonderful job of handling all of that by yourself. Don't think I'm not proud of you.

It seems like a million years since I saw you last. Saturday when you came to the office, even though I looked at you, I don't believe I saw you. It was all like some horrid dream. I remember being happy cause you didn't cry and I walked away from the car briskly, but I could hardly make it to the H & S orderly room. It still seems like something unreal to me. Little girl, you know what I'd like you to do for me? I'd like you to send me a small wedding picture of us two, just about the size of the proofs. And I'd like you to send me that picture of you—you know, the one I like, the one I left in Raeford. You had better wait until I give you a definite address before you send it to me however, because right now you can only write to Ft. Bragg and hope that it will be forwarded. How does it feel to sleep until after the sun comes up? I bet that even though you may miss me, you won't miss getting up in the middle of the night to fix my breakfast. I guess your mama will see that you take good care of yourself. You had better, cause—well just because. The next few years aren't going to be happy ones, but we did crowd lots of happy years in our three weeks at Raeford and there's going to be lots of happy years after this war is over. So be good and keep a stiff upper lip, just like the way you did when I saw you last.

February 24, 1942

Expect to leave here for New York in a couple more days. Today is the first easy day in the past week and a half. There is a feeling of restlessness present throughout the Battalion. I have a suspicion that we will not sail to San Francisco from New York even though we are having our mail sent there. Our trucks are supposed to be en route to San Francisco now, but I believe that that is a "secret" which is supposed to leak out. Am well rested now and ready to move out. Everyone's nerves are tense.

No date (postmarked February 26, 1942)

Dearest Hymie,

I got your card from Washington this afternoon and your folks got your letter from yesterday. They were very anxious to hear from you so your letter was just what they wanted. I'm glad you got plenty of rest. You didn't look like a fresh daisy when I left you and I was hoping that you'd be able to sleep that night. I wish I would have known you weren't leaving that afternoon. I'd have waited until Sunday morning and maybe I'd have had a chance to really see you. I know you hardly knew what you were doing. But maybe it was better that we said goodbye really quick like that. I didn't have time to realize what happened. It all happened so quick.

I made good train connections and got home about 10 P.M. Sunday. I didn't wire or anything. I just came on home in a cab and I know I never saw more surprised people in all my life. I walked in on Aunt Shanie the next morning. I didn't call her first because I was afraid if I did I wouldn't have anyone to talk to when she heard my voice on the telephone. She was so dumbfounded that for a while she didn't realize what was happening. The hardest part was telling your dad all about it. I know it was a blow to him. All he does now is make more love to Tex. He's still got his dog. He keeps asking him, "Where's Hymie, boy? Where's Hymie?" And Tex's ears go way up and then he runs all around the house as if he's looking for you.

It's good to be home, little boy. Honestly I know there's one place I'll never miss and that's Raeford. There's only one thing I do miss about it and that's the happy days we had there. I think about them a lot now. I still feel as if you're very near to me, little boy, even though you're miles and miles away. Especially when I write you or hear from you. I hope that no matter how far away you'll go we'll always be able to hear from you cause when you're away like this I live for your letters. Well, good night for now, little boy. It's late and I'm sleepy. Write me soon and write me often. Take good care of yourself and remember, I love you.

February 27, 1942

Major Yoder joined the Battalion this morning as new C.O. [commanding officer], relieving Major Martin. Martin was doing a poor job—too big a task for an ex-insurance salesman. Hope Yoder will be better, but can't expect him to match up with Col. Pohl. All officers wish Pohl would come back, but the arrival of Yoder makes Pohl's return nearly impossible. It snowed this morning. I took control of the half-track awhile and enjoyed riding over rough country through snow and ice. Was very much moved by "The Star-Spangled Banner" during the review this afternoon. Tears flowed down my cheeks. Words had a lot of significance, "our loved homes."

No date (postmarked March 2, 1942)

Dearest Little Boy,

It seems as if everything happens to keep us further and further apart. I just came home and Momma told me you called this morning. God! I was never so disappointed in all my life! It seems every time I have a chance to see you or talk to you I always miss you. Its more than a person can stand. I think if you'd only call me again tonight. But I know you won't. Oh, little boy, I miss you so much. Honestly it's so hard not to. I have the darnedest luck. I'd have given my arm to have spoken to you this morning. Won't you ever, ever come to my arms to stay? I know I'm acting like a baby right now but I just can't help it, little boy. I just can't seem to be able to think of anything but my horrible luck. I went to Henderson's Point to forget about you a little. But that was so silly. There was everything at Henderson's Point to remind me of you. Every little corner; everything about every part of it reminded me of you and the fun we used to have there. I ignored all those little things, made myself enjoy myself in spite of all of that. And here I come home and find I could have spoken to you on the telephone, little boy. That's just one blow too many.

But you needn't worry, angelpuss, I'll be all right. Tomorrow I'll try to forget all about today—about this horrible nightmare. Try to forget about everything but that I have to take care of myself and of our little baby. I'm so happy every time I think about it, little boy. Honestly it's a wonderful thing for keeping my mind occupied. I've been walking three miles a day and eating meat once a day, at least a pint of milk, plenty of fresh fruits, and raw vegetables and all. And I can't wait til my baby starts getting big. I don't know what Momma means but she said you told her you wouldn't be able to write. I hope she misunderstood and that you will write just as soon and just as often as you can, and I hope that that will be often. Did you get the letters that I wrote you this past week? I addressed them to Fort Bragg and now that you've moved out so soon I hope that they'll be able to forward those letters all the way to San Francisco.

March 5, 1942, Brooklyn

Dearest Dora,

We are lying at anchor in New York and probably will not move out until tonight. I guess this letter—and all that follow—will be censored; so I don't know what to write. There are six of us crowded into a 12′ by 12′ room; and with all our baggage and equipment in here with us, there isn't much room to move around. And we are officers. The enlisted men don't live quite as comfortably. I just learned that you won't be able to get mail from me while the ship is at sea. So this will probably be the last time you will hear from me in a while. There's nothing to say. I can't write. So long, little girl. Be good. I surely love you. Don't know where we're going.

TWO

The Voyage to Australia

March 10–April 21, 1942

Because We Want It to Be

The little drop on the top of the wave,
bursting forth from the sea,
bursting forth from its watery grave,
must be filled with glee.
But I wonder how long that little drop stayed
down on the ocean floor;
and I wonder how long that little drop prayed
to see the light and air once more.
And why do you think it rose to the top
and splashed in ecstasy?
Because it was a patient drop
and wished the light to see.
For years you and I on Ponchartrain's wall[1]
have seen the Dipper[2] swing round,
have seen the dry Dipper come nearly to fall
and crash upon the ground.
But on deck last night as I watched the stars,
I saw it swinging fast
and work its way 'tween the ship's darkened spars
and quench its thirst at last.[3]
And why do you think it dipped down so low
and scooped water from the sea?
Because it wanted its thirst quenched so
and wished that it would be.
Why do you think there's a Heaven above?
Because man wants it to be.
And why do the flowers bloom forth in the Spring?
And the sun rise each day?
Because these are the things which happiness brings,

and people want it that way.
And how do I know, my dear little wife,
again together we'll be,
that together we'll be for the rest of our life?
'Tis 'cause we want it to be.

> —Aboard the *Santa Clara,* en route to
> Australia, March 10, 1942

April 4, 1942, at sea

Dearest Dora,

In another day or two we should be at our final destination. I don't know yet whether we will be permitted to say where we are, but I cannot see why anyone should want to keep that a secret; so I might as well tell you that we are landing at CENSORED, Australia. Believe me, I am going to be a happy man when I set foot on good solid earth again. You don't know what wonderful stuff the land you walk on is until you spend five weeks on a troop transport. It isn't pleasant by any means. However, I would be lying if I said that I have not had a lot of fun. I guess I ought to be ashamed of myself for saying this, but I do get a big kick out of seeing everybody gripe about everything. It is amazing to see how some people are unable to adapt themselves to trying conditions. The group which is the most amusing is the doctors. There are about 200 of them on board, and they are the sourest bunch of men I have ever seen. Of course they hate this kind of life. It is a lot different from what they planned to do. But they—oh, well, why talk about them? How are you, Stinky? You know what I'd like to do. I'd like to sneak up on you tonight while you're asleep, just to see you. Then I'd give you a good kiss; I'd be careful not to wake you. And then I'd be satisfied to go away. I guess that's pretty much to ask for however, and I'll have to content myself with just dreaming of you. No joke. I have reached the point where I look forward to going to sleep, for life is much more enjoyable in my dreams than while I am awake.

There is a major on board from Australia, and he informs us that we should be able to send night letters when we get there. I will send you one just as soon as we arrive if this is possible, but I have every reason to believe that it I will not be as easy as the major said it was. I am going to close this letter now, but I will add more to it later, perhaps tomorrow. After we are in Australia, there will be plenty of news to write about, and I will write often. I wish there was some way of telling you how much I love you besides words. They just weren't made to express the way I feel. So I won't fumble around with them. If you love me, take care of yourself; I know of no better way you could prove that you loved me. Oh, little girl, I miss you.

April 4, 1942

Dearest Little Boy,

Aunt Frieda celebrated her 50th birthday and I guess it wasn't as big a celebration as the previous ones. There were only 50 people there instead of the usual 100, but it was really beautiful. There was a sort of sad atmosphere. I mean everyone there could have been a little more lively.

April 5, 1942, aboard the Santa Clara

It is Easter morning. I am sure that the men will be wearing the same fatigue clothes that they have been wearing for the past five weeks instead of the new linen suits and white shoes they would be wearing back home. Yes, it is a little over five weeks that we have been aboard the *Santa Clara*, and in another day or two the voyage will be over. It hasn't been a very happy five weeks, but it has been the kind of time which always grows more interesting and enjoyable when one looks back upon it. It was, I believe, the first day of March that we left Indiantown Gap for New York City. Half the battalion was in our swaying and groaning old train. The other half was to follow a few hours behind in a similar relic of the Reading Line. Just a little while after dark we got off the train. We were on the Jersey Coast, and just across the Hudson lay Manhattan. Each man, loaded with full field equipment, about 60 pounds including his barracks bag, struggled along to the ferry boat which carried us out over the black waters. King and I hung over the rail at the bow of the ship and were thrilled at all we saw and with the momentous experience we were going through. We docked at some warehouse in Brooklyn and from there we boarded the *Santa Clara*. It is from that time to the present that I am going to write about.

Tugging at our barracks bag and clothing roll and groaning from the way our straps were cutting, King and I reached our stateroom. Actually it was no stateroom at all, just an old office formerly used by the ship's physician when the *Santa Clara* made pleasure trips. The room must have measured 12 by 12 feet and shared the bathroom with another stateroom which was even smaller than ours. Each of these rooms had six bunks: two piles of three. Kyle and Berlinger, two officers from the 576th dump truck company, had already moved in and had occupied the top bunks. Their clothing and equipment lay in a disorderly heap in the center of the floor. King's and mine were added to the pile and we immediately staked out claims on beds. A little later Eddy and Eardley, the remaining officers assigned to 96th came in. By this time, the pile of clothing and equipment in the center of the floor was half way to the ceiling, but that could be straightened out in the morning. We needed sleep! The toilet had been stopped up and the bath room was flooded. About 30 or 40 cigarette butts floated around in the water, and it was obvious when one opened the bathroom door that the workers who had been conditioning the ship for a troop transport had been urinating on the floor. As we wandered about the ship, more than our bathroom struck us as being downright stinky. In fact, the boat was no more than an unpleasant hole. We must have lain in New York harbor two or three days, during which time living accommodations were straightened out and we were adjusting ourselves to two meals a day. There is a big gap between breakfast and supper when the most entertaining thing one has to do is eat. There were a lot of old magazines and books aboard. These had been donated by the Red Cross, the U.S.O., the Jewish Welfare Fund, and so on. Many must have been collected five or six years ago, and the magazines made good historical reading. The only reading material I had brought on board was a pocket book of verse, probably thrown away by one of the colored boys of our outfit. That little book of poems has turned out to be my bible on this voyage.

The whole time we were in New York harbor we had to stay in our rooms and were supposed to keep all port holes closed. This was a precaution against the saboteurs on shore who might be interested in informing some enemy power that a troop convoy was just about to leave New York City. The seas were rather rough the day we left New York. After the ship cleared a certain island, I have forgotten its name, we were allowed on deck. Actually I had witnessed our coming through the submarine nets and mine fields from the port hole. But on deck is where we enjoyed a real thrill. Ships seemed to be coming from all directions. There were troop transports, destroyers, cruisers, two blimps, and airplanes. We zig-zaged so much that to this day I doubt that any of the movements were planned. It looked as if every ship was for itself. After a few hours the convoy took shape. It consisted of the following: our ship, the *Santa Clara*, flagship of the convoy, about a 12,000 ton craft, smallest and swiftest of the troop ships; the *Uruguay*, which I estimate was a 22,000 ton vessel, largest and ugliest boat of the convoy; the two sister ships, *Santa Paula* and

Santa Lucia, very handsome 18,000 ton steamers, and the *Panama*, a ship about the size of our own but with a strange silhouette. Our escort was heavy. There were two light cruisers, about a half dozen destroyers, and two blimps. Shortly after dark the blimps left the convoy and headed back for land. During the first night at sea, three more ships joined us. Two were freighters and the other was the *Hornet*, one of our new aircraft carriers. On the aft-A deck of the ship there had been placed about a hundred drums of gasoline. This constitutes as much a hazard to the safety of the ship as any German submarine. A careless person with a cigarette could cause this ship to be sent to the bottom. And if we should be attacked by an enemy airplane, his tracer bullets if they should strike the drums would beyond a doubt explode them. In order to avoid such a catastrophe, or at least attempt to avoid it, Company A was given the thankless job of furnishing a guard of two squads to be on hand at all times to toss over the drums if any emergency should arise. Officers were detailed from the 96th to be in charge of the guard: Humphries and I the first night we were at sea. He took the first four-hour shift from six til ten P.M. By ten o'clock, 75% of the ship's passengers were sea sick. Humphries just did make it down to the bathroom before losing his supper. When I went on duty at 10 P.M., there was an ugly old moon just above the water. The new guard relief did not show up. The men on the old relief were groaning as the ship rolled up and down. In a few more seconds, Sergeant Jenkins reported to me: "Sir," he said, "I can only get two men from my squad out."

"What do you mean only two men," I answered. "Get out your squad and get them out now!"

"Yes, sir," the ashen negro answered and left.

Half hour later he had still not returned. So I went after him myself. I found him, pale and nauseated, leaning over a sea-sick man whom he was trying to wake up. I could see that Jenkins wasn't going to be of much use to me, so I went to Sergeant [Lloyd H.] Smith, the first sergeant. Smith was as sick as the rest. I had to wade through vomit to get back to Jenkins. "Sergeant," I said, "You just show me your men and I'll get them out of bed."

We walked around and I gave a direct order to each man. These boys do understand the significance of a direct order from an officer and very few will ever disobey if it is humanly possible to do otherwise. In another 10 minutes they were at their posts, and the old guard was relieved. As I was explaining their duties and the method to be used in throwing over the drums, one man came close to vomiting in my face. Then I asked—it was a foolish question—how many were too sick for duty. They all gave some kind of indication that they were too ill. So I excused none. Then I made them start walking from one end of the ship to the other. I had heard that this was good for seasickness. But they groaned and grumbled and vomited. It was a pathetic sight, but I had to laugh anyway.

I was enjoying the heavy seas. It was my first time on the ocean. After a few days at sea, morale became bad and nearly everyone was quarrelsome. No one knew, or at least those who did know wouldn't say, just where we were going. Most rumors indicated that we were going to Australia by way of the Cape of Good Hope. This seemed fantastic to me. I thought Central America, perhaps South America, would be as far as we would go. I felt more sure of my predictions when I observed that we were traveling towards Panama. On March 11th, we pulled into Cristobal to take on fuel and water. No one was permitted to get off the ship, and peddlers were chased from the pier when they approached to sell fruit. There was grumbling among the men, and once they threw a barrage of banana peelings at a M.P. when he chased away a man who was selling them bananas. Naturally this sort of thing cannot be tolerated in the army, but I did think it was amusing.

The trip through the Panama Canal was an educational experience, and part of it was beautiful to look upon. We docked in Balboa while the remaining ships came through the Canal. Here we were allowed to go ashore for a few minutes, and we bought everything we could get our hands on. I should have said that the officers were allowed to go ashore, for none of the enlisted men have been permitted to set foot on terra firma since we left New York. The Pacific side of the Canal is very picturesque. There seems to be a thousand islands scattered around, obviously the tops of some sunken hills and mountains. There were no guns visible on these islands, but my guess is that they carry some of the world's biggest guns. And then we entered the Pacific, where we were met and accompanied by the cruiser the *Richmond*. For three days we sailed on a sheet of glass. Here entered a period of bridge, checkers, chess, poker, blackjack, reading—anything but thinking. I find that thinking of home at a time like this is the worst form of torture that I can subject myself to. It was hot, and we took long sunbaths. We all had nice coats of tan within a week. Some few got too much sunning and were sick. We exercised on deck and in all we led a fairly decent existence. Our escort now was small, only a cruiser and a destroyer. It is an impressive ship. Incidently, the two freighters were no longer with us when we left Panama.

On the morning of the 25th, land was in sight. To me it looked like a dreamland. Jagged mountains rose vertically from out the sea. The waters within the coral reef that surrounded the island were every shade of blue and green imaginable. I will not type the name of the island here, for it is a strict military secret. Although no one was allowed to go ashore, we were permitted to go swimming. Berlinger and I swam an hour and a half without resting. I was surprised at the excellent physical shape I was in. The natives came around the ships trying to sell things, but they asked ridiculous prices. All they knew was, "Two bucks" and "No." The only things they had to sell were bananas and coconuts, so there weren't many business transactions carried on. It gave me somewhat of a thrill to know that the name of the cruiser which met and accompanied us from here was the *New Orleans*.

We are now at journey's end. Within the next 24 hours—it may be only several hours—we shall be in sight of Brisbane, Australia. What our job in Australia will be we do not know. I hope that it will be constructive and that we will be kept really busy. If the rest of our wartime experiences are no worse than this journey, I shall be a happy man. And if this thing does not last too long, say, over 18 to 24 months, and that isn't an unreasonable dream, I think that it will all be good experience and should add a lot of interest to the rest of my life.

April 8, 1942, off the eastern Australian coast

It was on the morning of the 6th of April that we sighted Australia, just 25 years to the day that the United States had entered the War to end all wars. Australia's coast just south of Brisbane is not at all inviting, and I could not help think of the first settlers who had come but 150 years before. It took nerve to try to establish a colony on such a barren coast. Everything seems poached under the merciless sun. The sandy beaches were tireless and the distant, crooked peaks looked as if they were saying, "Stay away." But no one had set foot on land since Panama (and most of us not since New York), and here before us lay a piece of the solid stuff nearly the size of the United States; so no matter how barren it might try to pretend to be, we were happy to see it. It was to be our home for a long time!

As I strolled about the boat deck, I caught the sound of what might be a radio. Yes, there it was—a radio! I knew all along that I had missed the radio very much, but I didn't dream that it would sound quite so good when I heard it again. There was some one playing a piano sonata; and although I had not heard it before, it was beautiful.

The announcer was a woman, and I could not understand her English. She seemed to speak much too fast, and her voice sounded like a recording which is pushed around rapidly on a Victrola. Our route through the bay outside of Brisbane and up into the river was like a serpent's trail. Evidently the harbor had been carefully mined, and no one, unless he knew the proper course, had much of a chance to get through. Brisbane looked pretty from the boat. We crowded the rail. Our equipment and clothing were all assembled, and we were ready to debark. At last we were at journey's end. There was no telling what lay ahead, but that didn't matter. Then came a message. The 96th and the 576th were not to get off the boat! It had been a terrific anticlimax, and morale fell through the floor. Men had to carry their clothing and equipment back to their quarters; everyone had to return to the life which he had endured for five weeks and had hoped to be leaving.

What was the hardest blow of all was that I was appointed mess officer. The medical officers were getting off at Brisbane and the "old" mess officer was one of the Medicos. I had to take his place. It was a hectic night. Supper was late, for the kitchen had closed down, thinking that we would have supper on shore, and everyone was griping. The M.P.'s had got off the boat also; so there were none of them to help me manage the disorderly mess lines. But by 11 o'clock all 1600 men were fed and the mess hall had been straightened up. I went back to my room, where I fell across the bed and slept. I was glad that I had been extra busy; for if I hadn't been, I would have joined the other officers in griping about not being able to go ashore. Next morning we found out that because of the transfer of many of the troops aboard the *Santa Clara* to the shore and because of the transfer of certain troops to the ship, the entire cargo would have to be unloaded on the dock and then reloaded again. This would be at least a three day job, and the troops on the boat would not only be in the way but would be in danger of being hurt by the swinging booms. So an order was issued stating that all the troops would go ashore to be taken on hikes. We were unable to turn them loose in Brisbane, for already there had been a lot of trouble with negro soldiers in that city. However this setup meant that the officers would have the opportunity to go ashore in shifts.

Eddy and I left the boat about 10:30. Solid ground felt wonderful. There were camphor and chinaberry trees which reminded me a lot of good old New Orleans. I was seized with a feeling of happiness and loneliness all at the same time. On the corner where we waited for the tram (that is what street cars are called in Australia) there was a scale graduated in pounds and "st's." We never did figure out what a "st" [stone] was; all we knew was that 14 pounds were equal to one "st," a shining example of English simplicity. The tram ride to town was a lot of fun. There were no sides to the tram, and people got on and off at any point. Then the conductor walked around, picking up the carfare, which was two pence. We had nothing but American money, and it took a couple of minutes to figure out how much Australian change we should get for the quarter we handed him. Driving on the left hand side of the street was a constant bother to me. I am afraid that it would take a long time for me to learn to drive in a place like this. I had about $25 in my pocket, and I didn't care whether I had a penny of it left when I returned to the ship. First I stopped in a place to buy some sun glasses. The man explained that they were "dinkum" Wilsonite and that they cost—oh, about $1.50 in American money. I thought the word "dinkum" was a particular make of glass put out by Wilsonite and associated it with the word "dinky" which I have always used to describe something which was not very good.

"Why do they call the glasses Dinky?" I asked.

I was surprised to learn that the word dinkum meant genuine in Australian slang. This salesman spoke to us about half an hour. He was interesting, but so would any other Australian be. A little old dried-up Australian soldier came up to us. It was evident that he had been drinking.

"I say there," he started, "Are you entitled to a salute?"

"Yes sir, I think we are," Eddy answered.

"That's all I wanted to know," the little man replied.

He saluted us, nearly losing his balance and falling over. We stopped in a beer joint for some of that delicious beer which we had longed for so much while we were in the Torrid Zone. It was tasty but not very cold. We bought cake and candy and ate 'til our stomachs could hold no more. Then we dropped into a cafe for a bite to eat. We were acting the part of a couple of gluttons. But who wouldn't after the tasteless food we had been eating on the ship. Two girls sat at our table. As they gave their order to the waitress, it sounded as if they were speaking some foreign language. All of the Australians seemed to speak too fast and slur their words mercilessly. Finally we got into a conversation, and they proved to be delightful company. Eddy and I regretted that we could not accept the invitation to have supper with them at one of the girl's homes, but we were both on duty at night. We met about a half dozen other people and with all of them we had a lot of fun with money transactions.

The people are all friendly and seem to appreciate the arrival of the American soldiers. They seemed to look at America as a dreamland with more respect and admiration than for their own England. The men were a sturdy lot, not handsome but truly masculine. The women were thin and unattractive. They looked like good, honest people who would not want to harm anyone. They seemed to be very happy. Pure democracy existed everywhere.

Brisbane, Australia, 11 P.M.: It seems that this is not our final destination after all. Only the medical officers are getting off. Rumor has it that we going to Townsville, 800 miles up the coast. There should be a lot going on there. War news in the Brisbane paper seems favorable for the Allies. At least the Japs have not been making any enormous gains the way they did during the first two months of the war. Our troops on Bataan are making quite a name for themselves— wonderful work!

And now we are on our way to Townsville. The trip will carry us through a lot of islands and we may even get to see some of the Great Barrier Reef. Some of the fellows even believe that we going to see some of the Japs. I doubt it.

April 8, 1942, on the way to Townsville

Pulled out about 2 A.M. There might be some excitement. Much bridge tonight.

Hello, little girl. I dreamed about you a lot last night so that now I feel like telling you hello just as if we were never apart. Dreams are wonderful things, aren't they? We were in CENSORED for 30 hours or so, and the officers were allowed off the boat for a few hours. It was a very interesting experience. We are now making a short trip to our final destination. I say a "short trip" only when compared to the vast distance we have covered during five weeks aboard a fast-going steamer. It is in a far-removed, safe place and unless there is plenty of work, I am afraid we will be bored to death.

How have you been making out doing the jobs of both husband and wife? I guess there must be a lot of little things coming up which keep you more than busy. This coming summer won't be very pleasant either, but I hope you won't be too uncomfortable; and then after the baby does come, you ought to have enough to keep you busy. I really think that that will help. I do miss you an awful lot, but this cannot go on for long—perhaps another 18 months, maybe two years—but then, oh boy! Just think of the good times we'll have. We will take that honeymoon which we once planned and then a lot more. It is things like this that add variety to life and make it spicy and interesting. So let's just sit tight and wait 'til this is all over. Then we will have a big time.

April 10, 1942, Townsville

Ship is being unloaded. Tomorrow we debark and move inland. There will be many officers awake all night. My job is attending to the mess. Have to see to it that every man has a noonday lunch. Hear that Japs have taken Bataan. That is sad news. Got in a crap game this morning and lost around $15 — every penny I had. For some reason it made me feel awfully depressed. I couldn't even buy a box of matches now. This is barren looking country here.

April 11, 1942, Oonoonba, Australia

Am in command of H & S Company in absence of Miller and Hering. They had to remain on boat to help supervise unloading. This is a beautiful woodland. Many strange trees and birds. Also snakes, so the men told me. I told them that they were not poisonous (I don't know) and that they should sleep on the ground anyway. There was no alternative. Sgt. Lewis did a good job in getting supper prepared. We all enjoyed it after a hard day and no food since breakfast.

April 12, 1942

Working hard. Miller and Hering still away. Company is in good shape but Battalion is not so well off. Wish they would give me a free hand in segregating supplies. Had officers meeting today; principal topic of discussion was schedule of command car which is to carry officers to and from town. It seems that the only thing Yoder worries about is the morale of the officers. And he has the idea that the way to build up their morale is to let them go to town whenever they desire, including duty hours, and buy and drink all the alcoholic beverages they can. He seems to believe that the Battalion will run without officers. Fortunately for him, he stepped into a well-organized, smoothly running outfit. At the present rate, it will be a wreck in another month. He seems to be living just as if we will all be dead two weeks from now. Perhaps he knows something I don't know.

April 13, 1942

Tired and disgusted. Wish Miller and Hering were here. Hardly any officers around and Battalion Supply in awful mess. H & S Company is in good shape. Rumor that we are to move out soon.

April 14, 1942

Miller and Hering out here at last. Things were really buzzing all day. Company A was attached to us for labor assistance. These companies of 283 men are huge outfits.

April 14, 1942

Dearest Dora,

I wish I could write a good letter which wouldn't have to be censored. But I can't. We have been working hard—that is, some of us are, but others—well, I can't say. It is a funny thing how some men crack up at a time like this and are willing to let everything go to hell. But I had better say no more! The Australians are a wonderful group of people. They are friendly and kind, more like Americans than you would ever imagine. On my birthday I was riding down the streets of one of these towns. I was in the front of the lorry and it was filled with troops. The people of the town cheered as we drove by, but I was down in the dumps, for there was no mail from home yet. The truck slowed down at a crossing. A girl on the side of the road looked at me and shouted, "Thumbs up, soldier!" She seemed to have her whole heart in it. It made me feel better for the rest of the day. I would like to describe this place to you, for it is very beautiful; but that is prohibited.

I love you, sweetheart. It seems that we have been apart so long already that you seem like a dream. In fact, all my life except that with the Army seems like a dream. That with the army is like a nightmare. I love you.

April 15, 1942

Company B attached to us. Lot of work accomplished. Major Yoder still not around and morale is dropping. Officers are griping and wishing Col. Pohl was back. There is no doubt that Yoder is a very entertaining talker if he would shut up after 10 or 15 minutes of his machine-gun gab and I must admit that he makes no pretence to cover up his foolish habits. But he should realize that he is the head of more than 1200 men and that he bears a marked influence on them all. Captain Behrens is no better than Major Yoder.

April 17, 1942

I was O.C. [officer in charge] Wednesday night and had to go to town to see about a fight. Over 100 of our men had been rounded up by white soldiers armed with bayonets and loaded guns. A corporal thrust a cocked rifle at me when I stopped his truck and gave instructions to his negro "prisoners" on the back of it. After this I loaded my own revolver. It is a dirty shame the way the white American soldiers treat our boys. The Australians are wonderfully tolerant, but the Americans, especially the Southern boys, are a problem. The only solution will be to send our battalion away from any town.

Yesterday, King and I went to Townsville to get paid. Afterwards we dropped in for a glass of beer before dinner. From four o'clock on everything is very vague. King says we had 15 or 20 glasses of beer. I remember lying on a lawn watching the Pacific; then there were two girls. They wanted souvenirs from us. One got away with one of my shoulder bars. I remember talking with a war correspondent in the Queens Hotel. I told him about the problem between the white and colored soldiers. All of the rest is very vague.

Later: Just heard news broadcast from Tokyo. It was in English. It was very democratic, very much like our own news broadcasts. They followed with some classical music. Music is wonderful stuff. It's beautiful even when played by the Japs.

April 18, 1942

Because of the fight the other night, the colored boys are not allowed in town. In order to give them some recreation, we planned a movie and beer party this evening. It was a horrible flop. We had bought only 1200 quarts of beer, less than one bottle per man, and of this we sold less than 25%. The men were for the most part broke. And even those who had money didn't like this kind of recreation. They want to be free, to be with a woman. The movie was a flop. The sound was poor, the films were old and the attendance was small. You can't force recreation on a man. It just doesn't work.

April 20, 1942

We moved 10 or 15 miles inland today. Camped on the banks of the Ross River, altogether dry now. We have a very picturesque place. It is pathetic how helpless the staff officers are. Morale is getting worse and worse. I thought that after we got off the boat, we would all work together, but instead everyone seems to be getting more and more selfish, less cooperative, and more unpleasant. Yoder is not around. Believe he has flown to New Guinea on a reconnaissance. Happy we are going forward, not back.

April 21, 1942

Battalion busy constructing runway for airfield. I am to fly to New Guinea tomorrow with two squads of men. I am to be "advanced" supply officer for the Battalion. Company B, Company D, and H & S are to follow in a few days by boat. Company A and Company C are to remain in Australia, attached to 46th Engineers. Williams and Behrens are taking command of these companies from Palick and Schwalbert—a very awkward situation, especially for Schwalbert who has been C.O. of C Company since the 96th was first organized. I imagine I'll be transferred to either B or D as soon as the Battalion is in New Guinea.

THREE

Port Moresby, Papua New Guinea

April 23–June 17, 1942

April 23, 1942, Port Moreseby

Company D furnished me with their two worst squads yesterday morning. I did a splendid job in getting the squads in shape. First I made them line up. Sgt. Tolliver reported two men absent. I made him find his missing men.

"How many men are not armed?" I asked.

Four men held up their hands.

"Lt. Matheson," I said, "I desire that these men be issued rifles immediately."

I could see that he was embarrassed. He turned to Mouron and told him to issue rifles. Then I called off the list of equipment which each man should have. Whenever a man did not have what I called off, I stopped and saw to it that he obtained that article. When they were equipped satisfactorily, I called them to attention in a forceful voice, faced them to the right and had them march off. Two hundred yards down the road, I halted the squads and addressed them briefly: "My name is Lt. Samuelson. You will be assigned to me until you again join your company. You are going out on an important mission, and every man must put forth his best at all times. You will obey my orders like that." I snapped my fingers. "And the orders of your squad leaders will be similarly obeyed. You made a poor exhibition a few minutes ago in getting ready for this move. Such slow, unsoldierly action will not be tolerated."

When we got to the wharf my two squads got off the lorries so quickly and formed in ranks that we motored out to the first plane, leaving Capt. Thomas and his two squads to catch the second plane. Apparently, I am the only American Army officer in Port Moresby.

The town has been evacuated. Wreckage from Japanese air raids lies everywhere, although none of it looks serious. There are a few damaged planes lying around. The stores have been stripped, probably by vandals after the evacuation. I enjoyed the evening drinking and smoking with Australian Air Force men in the grass hut across the way. Capt Thomas and his 20 men have not arrived yet. I hear that they have had engine trouble and were delayed. I hope it is nothing worse than that.

12:30 P.M.:   I placed two squads of men in the woods, one at each end of the bay to unload some bombs from trucks. Then I went to the ship where the bombs were being unloaded. The captain invited me aboard for a cup of tea. I was sitting at the table when the alert was given.

"That's an air raid," the captain said, "We'll have to make a dash out of here. You can stay with the ship or—"

"I'll go ashore," I interrupted. I climbed up the hill to a slit trench. There were some Australian soldiers there. In fact, I haven't seen another American soldier here.

"There they are!" shouted one.

Yes—eight bombers. Our anti-aircraft guns went into action—a beautiful sight. It must take a lot of nerve to keep such a perfect formation with all those explosions around you. Then the bombs. We were way off to the side, so there was no danger to us. Our P-40s closed in on the bombers. They faded out of sight. I hear the bombs tore up the runway at the seven mile port. Guess we will move there next to repair the damage.

Later: Thomas has arrived with 20 more men. Thomas says the reason I am here is that Major Yoder thinks I'm his best lieutenant, "So capable of meeting any situation," as he puts it.

What a joke! I didn't believe Yoder knew I existed. I'd like to hear the same compliment from a man whom I thought more of.

April 24, 1942

Thomas and I are on an all day reconnaissance. This is beautiful country. The mountains make one feel so small and insignificant. Man! So wise and yet so foolish! The Japs had a good day of it. They got a Catalina in the harbor and a couple of our Kittys. We *think* we got one Zero.[1] What a score!

April 25, 1942

The Australians are wonderfully hospitable, but a bigger bunch of blundering fools I have never seen, as far as fighting a war is concerned. They will promise to give you anything at any time and at any place, but you will get nothing. When you make any kind of requisition, they will get on the phone, call somebody who is denoted by a long series of letters, then send you half way across New Guinea where so-and-so will take care of you. When you find so-and-so, he will look amazed, "Must be a mistake. You will have to go see _____ at _____." And then the rat race begins. I became darn rude when I had trouble procuring food and shovels—such necessities—and probably made a bad impression on the Aussies.

"I don't know whether you have too much red tape or whether you simply won't cooperate," I old Mr. Weber, the RAAF mess officer. I got everything I wanted.

May 4, 1942

Last Monday night we had a party at the officers' mess which I shall never forget. It seems there were two chaps who were leaving the next day on the *Taruna* for Australia, and the drinking went heavier than ever in wishing them bon voyage, good luck, and so on. Before 9:30 the whole lot of us was stinky drunk, all the way from Colonel Pitt down to me, the lowest ranking officer here. Then followed one of the most entertaining evenings I have ever witnessed. Everyone had to do something in the line of entertainment. Some officers played the piano, others sang, one told of his escape from Rabaul, another improvised poetry, beautiful stuff, too. There were native dances, mock speeches of Hitler, Mussolini and Konoye. Major McKenzie played the mouth organ. Some of the fellows, for their part in the show, led the rest of us in song. The party grew wilder and wilder. We danced and sang: American songs, Russian songs, Scotch tunes. Then we joined hands, sang and danced around the room, up over chairs and tables. There was a messy heap of broken bottles and glasses, bruised arms and legs, cigarette butts, sweat, song, and laughter. Then we got up, very solemnly sang "God Save the King" and concluded the evening with "The Star Spangled Banner." This was around 1 A.M. and Thomas and I stayed up another hour discussing plans for the next day when the *Taruna* was arriving with over 600 of our men and 650 tons of cargo, all of which had to be cleared from the ship during the night.

The next day shall long be remembered. I made the plans for unloading the ship, wrote them up, placed the road guides, etc. Heavy rains made most of the roads impassable, and I had to cover a lot of ground on foot, walking through mud up to my knees. That night we worked, right on through 'til dawn, in a cloudburst of rain. I had placed D company on the job while B company tried to get some rest. At dawn D company was dismissed and allowed to retire in the deserted Papau Hotel. They had done a good job, for as I drove out to Six Mile [airdrome] to pick up B company, I saw the *Taruna* putting out to sea in the gray dawn. The next day I worked with company B, assorting and distributing equipment from the Sports Grounds to the various sites of the companies. I finally went to sleep at midnight. I hadn't had a wink of sleep for 42 hours, but the job had been done well, and I was happy over the success which resulted from my planning. Five hours sleep that night was sufficient to keep me on the go the next day. We were handicapped by lack of transportation, bad roads, and the Japs were becoming a bloody nuisance with their ground strafing.

Now everything is in pretty decent shape. Miller and Hering are still in Townsville, and again I am in charge of H & S company. Incidently, Col. Yoder (He received his promotion the other day) told me that I am to be transferred to Company D. I told him I would rather be assigned to fly one of these Cobras than serve under Matheson, and followed with what I thought of Matheson: the same thing I told Matheson to his face the day before. Yoder seemed displeased with what I had to say, but I don't give a damn. I like to work under a man, regardless of how mean and ornery he may be. I don't want to take orders from a spoiled, selfish, uncooperative kid.

The other day 27 Cobras arrived and we have been giving the Japs hell ever since. He still comes over, however. A thousand American troops, Anti-Aircraft Artillery and Engineers, arrived last night.

May 16, 1942

Miller and Hering have been in for 10 or 12 days, and there hasn't been much rest for anyone since their arrival, for they brought up with them the equipment with which we could go to work: trucks, graders, bulldozers, scrapers, tractors! All of it was purchased from Australian contractors, and most of it is fit for the junk pile. But we have been keeping at least half of it in operation, and have been accomplishing a reasonable amount of work. I have been called out to do various little engineering jobs, and all have turned out very

successful. Yoder apparently is giving me my way and not transferring me to D Company. Instead he has made me "heavy equipment"
officer, and I am in charge of road construction around here. I draw
men from Company D as I need them. It is a wonderful setup for me,
although I know Matheson's feelings must be hurt! But I am accomplishing a lot, putting in a half mile road in a day with only two
squads and headquarters seems well pleased. Mail came in the day
before yesterday. It was the greatest thrill of my life. The Japs sent 26
bombers over the day before yesterday, but they did such a poor
showing, dropping all the bombs into the sea, that I believe they all
committed mass harikari, for none came over yesterday or today.
Willie Hering didn't hear from his wife. Poor fellow gets some tough
breaks.

May 17, 1942

Came as close to being shot today as I ever hope to come. I had just
checked my squads and made sure that they and the equipment were
off the road we were building. I started walking back to our mess tent
where our telephone is so that I could get the "all clear" as soon as the
Japs had gone. Along the way I stopped to watch a dog fight which
was taking place a few miles over. Suddenly I heard a plane diving —
that unpleasant drone of the Zero engine. I turned around and saw
two Jap planes swooping down on our road. I jumped off the road
and rolled into the grass. As I did, the machine guns opened up. The
shadow of the first plane passed over me. Then came the second
plane. For another second or two I held my breath, hoping I could
shrivel up to the size of a dime. I lay there for five minutes after the
planes had passed over. Then up and back to work.

May 18, 1942

Thirty-three bombers today, and for the first time Bomana Drome
[airstrip] was bombed. It sounded as if hell had broken loose, for the
Japs' aim was good and he caught us flat-footed. He wrecked two of
our planes, a tractor and a road grader. Thank God no one was hurt.
Our camp is too near the drome and there are bound to be some
casualties. The amount of sickness in the Battalion is growing. That
can be expected, I guess.

May 20, 1942

Because our last "decent" grader was wrecked in the last bombing, I have had to build some road machinery. I built a scarifier, a drag, and a roller. It all turned out very nicely. I am anxious for the boys to finish putting material on the road so that we can use our new "machinery." I was much surprised at Sgt. Gates when he told me he couldn't build this equipment. When a sergeant tells me he cannot do a thing, I can think of only two excuses: either my order was unreasonable or the sergeant is incompetent. By making his squad do the job anyway, I proved that my order had been reasonable. Matheson simply has his men spoiled. He has no idea of how men should be handled.

May 24, 1942

Major McKenzie much pleased with my road construction around here. So is Major Martin. They both stink as far as I'm concerned. Right now I am putting in concrete slabs for the showers and for the men to do laundering. It is fun to be kept busy.

May 25, 1942

Had our first night air raid a few minutes ago. It was a colorful spectacle.

May 29, 1942

Tuesday there was an order that came out attaching me to Company B with two squads from Company D. My job, I found out Tuesday night, was the construction of some houses for the air corps. My material consisted only of wreckage from Yankeyville. The Company B officers laughed at me for they knew I had drawn a nasty assignment. But tonight, just three days later, I have completed one hut (20 feet x 16 feet) and have set the foundation for another. I hope to be able to complete one hut every two days. It is interesting work and the men seem to enjoy it. The Japs were over Tuesday and Wednesday nights but left us alone last night. But a deluge of rain was most disconcerting. It caused my shelter roof to fall in and dump no less than ten gallons of sky juice onto my bed. Talk about a mess! I ran over to the B Company officers' hut, yanked a blanket off King's bed, and went to sleep on the floor for the rest of the night. It's raining like hell tonight again. I'm in the officers' hut. Hope my tent doesn't fall down.

May 30, 1942

Still raining. Everything bogged down. Mouron's bridge over the Lakki washed out. He should have used piles instead of sills on the bottom of the river. Some of these brass hats around here can't see further than their nose. Water is water in peace or war, and if you want a bridge to hold, you have to design a foundation as well as the superstructure. Wish I'd get the job of putting in that bridge. Incidently, my housing project is coming along very nicely, and I believe we can easily reach our goal of a house every two days.

May 31, 1942

Homesick this evening. It is the first time I have been so homesick since I left the States. I guess the main reason is that I received five letters and a couple of pictures from Dora. One of the pictures was our wedding picture; the other was that picture of her which I have liked so much always and which I have always carried with me. I haven't written much in my diary about her but my mind is on her night and day.

A Town for the Bomber Crews

On May 26 there came out of Headquarters an order attaching me and two squads from D company to company B. There was a special job to be done. I found out that evening what the job was. It was the construction of a little village southeast of Seven Mile Drome to accommodate the bomber crews which came in during the late afternoon from Townsville and who stayed over until dawn before taking off on their bombing missions. Dellavia had started the job. He had had permission to tear down the buildings at Murray Barracks and was reassembling them again at the new camp site. But after tearing down two buildings, he got word that he would have to stop, that Murray Barracks were to be occupied again by some of the infantry troops arriving almost daily in Port Moresby from Australia. He would have to get his material from the wrecked buildings of bomb-shattered Yankeytown. Yankeytown was a little settlement of a score of buildings located at the northwest end of Seven Mile Drome. It had taken a terrible beating from Japanese bombings. Not a single building stood in condition to be used as such, and wreckage lay everywhere. This was the material which Dellavia had to use to construct a new town, large enough to accommodate two hundred people. And it was at this point of the game that I was called in. I knew I had a problem on my hands just to keep the man straightened out.

"You've got a helluva job," Mark told me, and he couldn't help laughing.

I went out to the site of the work that evening for I wanted to get an early start in the morning. I wanted to prove to the fellows at B company that I was a real engineer. The material which had been hauled from Yankeytown did not look nearly as bad as they had described it. There were a lot of two by fours, and many sections of walls had been delivered in good condition; these could be used just as they were. The principal job before me was to get the material sorted out in order to find out just what I did have to work with. We went to work the first day on two trucks. I called Sergeant Gates over to me and gave him his orders.

"Do you see that pile of wreckage? Your squad will start sorting it into neat piles. I want all lumber of the same kind put into the same pile. In other words, stack all your four by fours over there, and your two by fours over there, and your two by sixes under those trees. I also want the stacks to contain lumber of the same length. Do you understand? All right, then go to it."

Then I called sergeant Williams over and told him that his squad would start work on the first house immediately.

"I will work right along with you but I want you to pay strict attention to what we do, for on the next house that we build, you will have to work by yourself."

We laid out a foundation for a 20' x 16' building, just a one-room affair but large enough to hold eight or ten men. It took us two and a half days to complete the building. That is, our job was complete. The local Natives still had to put grass on the roof and sides. Next day I made the two squads swap jobs and stayed with Sergeant Gates's group while they built their house. At the end of five days' work two houses were finished. Each squad had built one. In addition to this we had a rather nice "Lumber yard" on the site from the work which the squads had done in sorting the wreckage. Next day I called my two sergeants together and told them, "You have each put up one house. Altogether we have to build about sixteen of these houses. That means that each of your squads has to build about eight houses. I want them all built similar to the first two that we built. I am turning you loose on your own. I will be in the area to help you out if you run into a snag, but I will not interfere with your work unless you ask me to. About two or three times a day I will come around and inspect your work; and if it does not meet with my approval, I'll make you tear it down and do it over again. In addition to your job of building houses, Gates, your squad will unload all lumber coming in on Smith's truck; and, Williams, your squad will unload all lumber coming in on Harper's truck. Are there any questions? O.K. Now let's see what you can do on your own." I might mention the fact that during these first five days we had an air raid alert almost daily. This caused us to lose no less than an hour's work each day. We had two night raids, which were disconcerting; and we were harassed by heavy downpours of rain.

Well, Williams did very well by himself. He got his house completed in two days, and the work was entirely satisfactory. But Gates fell down on the job. I had to have him tear down his roof rafters, for they were up horribly crooked; and when he finally did complete the house (after three days work) the building could almost be shoved over by hand. His men were griping and arguing back at him. They were pretty much out of control. I thought I'd have a talk with Gates.

"Sergeant," I said, "I am not at all pleased or satisfied with your squad. It seems to me to be a disorganized bunch of men without a leader. Now what do you plan to do about it?" "But, sir, they won't listen to me. They won't do what I tell them."

"I know that; that's what I'm telling you. And if they won't listen to you, their squad leader, to whom in the devil do you think they are going to listen?"

"Sir, I'd rather go back to camp and get another squad. I can't do anything with these men."

"Talk sense, sergeant. What squad would you go back to camp to get? Those men are your squad. It's up to you to make them work and listen to you. And when a sergeant fails to produce results from his men, we don't get new men for him; we get a *new sergeant* for those men."

"Lieutenant, I'd rather be a private than have to work with these fellows. But I don't know of anybody in the squad who could act as squad sergeant."

"I think you are the best man in the squad. All you have to do is convince the other men in your squad that you are. Now how are you going to do that?"

"I don't know, sir."

"Damn it, sergeant. What do you mean you don't know? I'll tell you what you should do. First thing tomorrow morning, line 'em up.

Give 'em hell for being so slow to get in formation, and then you tell 'em somethin' like this: 'I have you lined up this morning 'cause, I'm not pleased with the way you men have been working. From now on, when we're out on the job, you will do exactly as I tell you—yes, even if it's wrong. If you have any suggestions to make about the work, then make them. If I like your suggestion, we'll use it; if I don't like it, we won't use it. And that'll be the end of it. There'll be no arguing at all. Understand? We're going to work as a team, and we're going to get a lot done. And I'm going to be captain of the team. And you fellows are going to do just as I say. There's a lot of nasty jobs around here; and for those of you who don't want to play ball with this team— well, I'll just turn them over to the lieutenant; and he'll see that they get some of these nasty jobs. Now do you all have the set-up clear in mind? All right, then get on the truck and let's go to work'. Now, sergeant, if you tell them something like that, make them know who is boss, you'll see how they are going to listen to you."

The next house which sergeant Gate's squad put up was the best one on the whole job; and from then on there was no doubt as to who was boss in his squad. Altogether we put up seven little houses. Dellavia's men put up three. There were also the two large buildings from Murray Barracks and four completely native huts. We installed running water for the bath and kitchen, constructed concrete seats for the kettles in which mess kits are washed, built a grease-and-grit trap, installed over a thousand feet of drainage pipe in order to keep the area sanitary, and built a three-room concrete bath house which was the pride of the job. Actually, I had very little trouble from any of the men. When I left B company this morning to return to H & S all that Mark had to say was, "Sammy, you surely did do a damn good job."

But that didn't mean too much, for the job has drawn favorable comment from everyone, all the way down from General Brett to the Natives working on the job.

June 7, 1942

Food situation is rather critical. It seems that troops are coming in a lot faster than food. Consequently the ration is being cut again and again. This is a typical day's menu: breakfast—bread, jelly, cheese, and coffee, for those who can drink the stuff; lunch—bread, butter, salmon; dinner—bread, butter, canned stew or beans and canned peaches or foul-tasting bread pudding for dessert. That isn't much to keep a man going. Thank heavens we don't have much of an appetite.

June 8, 1942

It is almost a week since the Japs have been over, and the last couple of times he has come, we beat him back before he got over the drome. Only once since his 33 bomber raid has he been over during the daytime with bombers; and those bombs he dropped aimlessly into the sea. The field has dried up sufficiently to "take" our bombers, and 19 are on the drome this evening to take off at dawn and give the Japs a bit of hell in the morning. Our P-39s and P-400s are around here as thick as the mosquitoes, and they are really playing hell with the Zeros, whenever the Jap does decide to come over. Also more troops are pouring in. Perhaps there is a turn for the better.

June 9, 1942

Good news comes in about the battle of Midway Islands. Probably our claims are grossly exaggerated, just as in the Coral Sea Battle, but no doubt the Japanese Navy did take another beating. The Russians seem to be holding their own, too. England's 1,000 bomber raids over Germany are helping some, but won't win the war. She has to make a landing on the continent and push the Germans from the west while the Russians entertain the Huns on the east. I guess England is waiting for the U.S. to start its drive against Japan. That will come by way of Dutch Harbor, Kamchatka . . . Tokyo!

June 10, 1942

It feels good to put in a full day's work—before six in the morning until after six in the evening. With our scarce supply of materials it isn't an easy matter to construct a 70 foot bridge. We are making seven to ten foot spans, and there will be only a single stringer under each wheel. We do have some nice 12 x 8 for the stringers but only a very small amount. One of the local launches is being sent to Samurai for timber. Hope the bridge will be finished before it gets back. Steel and I and two enlisted men are going up to a place called Boston Island, about 40 miles from Samurai, to lay out a new airdrome.[2] Rumor has it that a company of the 46th will "work" the drome after we complete the survey. It also is in the wind that A and C Company are on their way up to New Guinea.

June 17, 1942

Captain Dubra, our chaplain, is the most interesting negro I have ever met. I enjoy talking with him very much. I like his views on religion. I like his ideas about race problems. He is one of the most intelligent men I have ever met. His grammar isn't very good, and a "picture" is a "pitcher," but his sermons to these colored boys are wonderful. I seldom miss any of them.

Capt. C. Herbert Dubra, chaplain of the 96th Engineers in New Guinea (second from left).

There is no other officer in the whole Battalion who has been affected more by our present setup than Jimmy King. I guess I considered Jimmy my best buddy back at Bragg where we were roommates who shared and shared alike. We felt that we were a lot alike, and we did like each other. But Jimmy is bitter now. Everyone irritates him. He complains and gripes at everybody. I spoke to him and told him that he wasn't acting just right toward certain people, but he still seems to be bitter. He and I had a wonderful time together that day in Townsville when we got drunk. I'd like to do that again with him. It seemed to have had a good effect on him then. Jimmy is still a kid, and he will be all right again as soon as he sees just a bit more of life. For he is made out of good stuff, and he can't keep on being so blindly prejudiced.

FOUR

Establishing an Air Base, Milne Bay

June 18–July 15, 1942

June 18, 1942

This morning, the Empire flying boat left the wharf at Port Moresby. We were headed for Boston Island. But Boston Island was not an island at all; that was only a "code" name. It is a coconut plantation located at the western end of Milne Bay. Later the name of this particular place was changed to Fall River. Actually there are no large rivers around either, but again that has no particular disadvantage. General Scanlan was the big shot aboard the flying boat. There was a reception committee at the Gili Gili pier to meet us. This consisted of Captain Rich, the local Native administrator, and a number of missionaries and other personnel from ANGUA [the Australian New Guinea Administration Unit]. I was amazed at the perfect rhythm with which the Natives rowed our boats from the plane to the pier. Never once did they look to see where they were going; yet they made a perfect land fall.

We drove out to the site of the proposed airdrome. The place looked reasonably level, and for nearly a mile along its length it looked well-drained. The eastern extremity seemed to be poorly drained and presented a problem which could be solved only by months of work. However, there was very little clearing and grubbing to be done; perhaps a hundred coconut trees, that was all. And already the Natives were busy cutting the grass along the proposed landing strip. The women worked as hard as the men. They swung their knives wildly, apparently without any regard for the welfare of any of their co-workers. They all seemed to work faster and faster, and their chant grew louder and louder. It had a sort of rhythm which was different from the kind we are used to seeing in the movies. At length they broke into loud shouting, and they swung their knives very vigorously at the grass. Then altogether they stopped work and let go a wail which was a single note and faded into nothing. Then after a few minutes rest, they started the cycle all over again. They produced amazing results. A new pier had to be built. We were told that the first ship would arrive in one week.

The first night I slept at Fall River was the first time I had slept in a house since I left the 'States. Something stung me on the knee. My knee became swollen and full of pain. Greenberg cut it open the next morning, and drained off about a teaspoonful of puss and blood. He then took a small piece of wood and dug out some rotten flesh. After a fortnight the wound stopped running puss and blood, but simultaneously a similar ulcer broke out on the side of the original bite. This second opening has been running blood and puss ever since, and even now I go around with a bandaged, aching knee. It is amazing how some of these tropical insects can cause so much infection.

The morning of the first day we were in Fall River we went out to see about constructing the new pier. "Yes, I've had some experience in pier construction," I told them, "but I don't think you will ever be able to put in a pier within a week. And it will take a devil of a lot of material. Anyway, I don't know what can be done with this Native labor." While I was thus beating my gums and looking around for material and at an old pile driving rig, the ANGAU got busy with the Natives. They shook piles into place, forming a rectangle 40 feet by 80 feet; this jetted out into about eight feet of water. Then they placed coconut logs on the inside of the piles, forming a wall. Finally the Natives came along with rock and coral, all carried by hand, and filled in the rectangle. They put on a smooth surface of beach sand. In the meantime, another group of Natives under the supervision of Mr. Latterman, the local carpenter, commenced work on an oil-drum pontoon—about 25 feet x 50 feet. This thing when floated into position at the end of the rectangular quay reached out into fifteen or twenty feet of water. Presto! There was adequate unloading facilities!

These Natives gave a good demonstration to a college-graduate civil engineer of how to build a pier—quickly! The whole job was completed in less than four days; but to look at the Natives working at any one particular moment, you would swear that the job would never be done. For instance, you might see fifty or sixty of the strongest men tugging at a palm-tree log, all of them shouting "oh—oh—Op!" And the log doesn't move. And they just keep tugging, keeping up that "oh—oh—OP!", each time pulling just a little bit harder than the time before. Finally the log gives 'way. They all look very much surprised. The women are used for carrying lighter stuff, such as basketsful of rock and coral. But if you observe closely, you will see that the women's baskets are always fuller than those of the men.

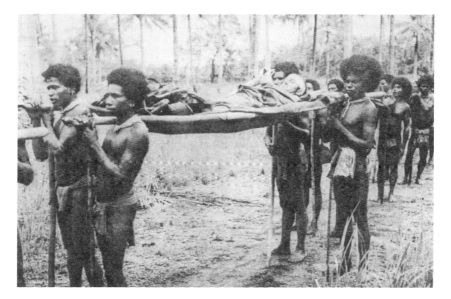

Papuans carrying a wounded soldier to a first aid station in the rear area. Aside from their crucial support role, they were organized into the Papua Infantry Battalions. The Allied victory in New Guinea would have been impossible without the Papuans, who were well trained and equipped, acclimated to the area, and armed with modern weapons.

All of the Natives go barefooted. The men wear a small band around their waist. Attached to this waist band at the small of the back is another piece of cloth (or leaf) which runs down the man's back between his legs, around his genitals, then up under the waist band at about the navel; the cloth then flops over the front. Some of the men wear a skirt over this attire, but most of the laborers do not. The women wear grass skirts. That is all. Most of the Natives, men and women, are well-built although of small stature. They seem to be reasonably energetic but suffer skin diseases. They work all day for their food and a stick of tobacco. This labor is not compulsory, but nearly all of them work. Their food consists of rice, some kind of meal, and whatever fruit they can find. They smell of copra, and look very unclean. Everyone lives in the same hut—husband, wife, children, dogs, and pigs. I have already seen a dog come up to the pot in which a Native was cooking and eat out of it. The Native went on stirring the food and made no attempt to chase the animal away. The Native wasn't affected, although I almost vomited. I have even heard that the women nurse the baby pigs. Seeing how they live, I wouldn't doubt it. Well, I mustn't talk too much about the Natives. Volumes have been written about them, but I doubt that anyone has ever written about Fall River.

Friday night I was full of fever. I thought it was caused by the bite on my knee and that it would clear up by morning. But Saturday morning I was no better. I walked up to the "big house" for breakfast, but I could eat none. My head was spinning around. I strolled back to cottage No. 3, made it to my bed and flopped across it. I was burning with fever and ached all over.

Later: Greenberg diagnosed my case as dengue fever. I didn't care what I had. All I wanted was a sour pickle. I lay in bed all day Saturday, unable to sleep. When night settled in, the Native tom-toms started beating. It had been raining intermittently, and everything was stuffy. I felt quite miserable. The tom-toms and the Natives' wailing were absolutely maddening. Later in the evening Greenberg gave me a pill to make me sleep. Sunday I was no better. I lay in bed and thought—and thought—and thought! Oh, if I could only stop thinking! I knew that I couldn't stay in bed another day without going crazy. So Monday morning I got up. Much to my surprise, I could not get around the way I had expected. The limit of my navigation was from one chair to another. Toward evening I was feeling much better, however; and I decided to start my mapping of the roads of the area the first thing in the morning. I had been sent to Fall River to do work, not to get sick! Gadsden, Turpin and I started out immediately after breakfast on our mapping task. It was an excellent bit of work, and Turpin should be proud of his accurate pacing. On Wednesday, we received a cable that two ships were due the next day. It was a good thing that we had the pontoon wharf completed. I was happy to see the ships arrive the way Commander Hunt said they would. I had a fear that they would be a few days late, and then supplies would be a few days later, and so on. This early arrival of the two ships made me feel that perhaps the brass hats really thought something of the Fall River Project after all. Thursday morning four ships pulled into Milne Bay. It is funny how all the women disappeared today upon the arrival of all the troops. They must have some degree of modesty after all. We learned that the *McDewey* which was hit the day before we left Moresby was hit again the next day and foundered in the harbor. Roads around here are no more than mud holes. I'll be glad to leave.

I was very much surprised Friday when Steele told me that I was to act as platoon commander of the second platoon of the 46th until Lt. Carnes arrives from Townsville. "They're out on the job now trying to open up the road for traffic. Go out and supervise their work," he said.

"Who is the sergeant in charge?" I asked, "And do they know that I am supposed to take over command of the platoon?"

"Oh, quit acting like Jimmy King, and go out and see what they're doing."

"It's very irregular, but I'll go." I did not feel like going up to the sergeant and say, "Sergeant, I am Lt. Samuelson. I have just been put in charge of the second platoon. You will take orders from me from now on." And I could think of no better way to say it. So I said nothing. After a couple hours work I became so exhausted that I had to leave the sergeants on their own while I came up to the house to lie down awhile. This complete lack of energy is an awful feeling. If I could eat I would feel better, but the food tastes horrible to me. Thank heavens for the citrus fruit around here. Starting Saturday the second platoon worked on its own, and they worked without an officer through Monday.

Over the weekend I felt bitter. Everyone seemed to irritate me, and the food seemed to be getting worse. Rains continued without a let-up, night and day! The war news, especially the fall of Tobruk and Rommel's push into Egypt, is particularly depressing. Jumping off a running truck while wearing heavy boots, I nearly tore my groin open and now limp around like an old man. It seems that everything is going wrong with me. My teeth are now giving me trouble.

June 28, 1942, Milne Bay ["Fall River"]

Ten days ago the Japs could have taken this place with a dozen well-armed men. Today we could hold out against nearly a thousand. In another month it will require a formidable Japanese landing force to take possession of Fall River.

June 29, 1942

A radiogram arrived stating that we must increase dock facilities, that more ships would be up *soon*. That means more troops and supplies are coming. A thousand tons of engineering equipment, for instance, will be up in less than a week. The "Burma Road" must be opened for traffic.

"Sammy, there's a job for you," Steele said, "You can get a platoon of the 46th, and I am sure that Major Margetts will give you all the help from the Infantry that you need."

"O.K. That's fine. Will you make arrangements for the staff sergeant of the second platoon to report to me at 6 A.M. at the fork in the road opposite cottage No. 3?"

I wanted no more of that stuff where I went out on a job and reported to the sergeant. I wanted him to report to me. Tuesday it rained. But we worked. Sgt. Shoemacher reported to me, and I had the three squads well under control. One had to construct a 70-foot bridge over Gili Gili creek; another had to load trucks with rock from the creek bed; and the third squad was digging ditches alongside the road and unloading the rocks off the trucks. When I came home that evening, I felt good. A lot had been accomplished in spite of the rains.

July 1, 1942

Two platoons of infantry under Lt. Bill Ryan reported today to help with the road work. I chummed around with Ryan all day long and had a real workout. He is chock full of energy.

"Come on, Sam, let's run over and take a look at that hill." And once we were there, he would exclaim: "Look at that field of fire! What a place for a machine gun! Look, let's go take a look at that hill." And we'd be off again.

"Let's sit down and enjoy a cigarette," I suggested, but he didn't smoke. In the meantime his troops didn't do 50% of the work they should have. The platoon from Company A had no officer in charge. I told Ryan what had to be done and showed him the section of the road that I wanted his platoon to get in condition for traffic. I told the sergeant of the other platoon what I expected of his platoon.

"Oh, we'll get that finished early this afternoon," Ryan prognosticated.

"I'll be satisfied if you get it done three days from now," I answered in a pessimistic tone.

"Oh, you don't know how these men work. But you'll see." Ryan then proceeded to give them a pep talk. They all picked up their tools and tackled the job vigorously as soon as he finished. Ryan and I then went for a stroll around the rest of the job and especially down to the creek where Sergeant Yaeger's squad was sinking piles by the "shaking-down" process.[1] About forty-five minutes later we returned to his job site. All his men were sitting around smoking, eating coconuts, and kidding. "What's the trouble?" I asked Ryan.

"Nothing. It's just the usual 'smoko.' They have one every hour—oh, for about fifteen minutes." I said nothing, but I thought plenty, especially when I saw how little work had been done.

For two more days we worked. And the heavens poured forth mercilessly. In spite of our efforts, the road could not hold a steady flow of traffic. We managed to get all the guns over, but the road was torn to shreds. The Infantry still piddled around with their section of the road. This platoon from the 46th is a really swell bunch of fellows. They are good workers and are reliable. Sgt. Shoemacher and Sgt. Yaeger are two of the best noncoms I have met. The bridge will be completed tomorrow—an excellent piece of work considering the material at hand.

Saturday was a hard day. I really drove my platoon of engineers. We built culverts, dug ditches, put rock on the road. I had 40 Natives working under me and I drove these too. I would not let them quit work during the heavy rain. Naturally the Engineers worked during all the rain. And they worked hard—a good bunch of soldiers if I ever saw any. But the two platoons of infantry were hopeless. The platoon from Company A had a rather easy assignment. Their section of the road was in pretty fair condition from the start. Most of their work was to prevent the road from "going out" under heavy traffic. But the section that Company C had was a different story. The road was in a flat pasture. Ditches had to be dug, deep ditches that would keep the water flowing. The road bed had to be built up. There was plenty of work to be done. And the rains weren't helping a bit. And trucks still came over the road, had to get through for one reason or another. I told Ryan that his platoon had a big job on their hands and that they would never get it done by tomorrow noon, the time when the ship with 1000 tons of engineering equipment and supplies was due. I could see that his feelings were hurt. I wanted that road to be in good condition by the time the ship had to be unloaded, and I didn't care whose feelings I hurt. In fact, I no longer cared how many men's backs I hurt. It is funny how hard and cruel a fellow will become when he has a job to do and is not getting it done.

That night as we sat down to have a drink before dinner, I offered a toast for "no rain." Fall River has had no rain since that night. Sunday morning the sun was shining. Oh what a wonderful sight that was!

"Let's go to it fellows," I told the Engineers, "There won't be any traffic on this road for seven hours. We got to get it in shape by then.

Remember, no work that is unnecessary. Get all the bad spots first. If we have time, we'll get the other places."

I went out to where the Infantry platoon was working. They hadn't arrived on the job yet. I paced up and down their section of road, looking at all the bad spots, trying to figure some way to get some kind of base to hold up traffic. Rock was out of the question; no time for that. At last Company C arrived. Lt. Ryan wasn't there. It was already nine o'clock. The ship was due at twelve. I came up to the sergeant in charge of the platoon and told him what I wanted done.

"It looks as if we might have a bit of dry weather. Anyway, we'll have to gamble on that assumption. Consequently, I want all work on the ditches to cease. I want you to have your men carry coconuts, and we will place them all over the road, especially down in the ruts. Then we will take palm leaves and place them over the coconuts, and finally we can throw a little dirt over the leaves."

The sergeant started arguing that it was impossible to build a road there, and that my method wasn't any good any way. I told him to do what I told him anyway. Reluctantly he told the men. Some wandered off and started gathering coconuts which were scattered all along the side of the road and placing them in the ruts. I watched the work. It was the bottleneck of the whole "Burma Road," and I thought I should stay there and see how the men got along. I noticed two young chaps off on the side, eating not gathering coconuts. I watched them for a few minutes. They saw me watching them but went on eating, almost as a gesture of defiance to my demands on them. I could stand this for about ten minutes. I was boiling with anger. I tried to control myself and act the part of an officer.

"What are the names of you two men?" I asked as I approached them.

"What do you want to know for?" one of them answered.

"That is none of your business. I asked you your name. It is your duty to tell it to me. It is *my* business why I want it."

"We won't give it to you until you tell us why you want it." I grabbed the identification tag on one, noticed his name was Corr, looked him in the eye. There must have been fire in my eyes.

"Do you know what kind of trouble you are headed for, soldier?"

Then I turned to the other soldier. I realized that I had done wrong by grabbing the identification tag of the first soldier and didn't want to repeat my error.

"Tell me your name!" I fairly shouted, then lost my voice. I could speak no more.

"Get it from the sergeant," came his reply.

I walked over to sergeant Wilcums. The two men followed close behind me. The whole platoon crowded around.

"Sergeant, what is this man's name?" I asked.

"Ask him what he wants it for!"

"He ain't our officer. You don't have to tell him anything!" came from another man who had crowded around. "You can't drive us like niggers!" said another.[2]

"We don't have to do this kind of work."

The sergeant held up his hand, told the men to keep quiet.

"What did this man do, sir?" he asked me.

I hesitated a moment. Should I have to explain to a sergeant?

"They—this man and that fellow there—were not working, and I want their names."

"Hollis, sir. The other's name is Corr."

"Thank you, sergeant."

I wrote the names down on a piece of paper. I couldn't keep my hand from shaking.

It was 2:20 before the ship was sighted, and shortly after 3:00 it tied up at Pontoon Wharf. The first thing to come off was a four ton truck.

"Can it go over your road?" they asked me.

"Sure, send it through." I rode in the cab of the truck, watching how the road behaved under this load. It held up wonderfully well. Then came another four ton truck. It got through all right. Then came a mobile air compressor. It went over in fine fashion. And then came word that there would be no more traffic on the road until morning, that they would leave the other trucks on the beach until dawn, when they would load them with landing mats and send them over the road in convoy. I went back to cottage No 3, had a bite of supper, and went to bed. I was burning with fever. Next morning I was very sick, but I had to get up and go out on the job. I knew what awful stuff these 2500-pound bundles of landing mats were and I had to keep that road open so that there would not have to be any rehandling of the bundles. If the road was not kept open, it would mean that the bundles had to be unloaded on the beach; then later when the road could be opened, they would have to be reloaded on the trucks and carried to the airdrome. That meant plenty of wasted energy. It had to be avoided. That road must be kept open. When I reached the "Burma Road" I found that it had been torn up. I asked Steele what had happened.

"We sent through one convoy of G–I trucks with landing mats and it got through all right. Then when the trucks returned, we thought we'd try again. This time they didn't make it."

Dispersal taxiway on an airfield in Port Moresby, New Guinea. The dispersal of airplanes on the ground was the most effective defense against Japanese bombing. Mud was a constant problem.

Two soldiers of the 96th Engineers laying steel Marsden Landing Mat. Although quickly installed by unskilled labor and used extensively to surface runways, it was only a temporary expedient.

"But I thought no trucks would use the road during the night," I protested. "We could have gotten trucks through if we had a crew on the road to keep it repaired, but there wasn't anyone on the road last night."

"We just gambled on it and we lost."

"Well, the road is out now. You won't be able to send trucks over it for several hours. You'll have to dump the mats on the beach in the meantime. I'll send you word just as soon as you can send trucks over the road."

"O.K. That's fine," was his reply.

I felt awfully low. The road had beaten me. It wasn't open, and mats were coming off the ship. Mats were being dumped on the beach. Each bundle would require reloading onto a truck, at least a fifteen minute operation. I had failed, and I was depressed. The sun shone down brightly. The road was drying out. Engineers, Infantry, Natives—all worked together to get the road back into shape. I had such a high fever that I hardly knew what I was doing. The men worked on their own. Around one o'clock I told Steele, who had been up the whole night before, that he could send G–I trucks through at two o'clock. I would give him further notice when the road would be open to all traffic. Later on I told him that if he could get me a platoon of Engineers for the night shift that I would keep the road open all night, that all trucks could carry mats over the road any time after 7:00 P.M. I went to work with this "night" platoon. I made up a system of traffic control, running three convoys of five cars each. My fever kept going up and up. Trucks rumbled by. The road was holding. I was full of chills. I had borrowed Olsofky's field jacket. Imagine some one wearing a field jacket in the tropics. But my body still trembled and my teeth chattered. I was nearly blind with fever. I staggered back to the ship and saw Jones.

"You working tonight?" I asked him.

"Yeah, I'll be on duty all night."

"Well, I'm going to have to leave that platoon on the road tonight. I can't go any further. I think they will be all right. The road looks good. Just remember that they're out there without an officer. See you in the morning."

I could hardly climb down the rope ladder over the side of the *Yochow*. I got into one of the trucks hauling mats and rode with the driver as far as the fork in the road which leads up to the "big house." From here I walked a few hundred feet up to cottage No 3. I felt so bad that I wanted to cry. I was just about stone blind. I fell in bed burning with fever and shivering. Throughout the night I heard the rumble of trucks going by—trucks carrying landing mats to the airdrome. The road was open! I must have drunk a gallon of water during the night. Gadsden brought me in a quart of water shortly after I was awake. I drank it all at one time. Shortly afterwards Lt. King, the medical officer of the 46th, arrived.

"You're hot as a fire cracker," he said as he touched me.

The thermometer revealed that I had 104.8. I must have had 106 the night before. They carried me to the Station Hospital in an ambulance. I hardly moved all day long. I lay in bed, feeling more dead than alive. I was in pain; yet nothing ached. I was hungry; yet I could not eat. The next day was the same. On the third day I felt better. On the fourth I was up and around, and on the fifth I was back at cottage No 3. I frightened myself when I looked in the mirror. I was thin and pale, must not have weighed much over 130 pounds. I was so weak for the next couple of days that I could hardly stand up. Walking was all right, but standing in one spot was murder.

News from Russia is grim. The day I arrived back at Cottage No. 3, (Saturday, July 11) a Jap bomber flew over Fall River. It was flying low, but apparently it saw nothing; for there were no Japanese reconnaissance planes over at any later date. And up until now there had been no enemy activity at all over the new place. If the bomber had flown over just a few hours later, it could not have failed to see the big ship in the harbor, a ship bringing in 400 troops, the first of a 6000-man brigade which is coming up to defend Fall River.

July 13, 1942

The advanced party for the new RAAF squadron flew in today. It looks as if they plan to bring up planes in another week. Steele is a bit under the weather. The hospital is overflowing with malaria patients. The dry weather is continuing and the drome is progressing nicely.

July 14, 1942

I am concerned. I am anxious to get back to Port Moresby and some real engineering work.

July 15, 1942

We learn that the Japs are pouring troops into Rabaul. The "lakeshore" road is progressing slowly, but it will be a good job when it is completed. It will be finished in another week. The airdrome will be ready for fighter planes on the 22nd of this month, and it will be able to take any kind of bomber by the 31st.

FIVE

The Japanese Land Offensive

July 16–September 17, 1942

July 16, 1942, Port Moresby

Col. Yoder came up to Fall River in the flying boat this morning with Commander Hunt, Major Tremble and Major Eads. We had a larger party returning. We had a strong tail wind and made the trip in one and a half hours. It feels good to be back "home" again, but I was very much disappointed in having no mail waiting for me. It wasn't that I hadn't received any mail, for Frank Eddy says I had a big pile of letters; but he put them on a ship which was going to Fall River, and the ill-fated vessel didn't get there. It was bombed twice and the crew mutinied, refusing to go to Fall River. Instead, the ship went to Townsville. God alone knows whether I'll ever see that mail. Willie A. received good news while I was gone. Not only did his wife pull through, but the baby is alive and well.

July 21, 1942

I investigated a case of larceny in the Company today. It was very much involved, but I finally got a written confession out of Mumford that he had stolen 22 pounds. However, he would not admit stealing the $5 bill which was with the Australian money. It was evident that he had stolen all of it. But stealing $5 of American money seemed to him a greater crime than stealing 22 pounds of Australian money. Really, 50% of these boys attach no value to this Australian currency in which they are paid. They have never bought anything with it, so how should they know?

July 22, 1942

The Japanese with 14 troop transports and 12 naval vessels are proceeding along the northeast coast of the island. We have been bombing them all day but practically without success, scoring only one direct hit on a transport. We sent out around ten P-40s this afternoon, each loaded with a 500-pound bomb to "dive bomb" the enemy ships. They then returned to Fall River. I don't know how these planes made out. Around dusk eight Douglas dive bombers (A-24) arrived on Bomana Drome. They ought to raise some hell tomorrow. We can expect more planes from Australia in the morning and a busy day all day long. Surprised the Japs didn't bomb us today. We will surely catch it tomorrow. Incidently, our fighter pilots claim to have killed hundreds of Jap soldiers in crowded barges as they were making landings on the coast from the troop ships. Matheson, who has been unbearable for the past several days with his fits of gloom and melancholy, went to the hospital today. Had a lot of company over this evening. It is good to get together.

July 22, 1942

Dearest Dora,

The men are having a prayer meeting this evening, and from down in the area I hear their spirituals. These colored boys really can sing. And to hear them like this—where all the spirituals seem to have so much meaning (Just select any one of them and see how well it would fit in with this kind of condition) is a real treat. They really do want to get home again. Whenever I get homesick, I think of them; and that always helps, for their condition is so much worse than my own. At least I know where I am. I'll admit that I don't know what tomorrow will bring, but these poor fellows have no conception of what part of the world they are in. The only thing that they know is that they can't "go over the hill" and expect to wind up home. It really is pathetic.

July 23, 1942

We hear all kind of rumors about the Japanese invasion fleet. It is evident that the figures I put in my diary yesterday were exaggerated. I like this rumor—two troop ships escorted by the naval vessels effected a landing of approximately 3,000 Japanese. We hit and sank one of the troop ships.

July 24, 1942

Willie A is really getting "bomb happy." During today's raid his teeth were chattering so much he couldn't speak. And the landing of the Japs across the Island has really upset him. He wants to load our truck full of food, ammunition, and gasoline and leave it near our tent so that "when the Japs come" we can make our getaway.

"Willie, don't be crazy," I tell him, "We can't run away. We have to stay and fight. And if we do have to retreat, I want to do it with the men of the company."

"Aw, Sammy, you don't mean that," he answers.

I can't tell whether he is joking or not. He speaks that way in front of the men, and that surely isn't good for their morale. The Japs bombed Bomana Drome. A piece of shrapnel hit within fifteen feet of me, tearing off some twigs and leaves from the tree I was standing under. Didn't do much reading today, was busy most of the time down in the supply dumps. Just came back from town.

July 25, 1942

Played lawyer again today. This time I had to hold a formal investigation against Albert Moore, Company B, who was charged with assault with intent to murder two men. I have been at Company B all day taking testimony, typing, getting signatures. The evening when I made my recommendation for the disposition of the case, I suggested that it be dropped for lack of evidence to substantiate the charge. I was glad, for I did not want to see another man get five years in jail because of something which we could easily stamp out— gambling! I don't believe I am ever going to gamble any more after seeing what the vice can lead to. Actually, I haven't even played checkers in over three months.

July 26, 1942

Mail! Four letters from Dora dated May 21, 22, 24 & 26. Gosh they were wonderful. My little girl has really learned to write beautiful letters. They inspired me to write her a five page answer this evening. Dora is well and the baby is kicking her—how wonderful! Everyone is well, but it seems that Beryl [his elder brother] will have to go into the army—nothing definite however.

July 27, 1942

The Japs are moving inland. They are 20 miles from Kokoda. We are putting all available equipment on clearing a road to Kokoda. You have to give the Japs credit for their bravery. They are advancing toward us when we have them outnumbered around five to one. I can't help but admire and like the Japs in spite of all our propagandists have to say. They seem to be fighting for a reason. I don't know why we're fighting. Oh yes I do. Because we are unfair and won't give the "other fellow" a decent break. We crush him but let him arm against us. What we should do is to give him a fair deal but destroy every piece of armament he has. Yes—everything. And we should keep enough to be able to put him right if he should attempt to do any arming whatsoever—yes, even to make a single machine gun.

July 27, 1942

Dearest Dora,

[FIRST PAGE HEAVILY CENSORED.] Do you remember reading an article in the June 1st issue of *Life* by Ralph Sherrod? I met him CENSORED twice in fact, once, I must admit, when I was so inebriated that I can hardly remember the meeting; but I do remember talking to him a long time and telling him all kind of things, mostly about the negroes of our battalion, about prejudices against the negro and so on. He wrote nothing about that kind of stuff in *Life*.

July 28, 1942

Had a real scare this evening. The Japs bombed us. We can always expect that when the moon is full. It was cloudy and we could see nothing except the flashes of ack-ack and exploding bombs. Then we saw about two miles east of here a number of pistol shots. Then came rifle fire. Then machine guns opened up. The firing increased for a minute or two, and it wasn't far away. I rushed into my tent for my revolver and helmet, found my ammunition pouch nearly empty; so I dug into my trunk for a box of .45 shells. I found my gas mask in the bottom of my barracks bag, the straps still adjusted so that it would fit over on over a coat. Then I rushed to the company, turning out all the men.

By this time the firing was loud and regular. The grass on several hillsides to the east of Bomana was on fire. I formed three squads from the men I could muster together, about 80% of H & S, and we all marched to "the Needle." Here we took up positions around the base of the hill where we could concentrate a lot of fire on the road from Bomana to John's Gully. By this time the firing ceased and ten minutes later I dismissed the men. Tomorrow I am going to get the company better organized for this sort of thing. A little organization may mean the difference between life and death for many of these fellows.

July 29, 1942

Seven of our dive bombers went out this afternoon with fighter escorts. One of them, badly riddled, limped home this evening.

"Attacked by Zeros," the pilot said, "Our escort ran off."

Gosh that is terrible news. The moon is full and old Nippo has been flying around since dusk keeping us in slit trenches. He comes in with three bombers. Searchlights pop up from everywhere. Ack-ack opens up. Perhaps a hundred bursts but never a hit. Then a few bombs come tumbling down and he is gone. Fifteen minutes later he is back again, and there is another performance of the same show. It is most disheartening. I guess he will be back during the night.

July 30, 1942

Around 3 o'clock this morning we had to tumble from bed and go to the slit trench. Two flights of three bombers each kept going back and forth for nearly an hour, dropping a few bombs at a time. The ack-ack must have fired several hundred rounds at the big Japanese bombers, but never came close to hitting one. It was a terrible display.

August 2, 1942

General Casey called together all engineering officers who could possibly come. He was the first man whom I have met in New Guinea who talked like a real engineer. He spoke in terms of planning, progress schedules, coordination of plant, labor and equipment—man hours! He spoke of the necessity of proper maintenance of machines, of good working conditions for the men (so they would work harder). He spoke of anticipation of supplies and equipment and of the necessity to improvise when the standard equipment was not available. He stressed the necessity of utilizing natural resources which were around. He referred to "we" as the United States—not as a combination of the U.S. and Australia.

"We have the help of only seven million Australians. The Japs have the help of 300,000,000. So our job is a big one." He stressed the gravity of the situation and made a plea for a special effort on the part of everyone: "So much depends on what the engineers do during this coming month."

August 4, 1942

The Battalion is being converted into a General Service Regiment. The "new" officers are on their way from the States.

August 6, 1942

A little excitement this evening. The hills north of here blazed up shortly after supper with a swiftly moving brush fire which imperiled our dynamite stores. I turned out all available hands, and with wet sacks and shovels we got the fire under control after several hours. The flames had got within 300 yards of our biggest dynamite pile.

Last evening we learned on the radio that the Japanese have captured Kokoda Drome, only sixty miles from here. They have advanced over half-way to Moresby since their landing at Buna some ten days ago.

August 7, 1942

All the mail which I had given up as having been lost turned up today—29 letters from Dora, two from Papa, two from Dotsy [his younger sister], and one from Gwendy [his niece, the editor of this book]. The first letter from Papa was so beautiful, there was so much written between the lines that I had to cry—it was for joy. My mind is intoxicated with Dora now. Reading all her letters makes me feel that I am right with her again. The Japs now hold Kakoda drome. There is feverish air activity around here. We ought to send a convoy around their backs and corner them.

August 10, 1942

Hear a lot of activity in the Solomon Islands. Hope we are getting the lead out of our tails at last. Investigated case against Wilbur Patterson of Company C. He is another man whose mind has gone back on him. These poor boys suffer so much that they can't help being disrespectful and disobedient at times. He has enough against him for a general courts martial, but I'm going to recommend a special court. So far Headquarters has upheld all of my recommendations.

August 11, 1942

Another man hurt today, run over by a tractor—broken legs, arm, and pelvis, probably will die. We surely have had a lot of men killed through carelessness.

The Allies in the Southwest Pacific have thrown in everything to capture Tulagi from the Japs. It doesn't look as if we are doing very well. Germany's drive to the Caucasus has been successful. The Mikop fields are being destroyed and what won't be destroyed will be captured. There is general rebellion in India. I hope that this is the darkest hour before the dawn. But it surely is dark now!

August 12, 1942

The report from the Solomons is not good: "Operations are still continuing." The Germans all up in the Caucasus now. When is the attack from England coming? Nine thousand troops poured into Moresby today. Many, some 1700, have kept on going right on up to Kokoda. In another month all of New Guinea should be in our hands. Reports claim that there is not a single plane at Ley and Salamau, and we have been pasting Rabaul daily—without any marked results, however. This selection of short stories by Damon Runyon is very funny. I am enjoying them a lot; even better than O'Henry.

August 14, 1942

Both the United Nations and the Axis are making wild claims of victories. One does not know who or what to believe. One thing which I do not like is the fact that Japan has landed another 10,000 men on the other side of the island. The struggle for Port Moresby should be soon forthcoming.

August 15, 1942

Dearest Dora,

We are permitted officially now to say that we are in New Guinea. I am perfectly safe. Remember I am an engineer. And they need plenty of engineers in a place like this. And they won't let us go out and get hurt. They use the Infantry for that.

August 16, 1942

Fighting continuing in Solomons. Apparently we're not doing as good as we should; otherwise operation would be complete by now.

August 18, 1942

Am reading a series of twelve pamphlets which I received from the Chaplain on "Understanding Human Nature." It is really a short course in psychology. It would do me good to understand people a little better—especially some of the ones around here whom I don't like.

August 20, 1942

We had a few courts martial cases. I blazed up like a lawyer in one case and actually eked out a verdict of "not guilty" from the Court. It was the first time this happened since being defense counsel. Yoder has been relieved of his post as Commander of Service Troops in Port Moresby. Colonel Mathews took his place.
Later: Willie A. is in bad shape. His mind is becoming badly warped. He is homesick and bitter.
"Let's go home, Sammy," he tells me a dozen times a day. I stay close to him as much as possible. I try to soothe him, but although he listens to me, his hands and voice tremble if I tell him anything which conflicts with his idea that everybody is trying to cheat him.

August 26, 1942

Worked all night Monday and Tuesday and I've been sleepy ever since. Large scale warfare going on around here now. Japs are reenforcing Solomons and have made a landing at Fall River. Glad I'm not there. Unless the Aussies have got in some better troops, the Japs will take the place without very much trouble. Moresby is alive with airplanes this evening. Well, there's no doubt that the Nippos are trying for this place, but we'll give them a hot welcome.

August 27, 1942

A couple dozen bombers raised hell with us today—knocked out four transports and five bombers besides a few trucks and a new C-12 road grader. There were some casualties, too. We still underestimate the Japs' strength. It's a shame we lost our transports. They were carrying food to our troops at Kokoda.

Many troops moved to the northwest of our camp. That was the way we planned to escape if the going should have become too rough. Perhaps the Japs might come from that direction. Fierce fighting continues in the Solomons, in Russia, in China; and now comes news of a British offensive in Egypt. The Chinese are going damn good. The Russians, after taking a big beating, are striking back. There are no definite reports from the Solomons, but it is big stuff. We still hold the drome at Fall River.

August 29, 1942

The Japs torpedoed one of our supply ships just as it was leaving the Port Moresby harbor. The ship is still afloat and we might be able to save it. Activities in the Milne Bay area aren't going so well for our side. Well, I got my new job as assistant S-3 [operations officer]. Will move to Headquarters in the morning.

August 30, 1942

Pres tells me one piece of flattering news. He says there was a cloudburst at Fall River about two weeks after I left. He says my bridge didn't wash out, but the lakeshore bridge just a mile further down the river did. And they had bolted their bridge together and took two weeks to build it. Mine was put up in a few days without a single spike or bolt.

August 31, 1942

Yesterday was the first day of my new job, assistant operations officer. I reported to duty at ten in the morning, and Kalman immediately invited me to take a ride with him to the various job sites. All day long we went from one project to another. It seemed to me that very little work was being done on any one of them, but that is the way it always seems to the man not on the job. Late in the afternoon as we drove back toward Headquarters, Jack Kalman asked me, "Well, Sammy, how do you like your new job?"

"I'd like to get to work." I had made the reply without a moment's hesitation and really without any forethought.

"What do you mean?" I could see that Jack was astonished by my rude reply. "What do you call work?"

"Oh, I mean making plans—definite plans, preparing tables for the distribution on machinery and man power—all the sort of stuff which normally goes on in an operations office."

"We're doing all that," came his challenge. "I'll show you all the charts we have. Every week Temple and Holtzclaw go around and find out where all the men are and where the equipment is."

"Yes, but you don't know. I don't mean *you* as an individual. I mean that operations cannot call the Motor Officer and tell him 'Send truck number so and so to C Company tomorrow morning at eight o'clock.' And the reason is that operations doesn't know where the trucks are. In other words the things are working backwards. Operations usually asks permission to give an order to a company. Take for example today when you asked Farley whether he could furnish a couple of men to help load some trucks for Major Farington, Farley told you 'no.' Then you went to see Schwalbert and told him how Major Farington had helped us and all that kind of crap, and naturally Schwalbert agreed to furnish the men. Now what you should have done was call Farley and simply told him this, 'Major Farington will send two trucks down this afternoon to obtain rock from the stock piles on the ground. Will you see to it that he has two of your men to help him load the rock.' And if Farley would give any argument, then the next time you should make your request in the form of an order." "But—"

"Now actually Farley has a legitimate reason to gripe. Why should he have to pull any of his men off the quarry for a little shit-detail like loading rock for the major. The major should have been refused in the first place."

"But, Sammy, you can't get along that way. You've got to work *with* people not against them, especially in a time like this where you are always needing the help of other troops."

"The hell with all that kind of diplomacy," I went on. "A man likes an order—a direct order to do or not to do something. He doesn't like to be told that he is doing a job for so-and-so because so-and-so did something for someone else. If he is an engineer—or any kind of man—all he wants to know is what his job is, what he will have available to do the job with; and then he likes to be left alone."

"That's too idealistic."

"The hell it is. It's idealistic all right. But it is practical. It is the way to get the highest degree of efficiency. Operations should *tell* companies what to do, but then it should leave them alone. Before a company is given a job, operations should present that company with definite plans, preferably written plans, with every detail of the job carefully thought of and worked out."

"But this is war."

"All the more reason that we should have more careful planning."

"Do you mean that you think operations isn't run right?"

"I didn't say that."

"Even if I must say so myself, since I have been operations officer things have improved a lot. I think I am doing a pretty good job. Don't you think so?"

"I think there has been a definite improvement since you have been operations officer, but there is a lot of room for further improvement. I have some ideas I'd like to discuss with you when things settle down a bit and we find time."

"Sure. That's the spirit I like. Yes, Sammy, I know that things aren't perfect yet, but a lot of progress has been made. And we will make much more progress. I am counting on your full cooperation."

I think I'm going to like this Captain Jack Kalman.

Sepember 1, 1942

Am trying to consolidate all surveys that have been made around Seven Mile Drome. It is practically hopeless. It would be better to start all over. Not a single bench mark! But once on the drome, I have little time for any mapping. Putting in grade stakes for a dispersion road, setting culverts to grade. I did manage to make a profile of bomber and fighter strips.

September 2, 1942

Things at Fall River are well under control — our control.

September 4, 1942

The air force has been fumbling around for two weeks trying to figure a way to move a 16,000 pound gasoline tank from Port Moresby to Six Mile Valley. I was ordered today to tackle the job. After dinner with a squad of men from D company, I rigged the tank

so that in the morning we can pull it out onto a trailer. I am anxious to
see how we make out.

September 5, 1942

The job went off beautifully. We pulled the tank onto the 25 foot
air corps trailer, then turned it into place with pulleys. We locked and
tied it into place, then started the perilous job of delivering the 16,000
pound giant. The first quarter mile of the road down the mountain
side was the hardest. And after it had been negotiated, I breathed more
easily. Tomorrow we will put the tank in position in Six Mile Valley.

September 6, 1942

Moved the tank into final position today. Notices that the outlet
end is 2 feet 3inches lower than other end. The bed hadn't been prepared properly. If I'm still on that job tomorrow, I'll have to rectify that.

September 7, 1942

Jap bombers over today. They tore up a runaway but damaged no
planes. Our recent job of dispersal bay construction was a big factor
in saving the planes. Yoder had eagles on his shoulders today. Perhaps
he is pretty good after all. He is the only officer in the Regiment who
has received two promotions.

Kalman sent me out to inspect works and make recommendations.
I had two recommendations: first, extend length of Seven Mile Drome
in NW direction 600 feet; second, have Warrant Officer Nichols stop
construction on his road until a more favorable location can be
secured. Kalman told me to make a survey for the new road and stake
out the center line. He also liked the idea about the Seven Mile Drome
extension, for it really is too short to be safe for the B-26s. He told me
to make the survey and put in the grade stakes as soon as I found
time. I like that. I like a man who will send you out to see what has to
be done and who will listen to your recommendations. It makes you
feel that he has confidence in you and hence you will do good work to
maintain that confidence.

September 8, 1942

Been surveying today. Am really making a first class highway out
of the remainder of Nick's road. No kinks or sharp curves, nothing

but long, gradual curves and tangents. Japs are 44 miles from here. They have crossed the Stanley Mountains and are in control of the pass.

September 11, 1942

With the Japs less than 40 miles away some peoples' thoughts turn to the defense of Port Moresby. Major Martin is in charge of the Pitt Street Sector. He has selected me as his assistant. Willie A is mad because he wanted me to help him fight with H & S. Both think I'm some kind of fighting fool who doesn't care if he gets killed or not. They don't know that the thought of being run through with a Jap bayonet makes me unhappy too. But I'm not scared. I probably would be when the time came. But I'd surely fight like hell.

September 12, 1942

The Japanese have crossed the Owen Stanley Range, and jungle fighting is going on some forty-odd miles northeast of here. The invincible Range proved to be another impenetrable Malayan jungle. But the real show hasn't started yet! Nevertheless, we do not have a devil of a lot of man power here—perhaps six or seven thousand Australian infantry and a battalion or so of light artillery. Our antiaircraft defenses are relatively strong and nearly one hundred Brem-gum carriers are a big item in our favor. But the bulk of the troops in this area are service troops—engineers, quartermaster, ordinance and ground troops for the air corps.

"Now we do not expect to call on these troops," Major Walker told us the other evening, "to go out into the pass to fight the Jap, but we do expect these troops to defend their own areas, to take up positions on controlling ground and provide for an all-around defense of their own camp sites."

Colonel Yoder was designated to be in charge of all the service troops in this, the Pitt Street Sector. Now Yoder makes no pretence of being anywhere near Port Moresby if and when the going gets rough. On the last "stand-to" which wound up in the Coral Sea Battle he was ready to leave with certain other brass hats in a launch. Now, I have no proof of this, only the Chaplain's word; but knowing the Chaplain as well as I do, I can accept this as a fact. So our colonel delegated this responsibility to Major Martin. Major Martin is a good insurance salesman but he is no tactician. He is frightened by anyone who ranks him, and his voice trembles when he gives an order to a subordinate for fear that he might hurt his feelings. For the past few days he has been rushing around trying to coordinate plans for defense of the various units around here.

Two days ago he came to me, his eyes bulging out half an inch from his face, and said "Sammy, you've got to help me."

"Yes, sir, major. What is it?"

He went on to explain the situation and requested that I put in reserve supplies of food, gasoline, and ammunition. I asked him where he wanted it and how much of each item and then told him I'd take care of it. Yesterday he called on me again to go over the ground with him, Captain Smith (H & S, 91st Engrs.) and Willie A. First we went up on the hill which was to be occupied by H & S Company, 96th Engineers.

"This will be your hill, Willie," the Major said. "Put one of your machine guns on it and dig for holes and string barbed wire all around it."

After awhile I interrupted. "Major, why not string barbed wire from here over to that knoll on the other side of the road (I pointed to the hill which was to be occupied by the men from 96th headquarters). A machine gun in this position could cover it, and the Japs would have a hard time getting through." "That's a good idea. Do it Willie." The Major sounded nearly hysterical. "Yes, that's a good idea. Good idea, Sammy. You know Sammy will be my right hand man in this defense."

"I thought you were coming over to H & S," Willie said.

"Oh, no we need him at headquarters."

They sounded ridiculous. I was flattered but embarrassed. Here were two *leaders* fighting to see who's side I would play on. They think that I am a reckless fool who could break off a Jap bayonet and eat it. They think I'm not scared of the devil himself. They look up to me as an example of a fearless officer. All I can say is if I am such an example, God help us if the Japs get up to here!

September 12, 1942

Japs are temporarily halted.

September 15, 1942

Completed a survey to see whether it is practical to construct a causeway from Tatana Island to the mainland. Tatana has six fathoms of water within 250 feet of its shore, and there is a stretch between it and the mainland, about 700 yards, where the water is hardly more than six feet at its deepest. Colonel Mathews' idea may have merit after all. I think I'll try to get permission to make a reconnaissance in an attempt to find deep water, with a deep approach, within 300 feet or so of the mainland. That would eliminate the causeway construction, might mean building approach roads. The most interesting part of the whole survey was the coral reefs and marine life—What beautiful color and shapes!

I almost burned to death. Our launch was tied up to a pier whose deck was loading with gasoline drums. One of the drums had a leak, and gasoline had poured down under the pier and onto the water. When we started the motor of the boat, a spark ignited the gasoline. We were momentarily enveloped in flames. When the blast went off, we saw the pier and ground under the pier on fire. Thanks to some brave, quick-minded Aussies who rushed out on the pier and rolled off the gasoline drums and then put out the flames with a nearby fire extinguisher the day was saved.

The 4½ mile bomb dump blew up this afternoon. All Moresby rumbled under the explosions. More damage was done than during all the Japanese raids. Fortunately it was in a deserted, valueless area.

September 16, 1942

Made survey for new fighter dispersal area on NW end of Seven-Mile Drome. It was interesting work. If all work on Seven-Mile Drome had been given a careful survey like this proposed job, they would not be confronted with the drainage problems that now exist. Capt. Thomas wants me to stay down there and work regularly with his Battalion. It is very flattering to have people want my services. What is more flattering is the way most of them listen to me. If I say I think a ditch should be put here and this culvert taken up and put there, it usually is done. I'd really like to work on Seven-Mile Drome awhile and see if I can't get some of their problems straightened out.

September 17, 1942

Am leaving Moresby in the morning on an expedition to Abau with General Casey and Colonel Sverdrup. It should prove an interesting adventure—all secret, of course. I hope it turns out as successfully as did the Fall River affair. Spent the whole day getting supplies and equipment ready. I get a big thrill out of preparing for these things.

SIX

Outflanking the Japanese

September 18–October 26, 1942

September 18, 1942, Port Moresby

The Japanese have complete control of the northern coast of New Guinea and are more than half way across the island from Buna to Port Moresby. We have a fair size force at Port Moresby but with the limited shipping facilities, crowded harbor and Japanese bombings, it is not a good policy to keep pouring in more troops. Our force at Milne Bay is kept busy by Japs who have retreated after an unsuccessful attempt to take the place. We can't pull out any of those men to help relieve Moresby for fear of another Japanese attempt to capture Milne Bay. But there may be another way. If we can land a strong force—secretly of course—at Abau, let them push well inland and finally drive to the west severing the Japanese supply lines outside Moresby, then close in on them from the rear—if we can do that we might win a great victory, for if we can recapture Kokoda, Buna should not be too difficult an objective. And Lae and Salamau would be ours again within a month after the fall of Buna. All of this sounds good, but what about getting ships into Abau? What are the chances of getting a strong force inland? Is food available along the way? Water? Will large rivers and steep mountain ranges have to be crossed? These are the questions to which we must supply the answers.[1]

September 18, 1942, Abau

The flight from Port Moresby to Abau went without incident. The gunners did not even man the guns during the flight which lasted only one hour. The tide was out, and the coral reefs shone in beautiful iridescent color patterns. The plane descended between Abau and

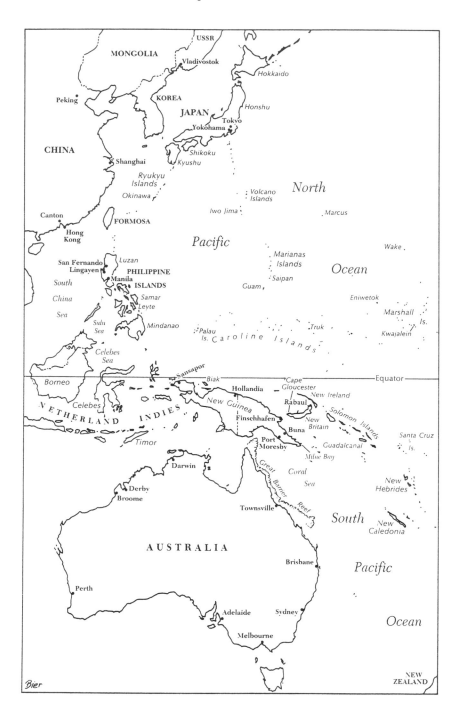

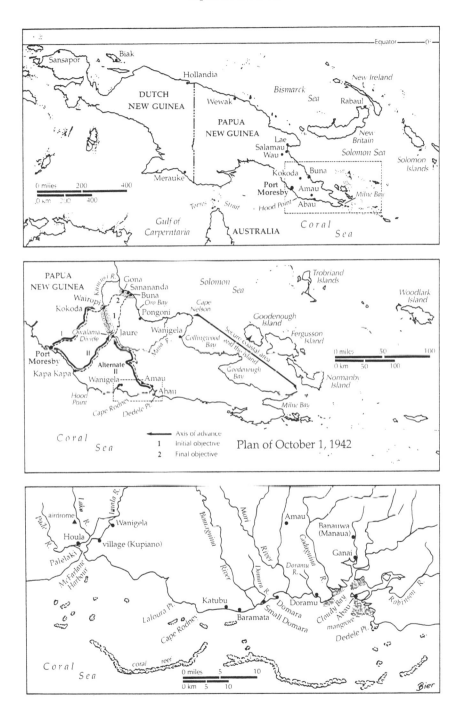

Plan of October 1, 1942

Abaui. A group of natives in a two-canoe boat came out to us. We loaded our rations and supplies onto the primitive boat and after getting on ourselves had the natives row us to the small pier on Abau. The *Jean L*, a 30 or 40 foot launch was tied up at the pier and we unloaded onto her deck and from it onto the pier.

The gardens of Abau are beautiful, and the walk up the hill to the big house, through rows and rows of sweet smelling, almost nauseating flowers, was like walking through a fairy land. It was good to see women and children and cats and dogs again. These primitive people in their grass huts gave me the impression of civilization. Yes, here was civilization. And here were we, ready to instigate plans which would soon destroy it. Well, better us than the Japanese. Mr. Bilston met us at the big house and immediately invited us to breakfast. It was a six or seven course affair, deliciously prepared, the best food I've eaten in a long time.

September 19, 1942, aboard the Lucy L

We divided into two parties and around noon the first party left alone in a small launch with Colonel Sverdrup in charge, Lt. Fryer, Australian surveyor, Warrant Officer Marsh a twenty year old Australian chap who knows the trails, languages and customs of the natives; Sergeant Dawson an American medical corpsman, and a dozen native carriers. They are going to Doramu by launch, then up a river by canoe. They will land about seven miles from Amau whence they will proceed on foot. Their assignment is to investigate Trail Number 4's possibilities for moving troops and artillery supplies. It will be about a two-week job and will be quite dangerous, for not only will nature pose a tough obstacle but Japanese patrols have been spotted in part of the region through which they will have to pass. Of course the natives are on our side, and that is a big factor—more about that later. The second party consists of General Casey, me, and two boys from the 898th Engineers—Corporal Parsons and Tech 5th Shipley. Our task is to find the best way of getting into Amau.

September 20, 1942

Just before Colonel Sverdrup's party left for Doramu, another launch under Major Bilston left for a point down the coast where the Jap dive bombers had made a forced landing. They were supposed to be some kind of new plane and the major wanted to bring them into Moresby for our intelligence department. Incidentally the six Japanese airmen who came from the three planes were all tracked down and killed by natives. They brought back the ears as evidence. The natives' explanation is simple: "Him resist, I kill."

All of the fighting in this area is to the death. No one is permitted to surrender. For instance, in the recent battle around Milne Bay we killed one thousand Japs; yet we didn't take a single prisoner.[2] There is one tale which might be worth while repeating. An army chaplain was performing the burial services for some sixty or seventy Japs who had been pushed into a hole with a bulldozer when one of the alleged dead men started to get up. The chaplain took out his revolver—BANG! —and then went on with the services.

All Friday afternoon we studied maps and charts of the area, questioned nearly a dozen people on what they knew of trails, harbors in this area. The inconsistencies were remarkable, even on government charts. It was very interesting trying to piece together all this information into something which was intelligent, but the only way to really find out whether a harbor or landing is good is to go out and see for yourself. So around five o'clock the General put an end to his interrogations and made plans for a trip along the coast.

Mr. Bilston served us a delicious supper—roasted chicken, fresh fruits and vegetables, sea food. We sat around after supper and chatted until nearly ten o'clock. We were up the next morning before daybreak, and before the sun had crept over the edge of Abasu we were heading out to sea. We traveled lightly, but even so we each had a heavy load. Take mine for instance. Besides what I wore (shirt, trousers, shoes, socks, leggings, and sun helmet) I carried three other pieces: a belt; a dispatch case which had a message book and this small diary, pencils, maps, mess kit, cigarettes, matches, mosquito oil, rule and tape, several packs of gum, a pace tally, a field book; and a clothing roll.

The trip from Abau to Mc Farlane Harbor took six and a half hours. The seas were very rough but the winds were with us. We sounded the approach to the harbor and found the deepest water to be around 2½ fathoms. This was too shallow for anything but a small ship and there were no good anchorages outside the harbor. The *Jean L* pulled into the harbor for a mile or so and then anchored. The tide was out so we could not go up the Paile River. We hailed some natives and told them to bring us up the small river in their canoes. There were five of us: the General, Lt. Clarke (Australian), Shipley, Parsons and me. Captain Willis stayed on the *Jean* to question natives about the trail to Debana. About a mile or so up the Paile we came to a little pier. Here we got off and walked inland for 3½ miles up to the Paile plantation house where we had some tea before starting back again. We observed several good sites for dromes. The soil is a silty clay and the only nearby rock is from the Lako river beds—very poor stuff, all smooth stones ½ inch to one inch. And the problem of supply would be difficult. In other words, the place is not suitable for an operational drome. However, with native labor alone, an emergency landing field could be cleared. And small quantities of gas and oil could be readily brought in.

Mr. Willis could get little information about the trail to Debana. Only two natives had been there apparently, and the trip had taken them six days—all over rough country. The General abandoned the idea of my going overland to Debana; for if it took the natives six days it would require two weeks for army troops to make the journey. A better access route to Amau had to be found.

Earlier in the day we picked up 8800 pounds of rubber—very valuable cargo these days. We picked up 13 natives who had escaped from the Kokoda Road north of Moresby. They claimed that the war was getting too close and they would get killed. Mr. Willis decided to send them back the first thing in the morning with a hundred more natives just recruited for work on the Kokoda road as carriers. We had a delicious supper aboard the *Jean:* another roast chicken along with half dozen other courses. Then we went ashore in the dinghy and climbed the hill to the mission house where we spent the night.

Aboard the Jean L: This morning as we weighed anchor and started out toward the Coral Sea, we saw 20 or 30 native boats all heading toward Palelaki. It was the native women all going down to cry while their husbands went off to war.

"It's the awfulest wailing you've ever heard in your life," Mr. Clarke tells us, "They scream and carry on something frightfully. Half an hour after the men folks have gone they'll be giggling and laughing as usual. The seat of their affections, which is in their stomachs, is not very deep."

We stopped at Palelaki to pick up some machine guns and ammunition which had been taken off a B-26 that had crashed recently in the harbor. And now we're out at sea again, bucking the wind and the waves. I get the smell of boiling crabs—delicious! I look forward to seeing a new airdrome here at Mc Farlane harbor within two months.

September 22, 1942, a native hut in Ganai

The wind blew harder, the seas became rougher, and the *Jean* bounced around like a rubber ball. The waves splashed over the deck. It felt good. Around three o'clock we anchored off Doramu, waiting for the high tide so that we could get over the bar which crossed the mouth of the river. Mr. Brewster came out to us in his small launch: about 25 feet long, eight feet wide, with a very shallow draft. We decided to let him lead in the *Jean*. We took soundings as we went, and in some places found only one fathom of water. The *Jean* was drawing 5½ feet so her bottom must have barely cleared the bar. Just at dusk we pulled into the mouth of the Doramu River and anchored. We had a delicious supper, and for the first time since I left home, I had some boiled crabs. They weren't nearly as good as the Lake Ponchartrain crabs but I enjoyed them anyway. Around 9:30 Parsons and Shipley took the dinghy ashore to spend the night in a native hut.

At the first sign of dawn we bade farewell to the *Jean* as she pulled out to sea to bring her precious cargo to Moresby. We then proceeded up the river in the smaller boat. It was a beautiful river with its hundreds of different kind of trees and birds. I chatted with Mr. Clarke most of the way. He has lived in New Guinea for 34 years and is very interesting. He has a wonderful sense of humor and knows a lot more than he impresses you with knowing. At length the river narrowed into no more than a creek. So we stopped and went ashore. An old Studebaker truck was parked where we landed and with some difficulty we got the engine to run. We proceeded eight miles inland on the truck, pushing the broken down vehicle ten percent of the way.

On the way to Amau I noticed a very interesting type of tree. It grew to great heights, much larger than any other tree I have seen in New Guinea. Yet the width of the tree's trunk at the base is not much larger than at any other point; and if someone would cut off its stabilizing flange-roots (which I will describe in a minute) the high giant would blow over in the first strong wind. But the tree has a strange, above ground root which gives it great stability. Generally there are three of these roots, each like a large sheet of steel plate. Sometimes there are more: four or five, and on some trees I counted up to twelve. On the larger trees these plate-roots are reinforced further by fins which are very much like the stiffeners on plate girders. In a few cases I saw where these fins were themselves strengthened with other fins. Occasionally the fins from one main root joined with the fins from another main root, resulting in "root bridges" and many beautiful patterns. The Quata Mission House is a four-story affair. It is owned by a Mr. Abeli, who was not in when we arrived. The house looks very much like a ship.

Finally we arrived at Amau. What a beautiful little village. Flowers and cultivation were everywhere. It was a new village, not over four years old, and remarkably clean. The General decided that I should go overland from here to Ganai to see the condition of the trail and in particular whether it could be made into a Jeep track. Around noon Shipley and I and six natives set out for Ganai. General Casey, Mr. Clarke and Parsons went with us for the first two miles. Then we proceeded without them.

From Amau to the Godaguina River there was a well defined track and the going was fairly easy. We found an excellent place to ford the Godaguina: about one hundred feet of rock bottom not over thirty inches deep. We had feared that the Godaguina would present a difficult problem, and this easy crossing made my hopes soar, for I felt certain that if the trail did not become more difficult, a Jeep track from Ganai to Amau would be highly feasible. But on the other side, the eastern side, of the Godaguina the trail narrowed and finally disappeared. About six miles from Amau the ground became hilly. There were some difficult stream crossings which would require bridges, but the soil conditions were favorable and the grades were not severe. Another two miles and the going became quite rough. We climbed slowly, perhaps to a thousand feet, and some of the grades could not be negotiated by a jeep. Our guide kept telling me about another trail. He knew only a few words in English. I knew none of his lingo. The only thing I knew was that I wanted to get to Ganai by the shortest and best route. I now learned that the guide had never gone to Ganai over this trail and that he was not sure of the way. I had kept close check on his course by compass the whole way and he had been heading in the correct direction.

"Find good camp," I told him when I learned there were no villages around.

We walked on for another mile or two, still climbing.

"This good camp" the guide told me.

"O.K. We camp here."

And with that I loosened my cartridge belt and let all my gear fall to the ground. Shipley and I flopped on the ground and enjoyed a few cigarettes while the natives built us a grass hut to sleep under. One native scrambled down the hillside to bring us water while another built a fire. One of my pants legs had been torn half way off, so I completed the job. We made hot coffee and warmed some canned stew and enjoyed a good meal. We put up the mosquito nets and climbed onto our bed of rago leaves. A few cigarettes and off to sleep with the humming sound of the natives in our ears. As soon as the first sound of dawn's breaking reached our ears we got up, packed, and started on our way. We climbed for another two hundred feet on a 60% grade.

"I hope it doesn't get worse," I thought to myself. "We have to find a road inland somewhere, and this is supposed to be our best bet."

We traveled along the top of the ridge for half a mile. And then we came to a point which made my heart sick: a 500 foot drop on an 80% grade. It was difficult to negotiate on foot. Mules would find it hard. For Jeeps it would be impossible. I looked around for a relocation as I had done at all other difficult spots, but although up until this point I had always been able to spot a new way to bring in a Jeep, here I found none. A side hill winding road was the only answer, but there would be no time for that.

"How far Ganai?" I asked the guide.

"Yeah" was his reply.

"Dododuro Ganai?" I believe that was what Mr. Clarke had asked one of the natives when he wanted to know how far it was to a place, so I used it. It must not have been the right expression, for the native guide did not understand.

"Me no go Ganai this way before" was the most information I could get from him. Well, we had better press on. I'll have to study this place for a relocation some other time. We stumbled on down and down and at length came to a mountain stream.

"We have tea here," I told the guide. We washed in the stream while the natives built some fires to prepare ours and their kai-kai. Ours consisted of hot coffee and canned hash. Theirs was roasted bananas. Feeling much better, we pushed on. A few miles more and the guide pointed out "Look, Taberer—Babaguina Riber—Ganai soon." Another quarter hour and we entered Ganai. The village policeman came up and gave me a snappy salute. He then led us to their guest house and spread weaved mats on the floor for us to sit on. I handed him a stick of tobacco and paid off the carriers with two sticks. I told the guide to stay with me until the launch came up the river to get me. I made a map of the area we had covered. After dinner, Shipley and I sat around smoking and chatting. Then we finally fell asleep, with all the sounds of the village in our ears: children crying, natives babbling, dogs barking, pigs squealing.

"Taberer, taberer—boat come!" a native awakened me.

I slipped on my shoes and socks, scratched my scalp, looked at my watch. It was 4 P.M. I had been sleeping two hours. I made a brief report to the General, then showed him my map. He was very complimentary. I told Mr. Clarke about the guide's telling me of another trail and asked him to see if he could get any information from him. After jabbering with the negro for five or ten minutes, Mr. Clarke turned to the General and said: "He says there's another trail. Much shorter. No hills. No swamps. He said Lt. Samuelson was a mad man for going the way he did. He told of a landing on the Binaguina River. You remember, sir, that river that took off to the left as we went past that island?"

"Yes, I remember," the General said. "Where we hit that deep stretch."

"Yeah. Well he said if we go up that river we come to some dry land where we can get off and go to Amau. He says it's only five or six hours across by that way."

"Well, we still have a couple of hours before dark. What do you say we have a look at this—what's the name of that river?"

"Bina—BI—NA—guina. The Binaguina River."

A trip up the river proved that there was deep water all the way. And right in the middle of the mangroves we came across the dry spot. This might be the future landing spot of thousands of troops and tons of supplies.

"I don't believe a white man has ever been up here before," Mr. Clarke said. "You never know what you're liable to find." A report from Colonel Sverdrup indicates that he is running into very difficult country. Unless we run into some better luck, this whole plan might fizzle out.

And here tonight at the government station we have a correspondent brought in by two missionaries named Newman and Salzman.[3] He has been in the bush for thirty days. The poor devil is no more than a skeleton with skin covering his bones. He is quite delirious and talks incessantly. We have radioed Moresby for a plane to pick him up. If he stays here, he will be done for in two more days. Can't get a particle of food into him. I'll jot down what he is saying now—

"Trees, trees, trees, trees, up, up, up, up, trees, trees, up trees—oh-oh-oh-oh-oh-oh-red-trees—red-red-red-red—trees-red trees-red trees-red-red-blood-blood-blood-red blood-red blood-red blood-oh-oh-mother, mother, mother, mother, mother!"

He hasn't stopped for more than two minutes during the past two hours. It's horrible. He is sleeping in the bed I slept in two nights ago. I guess I'll bunk on the floor.

September 23, 1942

Dedele Point with its natural fan reef breakwater is the only protected deep-water anchorage we have been able to find. But lightering from Dedele to Ganai or from Dedele to X through sand bars and narrow channels where the water is hardly one fathom during low tides presents a serious time-consuming problem. If an overland route could be found inland from Dedele this lightering operation could be wiped out.

"I remember," Brewster tells us, "about eight years ago a woman and her husband walked from Dedele to Robinson Plantation; and when I offered to take them back in my launch, they refused to go; they had enjoyed the hike so much that they wanted to return on foot."

"Quite impassable!" says Mr. Clarke. "Dedele Point is virtually separated from the mainland at high tide. I've never been over the track myself, but all reports indicate its a foul affair."

"Well, Samuelson," the General told me this morning "there's a little walk for you to take this afternoon."

With two Abau policemen and a native boy from the Robinson Plantation, I started from Dedele at 2:50. We had to come to Dedele Point in the launch with the dying correspondent to put him on a plane which had come up from Moresby and landed on the beach. Mr. Brewster said that he would meet me at the Robinson River Plantation wharf in four hours with my equipment and rations. I had received instructions from the general that if the Dedele-Robinson Plantation trail was satisfactory I should proceed on to Babaguina and then to Ganai; otherwise I was to return to Abau that evening in Mr. Brewster's launch.

The first two miles were easy going along the beach to the east of Dedele. This we covered in 30 minutes. Then we headed inland crossing the east tip of the Dedele coconut plantation and immediately ran into a mangrove swamp. Two-tenths of a mile of this swamp convinced me that a road was impossible; so I put away my tachometer, compass, and field book; and with my hands free, I could scramble over the twisted roots with much more speed.

But it was impossible to keep up with the three natives. They swing along like monkeys, making better time than they would have on flat ground. I thought it was great sport at first, but after a mile, my arches began to ache. At length we came to a clearing, where we ate a paupau. But then there were more mangroves. The boy-guide with one policeman got so far ahead that I lost sight of them. The policeman behind me moved up ahead to show me the way. He moved swiftly trying to catch up with the first pair, and I had my hands full to keep up with him. Part of the time, whenever we found a log lying on the ground or across a stream, we actually ran. The tide started oozing up through the ground. The mosquitoes and red ants bit voraciously. The woods were getting dark although it was not quite five o'clock. And then my policeman got lost! I was wringing with perspiration and exhausted. We had been going three or four miles an hour through mangroves, and that is really stepping. My policeman called out again and again and finally got a reply from the advanced two. We guided our way to them by the sound of their voices. Every time we crossed a stream now, water was flowing swiftly, for the tide was making fast. The going became harder, for now one had to stay on the roots or fallen logs or high ground, for to step in the mud meant going down to the knees. Only twice on the ten or twelve mile stretch did I stumble—once on dry land over a root and the other time trying to change from one submerged log to another submerged log while crossing a stream. I slipped off and went down to my seat in the mucky water, glad that it wasn't deeper. After three hours and fifty minutes we reached the wharf. Brewster had just pulled in. I paid the native a stick of tobacco and got on the launch. It was night now. A beautiful full moon lit up the river. We chugged along down stream against the "making" tide. Brewster made some hot tea, which was greatly stimulating. I slept most of the way back to Abau which took over two hours to cover the ten mile distance.

September 24, 1942, Abau

The General, Belston, and Parsons have not returned from their journey investigating the Banauwa[Manaua]-Amau track. I believe this trail will be the approved solution.

September 26, 1942, Domara Village Rest House

We spent most of yesterday drawing sketch maps of this area and making reports on our findings. The best route which we have been able to find is pretty close to what we anticipated before we arrived. Large ships can anchor off Dedele Point. Lighters can carry troops and cargo to Banauwa Landing, about a twelve mile haul, and from Banauwa to Amau a thirteen mile Jeep-track can be readily built. Before the General left this morning he told me to investigate around Doramu: "See if you can't find a place where we can have deep enough water to bring a lighter in. If you can find such a place, investigate further to see if you can build a road from this lighter landing to the road which leads to Amau."

Shortly after he left, a messenger arrived from Colonel Sverdrup. They are running into all kind of difficulties. Sverdrup says that a motor or mule track is impossible and that all maps which he brought inland with him are useless. He expects to return to Abau on October 6th instead of October 1st, as originally scheduled. It was a long dispatch. I took out the most important points to send a wireless to Moresby for General Casey when he arrives there. I know he is anxious to hear from Sverdrup.

Brewster, I and two natives left Abau shortly before 12 o'clock, heading for Doramu in the *Queen Elizabeth*, Brewster's 16-foot launch. It was an exciting, eleven mile sail, made in just a bit over an hour. All the way from the mouth of the Doramu River to Domara Village we took soundings 500 to 1000 feet from shore. We found no water over six feet deep and the tide still had another foot to drop. We crossed the mouth of the Mori River in our soundings, proving that an entrance to that big stream in a lighter was impossible. We stopped at Domara for some tea, salmon, and biscuits. By this time the tide was so low that we couldn't even get up the Domara River in our shallow-draft boat. So, we decided to wait for the tide before trying to proceed up the river to Baia Plantation where Brewster used to live before the war and where we decided to spend the night. We walked through the crowded village. One or two storms will blow this bit of land off the map. Most of it is covered now by high tide. Well, it is a few minutes past five and the tide has turned. A 20 mile an hour sou'easter is blowing, driving sheets of rain before it. We might not be able to come out of this protected spot and around into the river. But Baia is Brewster's old home and he is a fearless chap. My guess is that we'll be in Baia even if a storm should blow up. Frankly, this thing carrying on around us now is a pretty good imitation of a storm.

Around five o'clock Brewster reckoned the tide had risen high enough for us to "give'er a try." Coming around Domara Village and into the open sea against a 20 mile an hour wind was no easy task for our little launch. The waves covered her from one end to another, and steering her into the Domara River with everything: the wind, the waves, the tide, and her four horses pushing the sixteen foot craft along required a lot of quick action. The four mile journey up the Domara took two hours, and was a nightmare. Nearly ten percent of the way the water was too shallow for our boat and we spent most of our time pushing her off sand bars and submerged logs.

"I don't like to wade too much in this river, full of alligators"
Brewster said. That was enough to make me jump out of my skin
every time a piece of wood drifted by or a fish splashed. To make
matters worse it started to rain. And with that hard wind blowing it
got darn right cold. The only thing I liked about the trip was the
beauty of the phosphorus in the water. Whenever you would strike a
log, the water around it would sparkle with swamp fire.

It was around 7:30 when we reached Brewster's house. He had sent
a messenger ahead to tell his cook that we were coming; so when we
arrived, we had a hot shower waiting for us. Then came a delicious
supper, with all the formalities of a court banquet — just for the two of
us. I ate, as I have been eating ever since I came to this area, like a
half-starved pig. Brewster had given me a clean dry uniform of his to
put on, and I was quite comfortable. We sat around smoking after
supper until late in the night. Brewster is about 45 years old and is
normally a quiet chap, but on this particular evening he told me half
his life's history. I judge that it has not been a very happy life. His wife
died of black water fever, and he himself is one of the five percent of
those who get the disease and live. His life has been a struggle to make
money. Of course he doesn't tell it like this, but he has had a lot of
tough breaks. He has an unpleasant personality and suffers from the
feeling that everyone is against him. He is a talented little man, knows
a lot about motors and radios. He has no diplomacy or tact. His
human selfishness is so much on the surface that it is irritable. But he
treated me royally and showed me real hospitality. I rather like the
little bloke. There isn't much difference between his spoken word and
what's in his mind. His petty scheming is right on the surface. We got
off to an early start yesterday morning. We couldn't take the launch
because I had planned a trip to Rodney Point by water and back from
there to Baia by foot. Brewster made arrangements with some natives
who were going that way to take us as far as Cape Rodney.

I'd like to digress a moment here to describe the manner in which
the natives "tacked" with their canoes. But first a word about the
canoes themselves. They are made from two large trees, carefully
shaped and chiseled out. The two ends are covered with a "deck"
because they are always dipping down into the water and would
cause the canoe to fill up unless the water was made to run back into
the sea. The two canoes are lashed together with vines and spares
approximately ten-feet apart and a deck is placed over these spars.
Naturally, they are braced for stability. A large block of wood with a
circular groove is placed in the bottom of one of the canoes, and this
serves to hold the butt of the mast. The mast is simply a strong,

straight tree. The sail is of canvas, the only thing which the native has to buy.

Since the sail is not guyed from the outside, the ordinary method of tacking cannot be used; for when the sail would swing around, the mast would be pulled over. When they are about to "tack" they steer their canoe into a position which is exactly opposite to the direction they wish to go. Then they allow the sail to come around from the stern to the bow. And behold! The back of the boat is now the front; the front is the back—and away they go headed 45 degrees into the wind. And in this operation there has been no messy boom over the deck at any time.

When we left for Rodney Point in a native canoe, the tide was making up the river and it took nearly an hour for the natives to paddle the canoe two miles to its mouth. Here we found the sea a cauldron of boiling waves. The average person would hesitate going out in it in a medium launch, but these natives in their canoe did not hesitate a minute. First they crossed to the bar which covers the mouth of the river. Then they made a dash to the small isthmus which connects Domara Village to the mainland. At this point, protected from the waves and to some extent from the wind, they hoisted the sails. The canoe tore away from the mainland and dashed out to sea. Talk about a thrill! I estimated our speed at twelve miles an hour, and this was proven to be approximately right, for an hour after leaving the Domara we were off Cape Rodney. But what an hour! Two little boys bailed continuously, and we were all wet from head to toe. I mapped the shore line as best I could and took a few soundings. From Domara on past Baramata Point all the way to Ottamata (Cape Rodney) I found good depths of water, but there was no sheltered anchorage. And in heavy seas such as we were experiencing then, unloading from a large ship onto a lighter would be next to impossible. But at Cape Rodney the story was different. Although the eastern side of the Cape was hammered mercilessly, the western side was quite calm. I found that a ship of 16 foot draft could come within 1200 feet of the shore at low tide, but what was extraordinary was the fact that when we came closer to the shore the water became only 4 feet shallower in 1000 feet. In other words, a ship of 12-foot draft could get within 200 feet of the shore at low tide. This was not exactly what we wanted, but it might have possibilities.

At Ottamata we had some tea, hard tack, and corned beef. Then we hit the trail for home. The four and a half miles from Ottamata to Baramata along the beach is an excellent low-tide road as it is, and with a little work could be made into an all weather, high-tide roadway. We found a large garden at Baramata and filled our bellies with paws-paws and sugar cane before starting home. From Baramata to Baia a road could be built without any trouble whatsoever. The only large stream crossing is the Bomuguina, and that can be forded without difficulty. We reached Brewster's place a half hour after dark. I don't believe I'd like traveling through these forests at night. A delicious spring chicken added a lot to our meal—and off to bed early. I am tired and sleepy. I'll write of today's hike in the morning.

September 29, 1942

Brewster knew nothing of the trail from Baia to Amau and the only information he could get was from his "boss boy" who said it was ten hours of hard walking. Brewster interpreted this as being 20 miles or so.

"Impossible," I said, "It's less than eight miles on a straight line, surely not more than 12 by trail. My maps can't be that wrong."

Brewster only smiled at me. I could read his thoughts: "These damn Americans, here two weeks and think they know more of the country than a man who has lived here all his life."

October 1, 1942, Abau Government Station

I became a bit cross with Brewster about gathering up tools. I had made a request of Captain Lambden to make available all axes, shovels, etc. on these nearby plantations for use by the natives in clearing trails. Lambden had told Brewster to pick up the tools at Baia Plantation while he was up here. Well last Monday morning just before I started out from Baia to Amau, Brewster piddled around getting one or two shovels and a few axes.

"Will that be enough?" he asked.

"Get all you can find! They're not doing any good here on the plantation. Better use them where they can do some good than leave them around here for the Japs to capture!" He produced some sixty-odd tools.

October 2, 1942, on trail from Banauwa to Amau

It was nine o'clock Monday before we got away from Baia and Brewster's "boss boy" said we'd have to go very fast if we expected to get to Amau before dark. I thought this was quite impossible. For the first few miles we traveled on a course which was about 15 degrees west of north. I knew that this was 30 or 40 degrees off the course to Amau and was half tempted to tell the boss boy to go to hell and strike my own course through the bush. But at least he was on a track, and 20 miles is easier than five on a compass bearing through tangled wilderness. So I followed along. After six or seven miles we came to the Mori River, and the boss boy said we were half way. So I told him and Haila that we'd have kai-kai along the river's banks. Haila shot a bird and we would have eaten it if we had had time. But instead I took my knife and split open a tin of meat. This with a cup of tea and some bread was my dinner. When I had eaten all that I wanted, I gave the rest to the two natives. Then we hit the trail again. Incidentally I was traveling lighter than usual. In my hands I carried a compass, a pedometer, a pencil, and a notebook. Around my waist I carried a knife and a revolver. Actually I could have left the revolver behind too, except for crocodiles. I haven't seen these reptiles in action, but according to Clarke, Bilston and Lambden, they are very dangerous. Attacked by one in a river, you are helpless, and even on the shore, you don't have much of a chance unless you are armed with a gun.

"No, they won't eat you on land," says Lambden, "but they will attack you, and they will have you in the water before you know what hit you. Actually it will be the 'gator's tail that hit you. I remember the time two years ago when. . . ."

I had one close call on the trail to Amau. I stepped directly on a snake, just behind its head. It was a very small snake, but he quickly wrapped around my leg. I don't know whether I took another step forward or not, but I know that he was still under my foot when I looked down; and I crushed it to death under my heel. Haila thought this a very brave deed. He called me "hero." He doesn't know I was scared stiff. Haila is a little black man, not over five feet. He has a big head of hair, red at the top, black at the roots. He killed two Japs not so long ago in this area. He is very fond of me for some strange reason, perhaps because I always ask him to tell me how to say certain words in his language. I have learned a lot of words from him such as tree, river, rain, sun. He is very careful with me, washes my legs whenever we get to a cool stream. Yet when I lost my pencil, he thought nothing wrong with searching me for it, digging his hands into all my pockets just as if I were perfectly helpless.

It was round 4 o'clock when we reached Amau. It had rained very hard for two hours before we arrived and everything was full of mud. I was struck again by the beauty of the native village; so much cleaner than any other village I have seen around here. That night at the Quata Mission was wonderful. I slept on a bed in which I could stretch out like a spider. I slept for nearly 12 hours; and when I awoke, I lay in bed enjoying the wonderful luxury of that soft, big cloud. Brewster was to meet me at the Upper Landing at 1 o'clock, and that was a mere eight mile walk, less than three hours. So I spent the morning wandering around the village looking at the women and children. It makes me strangely happy to see women and children. Whenever I approach they act very shy, but I keep walking back and forth until they pretend not to notice me. I wish I could talk with the women and play with the children. I love to give them the colored candies from our C rations. They always run off and show them to their parents before they eat them. Gosh, what a wonderful time I'd have here with a lot of toys for all these pretty little children.

It was Dickson who picked me up instead of Brewster. He brought a note from an Australian lieutenant colonel by the name of Viol who said that he was leaving for Moresby by plane and would like very much to see me before going. I met him just before his launch left for Dedele Point where the *Moth* was supposed to pick him up. He asked me a lot of questions about the surrounding country. My "bushy" appearance, muddy and dirty (from the Amau-Upper Landing walk in the rain), five days without a shave—all of this must have impressed him, for he took my word on local conditions without question. When we finished, he turned to me and said, "You've ruined this report."

He had been scratching out parts of his report and adding other sentences the whole time I spoke. But then he turned to me and smiled.

"But thanks a lot. Better now than later, when it's too late."

"Yes," I told him, "you can hardly make a 'map' solution to any problem in this area. The maps are hopelessly inaccurate."

And I pointed out my sketch of the coast line from Doramu to Ottamata and showed him how the maps had it plotted. He said he would see to it that the maps were corrected in future printings. Next day (Wednesday) Viol and I made reports on the local situation. He had a long, thorough report. Mine was relatively simple.

Thursday was a day of rest. I started off with a novel, *God's Country and the Woman*, but after 80 pages of Josephine's quivering lips and clasping her hands to her fluttering breast, I laid the book aside to go with Viol on a little fishing expedition. We had a single line and no bait; we caught no fish. If there were any fish in the water, they would not be attracted by the white piece of cloth we tied to the hook. Viol had never seen a reef from close up; so he suggested going out to a fan reef in a native canoe. I went with him and a native youth, the chap who was my guide a week or ten days ago on my jaunt from Dedele to Robinson River. When we reached the reef, the waves swarmed the canoe and we foundered. Coral is beautiful to look at, but God have mercy on those who have to walk on it bare-footed. The coral cut like razors. But the hard calcareous formations were not nearly as bad as the soft "oozy" clusters which looked like brains. I had enjoyed dissecting a few star fish before we sank, but walking on their backs was not much fun. Next time I go for a canoe ride on a coral reef, I'll wear shoes—just in case!

And this evening I find myself on the strangest assignment of my life. I am a quarter of a mile from the Banauwa Landing, camped in an old native hut. I have with me a crew of 42 natives and we are starting work clearing the Banauwa-Amau trail for Jeep traffic. Clarke came out with me today and got things rolling. He gave me instructions for working and feeding the natives, and then he returned to Abau; he plans to return to the job the day after tomorrow. Until then things will be completely under my control. We are to commence work at the crack of dawn. Breakfast (for the natives) at 9 o'clock (1 cup of rice per man). Resume work at 9:30; quit at 3:30. Supper whenever natives want (one pack of biscuits and one cup of meal per man). Ration to be supplemented with anything natives can find—on their own time.

October 5, 1942, Dobbindorp, on the banks of a little creek, two miles from Banauwa

Col. Sverdrup and his party returned to Abau Saturday morning. I received a note late that afternoon from the colonel stating that he wanted to see me. So Saturday evening I packed up my mosquito net, blanket and toilet articles and went back to Abau with Corbett in the *Queen Elizabeth*. An otherwise enjoyable boat ride was spoiled by the constant talking of Corbett. The wind was blowing so hard that I could hardly hear what he was saying. But he kept on talking. I had to look at him; and when he smiled, I had to force myself to grin; and when he frowned, I frowned. The trials of the Colonel's 180-mile journey were clearly visible on him. He had lost a lot of weight and was cranky. Only his sense of humor had not suffered. And at dinner he was quite himself again, bubbling over with tales of places and people he had seen. He seemed to believe that a motor trail or even a mule trail from Amau inland was impracticable and said that I should abandon work on the Banauwa-Amau trail. This naturally didn't make me happy, for, being human, I hated to start something and then fail to push it through to completion. It isn't hard to picture my pleasure the next day when I received the following wire: "To Samuelson Abau from Casey Fletone Stop Abau Project Being Approved Stop Pending Arrival Engineer Bn [Battalion] Initiate Marking Approach Channel Clearing Landing Area and Improved Access Trail Abau Per Previous Direction Utilizing All Native Labor Procurable Stop Matthews to Furnish Hand Tools Stop Signed McArthur."

So when I handed the wire to Colonel Sverdrup to read there was nothing for him to do but countermand his order to abandon the road project.

Saturday, working alone most of the time with the natives, I succeeded in pushing through about one mile of trail. Mr. Clarke who arrived Saturday afternoon, worked the natives Sunday and completed about three-quarters of a mile. The work which he produced was better than mine.

Today we moved camp up to Dobbendorp (Our own name, named after Dobben Clarke's personal boy) and then pushed through two-thirds of a mile of new road. The country was more difficult than usual, and a reconnaissance this afternoon shows there is more hard work ahead. Clarke is just about down with rheumatism and I'll probably have to take over alone in the morning. I plan to set a goal for the boys, another creek about a mile from the place we stopped today. I am somewhat disappointed in the progress we are making. Originally I thought we could build the trail (13 miles) in ten days and build the pier at Banauwa and all the bridges in another ten days. I believe now that we will have to work flat out in order to complete the whole job in twenty-four days. Today is our third day, and we have completed only three miles of roadway. Our force has been increased to 54 natives.

October 6, 1942

Shipley arrived during the night. He says the Colonel is flying back to Moresby and that Parsons has gone with Marsh inland on a further reconnaissance. They will also recruit more native labor. Clarke was down today with rheumatism and Shipley and I took over the native gang. He worked ahead with the "mero ilapa"[4] and did an excellent job. We completed a mile of roadway by 1:30 P.M. up to "Corporal's Creek," another one of our own names. The boys worked as if under some strange inspiration.

"They're happy," Clarke says. "Plenty of kai-kai, plenty of work, plenty of rest."

October 7, 1942, Godaguina River

We moved camp today. I loathe the chaos and turmoil of moving supplies. Clarke beats the boys and curses them. But he does get results! Here on the banks of this river we have a beautiful camp. The clear-water, rock-bottom stream is full of fish, and its deep cool water (it's over ten feet in the middle) is a wonderful place to swim. Our native corporal shot a Gara pigeon which we fried for supper, a delicious treat. The country was flatter and the growth less dense and we cleared, I'd estimate, a bit over a mile today. The edge of the road is but two hundred yards from here; and we are a little over five miles from Banauwa. Today is our fifth day of work. We are slightly behind schedule but I feel confident that we will catch up on our proposed work. I am going to draw a progress chart this evening.

October 8, 1942

More natives arrived this evening, swelling the total to 98. Clarke wants to work all hands on the trail tomorrow. I think that is concentrating too many natives. But I guess Clarke, after having worked these buggers for over thirty years, knows what he is talking about and we will all work the trail in the morning.

October 9, 1942, Unea River

We now have 141 natives. I just strolled through our camp, and in a few hours the boys have converted this place into a little village. All the boys have gotten together and built their own huts. Altogether we must have about six villages represented. One of the huts was eighty feet long. One group was very proud of the twelve-foot long python they had caught and were cooking for supper. All of them seemed happy and were chattering like a bunch of monkeys. Reports from natives indicate that we are very close to Amau. At best I think we have two days' work left. Of course this is a good showing for I set a rather stiff schedule to meet, and we are beating it by about two days. The bridging schedule will be more difficult to meet, for there are numerous bridges which will have to be built which I did not include in the schedule.

October 10, 1942

Clarke and Shipley worked the boys on the trail today and pushed on within less than a day's work of Amau. The people of Amau, learning of the trail we are building to their city have mustered a few hands to come out and meet us. We learn that the trail they are cutting is so poor however that we will have to go over it. Our trail is a poor one itself, but at least we have taken out all the stumps.

October 11, 1942

I sent a note to Captain Lambden this morning requesting that he send the following wire to General Casey: "To Casey Maple from Samuelson Abau Stop Trail Clearing Complete 12 October Stop Estimate Completion of Bridges on Trail and Banauwa Wharf Sixty Foot Face Twenty One October Stop Appropriate Time By Jeep Banauwa Amau Seventy Minutes End."

The boys had a day off today. We paid them one stick of tobacco yesterday and another one today when they brought up their axes properly sharpened.

I wonder what Dora is doing now. If I guess right she is in the hospital, probably in labor this minute—poor little angel. If the doctor was right, I am a father already, but my guess is that today is the day. What a wonderful little baby we should have. I write very little about my little girl, but—well, a man doesn't write that he breathed today or that his heart beat today. My thoughts are always with her.

October 12, 1942

The two bridges I built today were put together without a nail and, I estimate, are good enough for at least four tons. One bridge was only thirty feet long and four large trees were used for stringers. There was nothing particularly interesting about this bridge. But the other was sixty feet long and required the construction of four bents. I would like to describe how these were made without a nail or a piece of lashing of any kind. First, three holes were dug in spots where the piles were destined to go. When these holes were three or four feet deep a 14-inch log was dropped into them. By eyeing from bridge seat to bridge seat, a mark was made on the loose pile to fix its top at the correct elevation. It was then removed and cut off with an axe. The top of the pile was then shaped. This was done to the three piles which held up the cap. A good piece of timber was selected for the cap and this was shaped so that it fit snugly into the grooves on top of the piles. When the cap was placed on the three piles and dirt tamped firmly about their bases with the handle of a shovel, the final result was a pier stable in any direction. The only refinement that I can think of which would improve this pier would be bolts driven through the two "lips" on top of the piles and through the cap.

October 14, 1942

It was around noon when I came in. I met Colonel Sverdrup in Captain Lambden's office. He had arrived a few hours earlier by flying boat. He gave me his usual big hello and then said the Banauwa-Amau project was off.

"Off!" I exclaimed "With the Navy in here checking channel approaches and all?"

"Yep," he said. "We're pushing the Japs back so fast that this place has lost all military value. Why we've got troops in Wanigela. I'm going up to Bibira to build an airdrome with native labor. Do you realize we will be in Buna in fourteen days?"

"Yes, sir things have been going our way a bit—air superiority. Then I guess I should cease work on the road project."

"Oh, no. Keep right on. It won't be used, but you have an operational order to build it; so until you hear otherwise, continue the work."

"And the Banauwa Pier? Build it?"

"Oh, yes. Keep on work just as if I hadn't told you anything."

"But, sir, the bridges and pier will rot out in six months. It is a shame to tie up all that labor for a job which will not benefit anyone."

"Well, don't let that worry you. I'm taking over half your labor with me. Plan to take over three hundred boys in with me."

"Yes, sir. Then I'll just keep on with the work until it is finished."

"Yes, and you'd better wire Yoder in three to four days for instructions. They will probably forget all about you."

"Yes, sir," I answered meekly and walked off to the house to lie down. "Buna in fourteen days!" I mumbled to myself. "Like hell! Just because the Japs have pulled off all their planes for an attack on the Solomons, we think we've got him licked, What fools!" I hadn't fallen asleep when in came Captain Lambden with four American officers. They shot questions at me fast and furiously. I think I was able to answer most of them. They wanted a guide to take them up to Banauwa; and since I was anxious to get back on the job, I told them

I'd show them the way. They were very complimentary on the work which had been done but I couldn't appreciate their compliments.

October 15, 1942

Morale is shot to hell. Clarke, who was always impossible in the morning, is that way all day long. "I told you they'd never use this road," he says. "Yes, and I still think they will in spite of what the Colonel says." I answered like that for the good of my morale as well as for anyone else's. My right leg is killing me. About ten pussy ulcers have me so that I can hardly walk.

October 16, 1942

Sgt. Galloway, who arrived on the job last Tuesday, left this morning with one hundred men, the best of our "little army," to join Colonel Sverdrup around Sapia. Corbett arrived this afternoon to take his place, and Clarke is very hostile. Clarke is impossible! The departure of the one hundred men today was a scene I shall never forget. As they started to leave, the seventy remaining boys (We have lost about 30 through sickness and desertion) ran up to the boys who were leaving; and they all started to cry. This went on for about ten minutes—the awfulest wailing I had ever heard. I sat down and watched and watched. Tears flowed in every direction.

"All right," I shouted *"Eta law gahara.* Let's go back to work!" Then all the boys who had to remain on the job rushed back to their work, and they plunged into it with songs and laughter. It was the greatest display of alligator tears I had ever seen.

My leg became so bad today that I had to quit work and go to bed. I plan to return to Abau in the morning.

"You're no good to anyone out here," Clarke tells me.

After seeing the scars on his legs and on Corbett's legs from New Guinea ulcers, and after hearing how long they spent in bed with them, I think it is advisable to return to Abau for treatment. The ford I attempted to build here is a flop. Clarke and Shipley found another place, a natural shallow ford. I failed to make a thorough reconnaissance.

October 16, 1942

Dearest little boy,

This is the first chance that I have gotten to write to you since the baby was born. He gets sweeter and more beautiful every day. He looks just like you, too. His nose is just like yours and when he cries or anything it reminds me of you. Oh, Hymie, it's so wonderful all this. And I am happy. I know you will be too just as soon as you hear about it. I love you so much, Hymie, that I ache all over. I can't help missing you until I find it unbearable at times. Your not being here all the while I was pregnant and all has been awfully hard to bear, but now that the baby is here I know that I'll have something to keep me occupied and pretty happy until you come home and fill the awful gap in my arms. I won't complain. I thank God every minute for that precious baby of ours. I thank God for all that we have. For we have each other, sweetheart.

October 17, 1942, Abau

I was a sad boy when I left camp this morning. Our "small army," crippled with thirty more deserters, had dwindled to forty working men. And these were small, sickly boys who won't last long. My leg was so full of pain that I had to limp along with a stick. I passed piles of idle tools, so precious, less than a week ago. I looked at my "fizzled-out" ford. I stumbled upon our road, a road which would be beautiful if we had labor, and a motive behind the work. The six mile walk to Banauwa was torture and when I reached the *Thistle* I had all I could do to climb aboard and lie down. Fifteen ulcers were throbbing on my right leg. Puss and blood were oozing from some of them. These didn't hurt. It was the puffed-up ulcers, the ones which had not broken, that were killing me. At the house I met the same four brass hats, still enjoying their visit. A boy behind me carried in a Gara pigeon which I had shot on the way to Banauwa.

"What did you shoot him with?" Colonel Myers asked me.

"My revolver."

"How long a shot?"

"'Bout eighty yards." I then removed the revolver and started to clean it. "I'll have to bring this thing into Ordinance when I get into Port. I aimed at that bird's neck, and the bullet hit him in the eye."

I was waiting for him to ask how many shots did it take to hit the bird. I was going to answer,

"Oh, I killed it with one shot" (Not to mention all the shots which failed to kill him.) But the Colonel never asked.

And this evening I find myself a damn bundle of pain. Oh, how I hate to be sick, and it seems that sickness always follows me. Well, at least I'll have some scars from the war to show my children.

October 18, 1942

For thirty minutes this morning I went through the most severe physical pain I have ever had to endure. About six of the ulcers had not opened. My leg was so swollen as to be almost unrecognizable. And in my right groin there seemed to be a fist under the skin—a fist full of knuckles. From seven or eight ulcers oozed blood and puss which would fill several teaspoons. In agony I sat down in the chair in front of the native boy who squatted on the floor with a pan of hot lysol water. He started bathing my legs. The water felt as if it were boiling.

"Too hot, taubara?"

"No—go on! Go on!" And I clenched my teeth.

I lit a cigarette. This seemed to help. Sweat poured off my brow. After several minutes of hot applications, he proceeded to squeeze the open ulcers. I grew weak from pain. Never before had I seen so much infection. He touched the ulcers which had not opened and said: "These bad, taubara. Full of puss. Hurt much?"

"Yes, yes, they hurt. Here take that knife and cut them open, squeeze that puss out. Go on, go on—hurry up."

I couldn't sit up straight in the chair any longer. I leaned over the back of it. Sweat poured off my forehead as he cut and squeezed, cut and squeezed. There was no longer any pain. The whole leg seemed numb.

"Don't bandage them," I told him. "Just sprinkle some sulfanil-amide powder on them."

As I stumbled on to my bed I passed a mirror. I was white as a sheet of paper. But this evening my leg is greatly improved. Most of the swelling has gone down and all the ulcers are either draining or are drying up.

A wire today from General Johns instructed me to return to Port Moresby by trawler which will arrive at Abau on the 20th. It will be wonderful to get all that mail. I hope all are well at home.

October 19, 1942, Abau Government Station

I spent the day lounging around reading the oldest magazines I could find. Not articles back in 1938 and '39 on "Can London Be Bombed?" or "Can The Philippines be Defended?" but 'way back there when people were writing on "How To Hold Your Husband" and other topics which nowadays seem very foolish. I laughed at the stupidity of some of our wisest men and marvelled at the accurate predictions and foresight of others.

October 26, 1942, aboard the trawler Bonwin *between Abau and Port Moresby*

It was an ugly dawn. The night faded and merged into a mass of grumbling gray clouds. Flashes of lightening snapped across the southern horizon, but there was no sound of thunder; the flashes were too far out in the Coral Sea to be heard. The Filipino crew stretched lazily as the mail and natives came aboard the *Bonwin*. The engines started up, coughed a bit, then started to whine. In a few minutes the ropes would be cast loose from the Abau wharf, and we would start the boat trip back to Port Moresby. Many women and children had come down to the wharf to say good bye to their sweethearts and husbands who were going off to Port Moresby as recruits in the Papuan Infantry Battalion, a body of well-trained, daring native warriors, equipped as modern soldiers with the added advantage of having spent all their lives in the New Guinea jungles. It was a big ceremony. The young recruits wore flowers in their hair, around their necks and arms, dangling from their ramus.[5] The women and children cried pitifully, some hysterically, and clung to the arms of their heros so that the boat could not pull away from the wharf. "Enough of that!" someone shouted. "Let loose there so we can take off!"

The recruits shook their arms loose from the women's hold. The crying reached a crescendo as the small trawler pulled away from the wharf. The young warriors, seventeen in all, stood erect and, in unison, gave forth a farewell cry. It was more of a loud moan. And then they sang their song of farewell—rising and falling in pitch— rising and falling. They waved their flowers over their heads, and those on the wharf returned the gesture. The trawler chugged on into the wind. The natives sang and waved their flowers. The singing faded into a humming as Abau grew smaller astern, and at length the humming ceased. All that was heard was the wind. The sunset was more colorful than the dawn, and a colorful fire-red sky set the stage for Hula Village as we sailed across the reef Hood Point. It was dark by the time we put ashore in the dinghy and walked up to the mission house. Shipley, Sgt. Troy, and I decided to go down to the beach and watch the natives dancing. There were about a half dozen girls and a couple of boys singing and dancing as we approached. When they saw us, they quit their singing and dancing and sat down. We sat down nearby and told them to keep on with their playing.

"You American?" one girl asked.

"Yes, I'm an American" Troy said. They started to giggle.

"You no American. These men American."

And the girl pointed to Shipley and me. All the others quickly crowded around and looked at us with great curiosity. They giggled and stared. It was embarrassing. Troy was angry by the lack of attention he was receiving.

"Sure I'm American! What do you think I am?"

"You Australian," one girl told him, and they all laughed.

"Just 'cause I got on Australian clothes doesn't mean I'm Australian. I'm American. See! American hat!"

"No, Australian hat." And with that they started jabbering to Shipley and me.

"Go dance, go dance," I said.

I felt ridiculous. They started to dance and sing. Gradually more and more natives drifted in. Here were no men; all have been recruited; and only few boys over twelve or fourteen years old. Some older girls arrived, girls of eighteen or twenty. I couldn't watch their dancing. The full moon shining on their nearly completely naked bodies, squirming, the other natives' singing was more than I could stand. Most of them had beautiful figures and just to look at them was all right. But they stood up there, wiggling like a snake, running their hands over their bodies with their bared breasts quivering like over-hard jello, their whole leg becoming uncovered through their grass skirt. It was enough to make a white man forget he was white. So I just didn't watch them. One girl offered me her grass skirt.

"Here, you dance," she said; and she took off the skirt and handed it to me. She had on another skirt underneath. "Put it on," she insisted.

I put it on, feeling absolutely absurd.

"You dance," she said.

"You dance with me," I told her. This was wrong, why I don't know. But her friendly manner stopped right there. It is all right for a white man to dance, but not with a native. She wanted to sell me the skirt.

"How much?" I asked.

"You pay."

I dug in my pocket. I didn't have even a threepence. I told her I didn't want the skirt. She was insulted. I offered her a piece of army hard tack, which she took and ate. Then I slid off to the side. Women are hard enough to understand when you can speak their language. A native gal—impossible! I did have a lot of fun with all the little boys and girls. They liked the way I sang base. For some strange reason natives never sing bass. I blew smoke rings for them which amused them to no end. But the main attraction was the hard-tack which I passed out to them. How their little teeth bit through the cement-like biscuits is a mystery to me.

We left at dawn the next day, sailed inside the reef until we came to the mine fields, when we had to stick our nose into heavier seas. It was around 3:30 when we tied up at Moresby where I learned the happiest news in the world. Dora had had a baby—a boy, Ian.

SEVEN

On Leave in Australia

November 5–29, 1942

Port Moresby, November 5, 1942

"Glad to see you back. I have a big job for you," the Colonel fired at me, all in one breath the evening I returned from Abau. Later in the evening he gave me a few details of the job: "The water supply here at Moresby has really become a problem. Troops spread between the Laloki and Ward's Drome have to cart every drop of water they need. The draw on the main line is terrific; and when the ships in the harbor are taking on water, the troops along the line can hardly get any pressure. Now with the increase in port facilities the demand for water will just about be doubled. I want you to take over the problem and see what you can do with it."

"Yes, sir. But has anything been done in connection with the water problem?"

"Oh, yes. Pipe and pumps have been ordered from Australia, and a whole plan has been drawn up by Captain Burkholder at Engineer Headquarters. I want you to go down there in the morning and get whatever information you can and attempt to coordinate all previous plans."

Next morning found me at the Engineer Headquarters fumbling through wires and radio messages, requisitions, scribbled plans for a water supply system. Everything was in hopeless confusion. None of the pumps which had been requisitioned were available in Australia, and this Captain Burkholder who had designed the water system must have never worked outside an office in his life. I concluded that this Captain Burkholder might know something about figures but he knew nothing about engineering. That evening I reported to the Colonel that I found the records confusing and that the present design was absurd.

"That's why you're on the job," he said. "But Samuelson, before you worry too much about this big job, we have to get water to these various camps who are now without water, some three thousand troops. Go over to Ward's Drome in the morning and see Flight Lieutenant Scott of the RAAF. He has been working on this project for about two weeks. Find out what he has done and see if you and he can't get together on some kind of program."

The next day was wasted trying to find Flight Lieutenant Scott, but on the following day I was able to contact him.

"Altogether we need about 27,000 feet of pipe," he said. "I have about 8,000 feet of my own pipe. Army has furnished some 10,000 feet, and I believe I can scrounge another 2,000 or so. That means I'll have to get another 7,000 feet of pipe. But we need tanks. I can get a 1,000 gallon tank from _____ but I'll have to lend them a bulldozer, and so-and-so said he would give me an old tank if I lent them a road grader for two days, and I think I know where we can get another one if—"

If! Always if! Next day I went back to see Scott and sat in his office for two hours while he called different people trying to tee-up some pipe or tanks. Everybody wanted all sort of engineering equipment in return for *their* pipe or tank.

"Mr. Scott," I said at length, "do you have to put up with all that kind of nonsense? Tell me, is this water supply an authorized project?"

"What do you mean 'an authorized project'?"

"I mean have any of the higher-ups said to go ahead with this project?"

"Well, not exactly. But if you wait for a project to be authorized," he argued, "you'll never get anything done around here."

"I know that. I mean simply this: Your men here are without water. They need water. Pipe and tanks are available. Why can't you get them for your job? Who are all these people who talk about *their* pipe? And *their* tanks? Doesn't that stuff belong to the Government? Hell, when we first came to Moresby when something was needed and the stuff was available, we could get it like that." And I snapped my fingers. "Who are all these brass hats that you have to beg for stuff? And haven't they got enough sense to know that you need your engineering equipment for airdrome construction? They can level off their tent floors with shovels. They don't need a bulldozer!"

Mr. Scott laughed. "It's not that easy. You have to be diplomatic."

"The hell with being diplomatic! I'm an engineer, not a diplomat. There's a job to be done, and I want to get started. I've been on this thing four days and haven't scratched. Now, if there are tanks and pipe on this island, I want to get them. And I don't want to have to convert myself into a diplomat in order to get them!"

"You will never get them like that. Things don't work that way."

"Look, I'll make you a proposition. You start laying the pipe you have, and I'll get the tanks. And whatever pipe you don't have or can't get I'll get it for you."

He accepted my terms. It was still early in the afternoon; so I decided to walk back to Headquarters cross-country instead of catching a ride along the dusty road. And as I walked along my temper quieted down and I realized what a big hunk I had bitten off. Tanks! Where was I to get them? Where? I kept my troubles to myself and next day went out to the area in which B Company is camped. Between their camp and the Laloki River is a hill whose top is about 170 feet above the River. B Company had installed two 2,000-gallon tanks on the hill and was planning to lead a pipe from them down into their area. Four thousand gallons storage! Not nearly enough for 3,000 troops. Where could I get more tanks? About ten more like these two? Tanks—hmmm—Damn it, why not build a reservoir on top of this hill? Not one like Burkholder designed, but one that would work? Yep, that was the answer—a reservoir! I found a good spot on the hill and quickly figured what storage capacity I could get—25,000 gallons! Good enough! All I hear at Headquarters is how we are all flat-out for labor. Maybe B Company will help me. I'll go down and see Mark.

Marcuson said "Hell no!"

Kalman asked me how I was making out on my water problem.

"It's still a problem," I answered. "But damn it, it won't be for long."

I lay in bed thinking. So far every time I have been given a job, I've gone ahead and got the thing done without having to cry for help. Should I go to the Colonel and tell him I needed a couple squads of engineers, and cement, and rock, and sand, and. . . . No, why should I? I need labor. Twenty men. That's what I've got to get. I'll worry about the other things later. I approached Capt. Glover of Company A, 208th Coast Artillery.

"I'm Lieutenant Samuelson, 96th Engineers. You don't have running water here, but you can get it in about ten days time if you will lend me twenty men for six days and ten more for four days."

"I can lend you forty men," he answered.

Here was a man ready to talk business. When I left him I made sure that there would be no slip up.

"And you'll have thirty men on the top of the hill ready to go to work at eight o'clock?"

"You'll never get the rock," Scott told me. "They're giving it only to the airdromes."

But I got the rock! Major Ross refused to give me the cement, but I went over his head and got it. We could do the job without sand I concluded. The steel mesh was easy to pick up from the airdromes, where it had proved a failure for taxiways. B Company furnished the air-compressor and one truck. The other truck came from C Company. The 208th tackled the job with energy. Lt. De Champs, Lt. Skinner, and Capt. Glover were on the job most of the time. They shaped the reservoir beautifully, throwing off by hand nearly 100 cubic yards of earth before they obtained a level surface and then excavating, again by hand, a square-shaped saucer into nearly solid rock large enough to hold 25,000 gallons. They placed the pipes and steel mesh as nearly perfectly as could be expected. And yesterday afternoon when they knocked off work, everything was set to pour the concrete today. I had said the thing would be built in six days; it was requiring seven.

It was 7:45 when I arrived on the job this morning. The concrete mixer was not there. I rushed to see Mark. He laughed.

"Your operator is there, but your mixer ain't."

"I can see that. What's the trouble?"

"The tong is broken. We couldn't pull it."

"Why didn't you let me know? You promised to have it on the hill yesterday. And when you didn't have it there by yesterday afternoon, I saw you about it and you promised to get it up before eight this morning. Hell, Mark, you can't tie up the work like this!" He laughed again. "This isn't funny, Mark. I'll have thirty men on that hill ready to pour concrete in fifteen minutes. Everything is set to go, water tank and all—and there's no mixer. You're getting as incompetent as the Aussies."

"Aw, keep your shirt on, Sammy. Sabastan is down at the bridge now, trying to get the mixer over here."

"O.K. then. There go the men from the 208th up on the hill now."

I threw the jeep in reverse, backed up, then swished forward—on up the hill. Skinner was there with his men, ready to go to work.

"There'll be a little delay," I told him. "Something wrong with the mixer, but it ought to be along before an hour or so. Here comes the water truck up the hill now. I'll be back in about twenty minutes; got to go see about that mixer."

I passed the water truck as it struggled up the hill. The tank was leaking like a sieve.

"Sir," the driver told me, "the water will all run out of that old busted down tank in ten minutes."

"I can see that. Take it back down the hill. That tank won't work. I'll have to get another one. Good job you did getting it up here on time. Sorry like hell that I didn't check the tank yesterday evening. All right, get it off the hill." I rushed down to the 374th Service Squadron and told Lt. Kelly why I needed their truck with a pump on it, and he said I could have it. That was a lucky break. I tore down the dusty road to where B company is building a bridge across the Laloki River. Here I found the mixer, deserted. The tong was gone. And Sabastan was not around. I picked up the field phone and bawled out Marcuson. He said, "Well, accidents happen now and then. I didn't break the tong. A Company did. You'll just have to put the job off for a day."

Company B of the 96th Engineers constructing a bridge over the Laloki River, assuring access to Laloki Airdrome. The river was subject to flooding, so the bridge had to be substantial. Port Moresby, November 1942.

"Like hell! We'll do it today. That's the trouble with people like you—always ready to put something off for later. I don't do business that way!" I hung up.

I went over to where the concrete mixer stood. There was a slight tremor in my body. There always is whenever I have an argument with somebody. Sabastan drove up with the tong in his hand. It had been broken completely in the blacksmith shop.

"I think we'll have to get a new one made," he suggested.

There was no point in losing my temper with him too.

"Hand me that rope." I told a sergeant who stood by. "Now tell that fellow to back his truck up to here. And get me some of that wire over there. That heavy stuff. Hurry up now."

Sabastan watched me. "You can't move that mixer without a tong. You can't steer it. You'll never get it up that hill."

I worked on with the wire and the rope, lashing the mixer onto the back of the truck.

"Well don't say that I didn't tell you when you let that mixer fall down that hill."

I worked on in silence.

"All right, now driver, pull ahead. Slowly! Now take it easy. You've got a long way to go. And the going is rough." The truck and the mixer pulled off. "So-long, Sabastan!" I called back.

Everything went along smoothly for over a mile. I sent word ahead to the men from the 208th and the fellow in charge of the water truck to leave the reservoir site but to be back at one o'clock sharp. Everything will be ready to go by then. But my rigging was not tough enough, and the mixer rolled into the back of the truck while the two pieces were rolling down a hill. There was no damage done; and in order to prevent this from happening any more, I fastened a rope to the back of the mixer and to the front of my jeep and then drove behind the procession. Getting the mixer up the steep 150-foot hill was no easy task. I must have lost at least a pound in perspiration alone. And without the volunteered assistance of many boys in the B Company area and the use of their half-truck, the mixer could not have been brought up.

It was around 3:30 P.M. when Colonel Matthews, Colonel Yoder, and a couple of brass-hats drove up to the work. Over half the concrete had been placed. The men were going at top speed, one gang placing the wet concrete, another bringing it from the mixer to the reservoir in wheel barrels, another filling the skip with materials for the next batch. The brass hats seemed highly pleased.

"You know, Samuelson," Colonel Yoder told me, "it seems that everything always runs along so smoothly on any job that you tackle. There never seems to be any trouble in getting materials or equipment. I wish all of our work went along at the same easy pace."

"Yes, sir," was the only answer I gave.

November 14, 1942, Sydney, Australia

Last Monday night Jimmy King came over and asked me to go with him on leave to Australia. He had been working without a single day's break for over six months. And what kind of work! On a sun-baked airdrome, on that dusty causeway! No wonder he wanted to get away from it all. Tuesday morning I put in my application for leave and then forgot about it. To my surprise, our leave came through at once. Packing was a simple matter. I believe I could pack in fifteen minutes for a trip around the world. And I could take a trip half 'way 'round from here without any packing at all. We hadn't had more than an hour's sleep when we climbed aboard the Lockheed Transport at Ward's Drome. It was after 4 A.M., and by the time we took off it was 4:30. The noise was deafening and the cold was painful. There were nearly 20 of us on the plane, and we were fairly miserable, especially those who, like Jimmy and me, hadn't had more than an hour's sleep. We landed in Townsville around 8:30. Much to our displeasure we found out that the plane wasn't going any further.

We went into town for a bite to eat. Townsville looked horrible. There weren't many soldiers in the street, about one person out of four, but the danger caused by the recent flood of soldiers which had passed through the city recently was evident everywhere. Big stores were closed with signs like this on the front door: CLOSED—NO STOCKS! Nothing was for sale. The bars were open for one hour: from eleven to twelve, and the beer was no good. The people looked at us with scorn if they noticed us at all. The waitresses in the cafes did not smile. They were impatient for our order, and downright rude. Townsville had really suffered from the war. We walked around, covered the town from end to end, had a lot of laughs out of seeing different places where we had such a good time seven months ago. It was around one o'clock when we got back to the airport and sat with grim determination to wait there until we could catch a plane to Brisbane. A happy surprise was in store for us. A plane was leaving at 1:30, a big Douglas Transport, D-C-2. It was an old crate and she bounced around like a kite during March.

From the airport at Brisbane we caught a ride in a G.I. sedan to the American billeting office, which directed us to the Oxford House on Ann Street where we could get accommodations for a night. The next day we started our eating campaign. We didn't pass a milk bar without dropping in. Jimmy kept complaining of bellyache, but he continued to eat right along with me. At the American Post Exchange we got the first good hamburger we had had since we left the States.

On leave in Australia, November 1942: Hyman Samuelson (left) and Jimmy King.

Night settled over the city. There was a general "brown-out," but the life downtown went on as strong as ever. Sailors, soldiers, pilots everywhere! Girls! Little ones, big ones, a few pretty ones, many ugly ones—girls in uniforms, in dresses, in slacks,—nurses, whores! Jimmy and I strolled down one street, up the next.

"Nice-looking stuff, there," I'd say.

"Yeah, let's go—oh, the Navy has taken over." There were two sailors already engulfing the maids.

Friday morning we bought tickets on the 11:10 train which was leaving next morning for Sydney. All day long we continued our eating, took in another movie. I weighed myself and found out I had gained four pounds since I had arrived in Brisbane. Our orders read that we had seven days leave commencing on our arrival in Brisbane at which time we should register with the base section commander. Naturally we were in no hurry to register; for once we did we were on our own time; and none could prove—or rather, none would try to prove—how long it had taken us to get to Brisbane. Or in other words, all the time we had spent in Brisbane so far was charged up to travel time: not a very honorable trick I must admit; but Shinn, just back from his leave, charged two weeks to "waiting for a plane in Townsville," and everyone else agreed that they were going to have all kinds of difficulty making connections. So why not us? I thought the train ride to Sydney was swell. Jimmy and I both had window seats and we enjoyed looking at all the beautiful countryside. We passed through mountainous country, full of rivers—quite an engineering fete, this railroad. It was an 18 hour trip. At night Jimmy complained of the cold, but I slept soundly. I had bought a book on animal and plant life in Australia before leaving Brisbane and read part of it on the train.

November 15, 1942, Sydney, Australia

We arrived in Sydney early yesterday morning. It was a dreary-looking day—cold! We heard music coming from around the corner and went to investigate. It was the Salvation Army Band. Two girls came up to us and showed us some pictures of army lieutenants.

"Do you know Lieutenant Rogers?" one of the girls asked as she showed Jimmy the picture.

"Nope!"

"Or lieutenant Evans?"

"I know several lieutenant Evans, but not this one." "Aren't you stationed—"

"No, just got in town today. We're strangers."

"Oh, I'm sorry—I—I'm sorry." And with that the two girls walked away. "Why so rough with them?" I asked. "I wasn't rough." "You were dern right rude. They only wanted to be friendly. I liked the little red head anyway. She reminded me of my wife. I wish she had spoken."

"I'm cold. Let's go back to the hotel."

"All right. Looks as if I have a dead head on my hands. But let's get some hamburgers first," I suggested.

So sure were we of not going out that we had them bury the sandwiches in raw onions. We started back to the hotel. And there are the same two girls again.

"Find who you were looking for?" Jimmy asked them. "Oh we weren't looking for anyone. We—"

"I thought you were looking for a lieutenant Rogers and—"

"Lieutenant Evans," I broke in. "No we were just—"

"What can a fellow do around this place?" Jimmy asked.

"Not much."

"It ain't like this every night, is it?"

"Oh, no. This is Sunday night."

"Ain't nothin' doin' tonight. Can't you go anywhere?"

"Luna Park."

"What's that?"

While Jimmy and the other girl were shouting at each other I edged closer to the red head, just in case we did go somewhere.

"Well, do you all want to go to this Luna Park?" Jimmy asked.

"We were on our way—"

"What's your name?" the little red head asked.

"Hymie Samuelson. Call me Sammy. And what's your name?"

"Peggy." Her voice was sweet. It made me feel good.

"How long have you been in Sydney?"

"We came in this morning."

"Just arrived in Australia?"

"Oh, no—last April. We're down on leave from up north."

"Townsville?"

"No—er—New Guinea."

"Much fighting going on up there?"

"Some." We walked along in silence. I found it difficult to make conversation.

"You like dancing?" she asked.

"Yes, pretty much."

"Any dancing in New Guinea?"

"No. No women."

"Oh. Any picture shows?"

More silence as we walked. Jimmy and Irene were walking up ahead, arm in arm, laughing and apparently getting acquainted right well. Peggy and I weren't doing so well.

"Homesick?" she asked. I looked at her and smiled. She was very pretty.

"A little bit, I guess." She took my hand. Her little hand was cold. We walked along without talking. At length we got to the quay where we had to catch the ferry which carried us across the harbor to Luna Park. As we sat on the ferry, Peggy noticed my diamond ring.

"It's beautiful," she said. "Your initials?"

"Yes."

"And this one—a wedding ring! Are you married?"

"Yes—"

"How long?"

"Eleven months."

"You haven't seen your wife much?"

"Not since we were married—about two months I guess. I have a son too—about six weeks old."

"Aren't you awfully young for all this: a first lieutenant, a father?"

"I'm nearly 24. Twenty-three and a half anyway."

"That's young."

"Not so young."

Luna Park is one of those places which are free to get in but which costs plenty of money to get out. The first ride we went on was the Spider. The man spun our carriage around so swiftly that even before the ride commenced we were both stone dizzy. I had my arm around Peggy and it felt good. We went on many other rides, and after an hour or so, we were well acquainted. We walked along with my arm around her waist, her arm around mine.

"You're awfully quiet," Peggy said. "Not much like most Americans."

"Sorry. What should I do?"

"Tell me about yourself. Tell me about—about your wife. What is she like?"

"She is about your height. She must weigh about ten pounds more than you."

"What color hair?"

"Red—something like yours. And her eyes are like yours. And—well, she looks a lot like you."

"Tell me more."

"Nothing much more to tell. I miss her. I miss her a lot."

"Did you know her long before you married her?"

"About five years. How 'bout telling me about you."

"Oh, there isn't much to say. I work in a box factory. I have two sisters, one older than me, the other younger. My father is at camp—"

At length we left Luna Park and rode the ferry back across the harbor. We stood on street corners and sang and danced, trying to keep warm. At last a cab stopped for us. Peggy sat down on my lap. I put my arms around her waist, and I must admit it felt good as the devil. We pressed our cheeks together lightly, and I got the whiff of the perfume she was wearing. I was just abut to kiss her when the taxi hit a bump and brought me back to my senses and I relaxed. I didn't kiss her; shook her hand when I said goodnight.

"Why in the hell did you tell her you're married?" Jimmy exclaimed back in the hotel room.

"She saw my ring and asked me."

"So?"

"Well, I told her."

"But you're not going to get anywhere with a girl telling her you're married to someone else."

"Well, I wouldn't offer the information to any of them but I'll be dern if I'd take off my wedding ring and lie to them. I'm bad enough as it is. But I don't lie. I don't always tell the truth, but I never lie."

"Well a lie is not a lie if it doesn't harm anybody," he argued.

"The hell it ain't. A lie is a lie no matter how you paint it. You know that!"

"Aw, I guess you're right."

November 16, 1942

We spent today in town eating, window shopping, taking in a movie, and winding up at the Sydney Zoo. Taronga Zoo I believe is its name. I enjoyed the zoo more than anything else we saw, but Jimmy was impatient as a little child the whole time.

"I don't like to look at birds and flowers. The big animals like lions and tigers and elephants are all right. But I don't like those little things."

At the Aquarium it was the same thing. The only thing Jimmy wanted to see was the big fish: the sharks, the sea turtles, the octopus. Whereas I was more interested in watching the anemones and star fish, the beautiful small tropical fish.

"If somebody offered you a sack of babies or a sack of kittens,"

Jimmy asked me with a disgusted look on his face "which one would you take?"

"Quit riding me. I can't help it if I like little things—little kittens, babies, even little girls—I like them."

"Well, I don't like kittens! I don't like babies! And I like *big* girls! Now let's go back to the hotel. I promised to call Irene at six o'clock sharp."

November 19, 1942

I had a date with Peggy again last night, the date which we had made last Sunday evening. She looked prettier than she did Sunday night, and I had put on a fresh uniform, brass all ashine, clean shaved, wearing a big grin. We looked like a decent sort of couple. Jimmy was in a bad mood, and he and Irene didn't click very well. But Peggy and I were right there. We went to see two British motion pictures, which turned out to be excellent productions. As we sat in a little tea shop on Pitt Street after the show was over, I realized that Peggy was at least twenty. Her lips were very pretty and her small, shapely body was quite feminine. The way she inhaled a cigarette proved she wasn't just a kid. While we stood on the corner waiting for a taxi, I put my arms around her. The streets are very dark with the "brown out" and making love in public is dern common on the streets. She leaned her body against mine so that I felt goose bumps rise all over. I said to myself, "I'll kiss her when we get into the taxi. Say she resists. You'll feel like a fool. You're married. You can't force yourself on a girl. Sure, I know, it's nearly nine months since you have kissed a girl. That's longer than you've ever gone in your whole life without kissing anyone. And sure you'd like to be kissed. That's what you'd really enjoy. Her mouth is very pretty. It is—but—oh, well, go on—I don't blame you. The drive to her house takes only ten minutes. This might be your last chance to take a girl in your arms until you get home— home—Dora! Gee, isn't it worth while waiting for. Just think of coming home and having her throw her arms around your neck and really kissing you. No other girl can kiss like her. This girl will disgust you. You'll be disappointed. And remember—you're married! You're not at college anymore! You're a man—a married man! Behave yourself— But no harm will be done by kissing her. I need it. She is clean and decent—It will do me good—"

"Why so quiet?" Peggy asked "What are you thinking about?"

"Oh—er—nothin! I'm tired I guess. I—"

"I'm tired too." We got into the cab. I looked at Peggy. She looked into my eyes, and I looked at her lips. I smelled the powder she was wearing. I leaned my face to hers and touched my lips gently to hers. She didn't turn away. We kissed. It was absolutely wonderful. Her lips were full and soft and she knew how to kiss. At her doorstep I took her hand.

"Don't guess I'll see you any more Peggy. It has been good knowing you."

She put her arms around my neck and gave me a big kiss. Then she started to turn, but I pulled her back to me and kissed her again. Then we looked at each other a minute.

"Have a good trip back. God be with you," she said half choked for some damn reason. She then gave me a quick kiss, and before I could take hold of her, she had turned and run into the house.

"I must be going crazy," I told Jimmy back in the cab.

"What do you mean?"

"I swear I feel like I have been out with my wife. I'm all muddled. I need some sleep. This is the strangest thing I have ever been through."

"Aw, snap out of it. Haven't you ever kissed a girl before?"

"Yes, but—aw, give me a cigarette." We drove a way in silence. "I don't think I've ever felt so homesick before in my life." Jimmy laughed.

November 22, 1942, Oxford House, Brisbane

In Sydney, Jimmy and I started off each day with a double-thick chocolate milk shake from the milk bar across the way. There is a little hamburger stand just around the corner from the Oriental. It opens each evening at six. Jimmy and I used to wait around for it to open and grab a couple hamburgers with onions before going into town each evening. It is a small place: six stools in a row alongside the counter and four tables. Thursday evening we came in around 6:30. Besides the girl who owns the place and makes the hamburgers there was another girl, an ugly hag in the joint. A half-drunk chap sat on one of the stools.

"Don't come in here," he said. "This place ain't open for business."

"Don't you listen to him," the girl in the green dress said. "What will you have?"

"Four hamburgers," Jimmy said. He always orders more than he can eat, but I manage to finish whatever he leaves.

"Fix me anything," I said. I hate to order. "You know—steak, eggs, tomatoes—something good to eat—you fix it and I'll eat it."

"You're going to eat one of her steaks!" the fellow on the stool laughed. "One man alone can't do that. Ha-ha-ha-ha."

"Quiet!" From way back in the corner table came the voice of a little dried up man. He was 70 years old if a day and not more than a pound of flesh on him for every year of his life. Another old bloke came in—a consumptive—leaned over the counter, and placed an order amid his coughing.

"Quiet!" Again from the little old man with his hat still on his head. Another person his size could be poured into the suit he was wearing. His blank expression never changed; but whenever the noise rose, he blurted forth with his "Quiet!" Apparently no one but Jimmy and me heard it though. The fellow on the stool flopped his feet on our table. A drunk American soldier came in, making all kind of noise. When he saw Jimmy and me, he politely asked for a match, then went on his way. Three soldiers came in, flopped on the stools and ordered something or other.

"Let's get out of here," Jimmy suggested. "I can't enjoy my food with all this noise."

"Sh—This is all right. Wipe that frown from your face and look around at the different people. You'll enjoy it. This is better than a picture show." Next a little Aussie soldier came in—a chap not over eighteen. He smiled at me. "How'dy" I said dryly. That was his cue. He flopped down besides me.

"Got a cigarette?"

"I think so." I gave him one.

"What's the things on your collars?" he asked.

"They designate our rank."

"Pretty high rank?"

"First lieutenant."

"Hmph—Look, lieutenant, I wrote a poem. Will you listen to it?"

"Yep—" He reached into his pocket and pulled out a piece of rumpled paper on which had been written in pencil his beautiful poem. Because of the local competition, he could hardly be heard; but he seemed to enjoy his poem anyway for he smiled while he read it and smacked his lips whenever two words rhymed. I grinned my approval at him every time he looked up at me although I hardly heard a word he said.

"Are you ready to make a break for it?" Jimmy asked.

"Keep still. This isn't so bad."

"I also wrote music for my poem," the little Aussie said. "Would you like to hear it?"

Without waiting for a reply he started in to singing his song. It was a mixture of opera and cowboy yodeling. What a racket! He would start off as a tenor, then switch to a baritone (or a bass—I don't know). And his yodeling—good Lord, what frightful music! And the sailors jabbered on! And the little old man in the corner shouted "Quiet!" And no one heard him. The steak and hamburgers sizzled on the grill. The man on the stool and the ugly gal with him laughed and made more noise than anyone else. The consumptive stood at the counter and coughed as he watched the girl cooking. A good looking girl came into the joint, but she walked straight on through to the back. At last our food! I gave the little Aussie another cigarette and he left us to sit with two old hags who had just come in and sat down at the table behind Jimmy. One of them slapped Jimmy across the back. Choking on his sandwich, he turned around when she asked, "Yes?"

"Got a cigarette?" the wretched-looking woman asked.

"No!" Jimmy was emphatic. We ate a little while. Jimmy looked so miserable that I couldn't help laughing. The hefty woman behind Jimmy hit him across the back again.

"What now?" he asked.

"Didn't you want something?"

"No—nothing." I was laughing almost out loud.

"Want a drink?" the woman asked me as she pulled out a bottle.

"No, thank you."

"All right. Be unsociable," she said and put the bottle to her lips and gulped down some.

By this time the little Aussie was reciting his poem to the two women behind Jimmy. They weren't listening to him, but that didn't matter anymore to the poet laureate than the way people ignored the little old man who still continued to demand quiet.

"Look," the woman behind Jimmy said to him. "I've got some pretty sisters upstairs. Would you like to come up and see them?"

"No!"

"I didn't ask you to come up to see me! I'm not in your class." What she meant by that we never did find out. "I've been married twice. I want you to come up and see my sisters."

"Look here, you. I don't want to see you. I don't want to see your sisters! Now quit pestering me. I'm eating!"

Then he looked at me pathetically "Can you help me with these hamburgers?"

"I think so."

Between the two of us we managed to finish the sandwiches.

"Cigarette?" I asked Jimmy. "Put those back quick! Wait 'til we get outside. These vultures will pounce on you if they see them."

As we walked out the door through the rumble of what seemed like a thousand voices we heard the little old man from 'way back in the corner. He said only one word: "Quiet!"

November 25, 1942, Mareeba, Queensland

Monday morning bright and early Jimmy and I went up to the air transportation office in Brisbane to see about a ride to Moresby.

"All planes going north are carrying cargo only, no personnel," the officer told us. "Perhaps in four or five days from now we might be able to take some passengers. But first we will start on those under orders. Are you under orders?"

"No. Leave orders only."

"They don't count," he said.

When we will catch a plane out of here, we don't know; but when we do, it should take us all the way to Moresby. But there are advantages either way. At Moresby there is mail. Here there is peace and relaxation. I'll take Moresby!

While we were in Townsville Tuesday morning at Garbutt Field we saw them bring in two Jap prisoners—two little kids, both so thin that they looked like skeletons with skin stretched over them. They were blindfolded—poor kids!

November 29, 1942, Port Moresby

Last Friday around one in the afternoon we at last caught a ride back "home." We flew in formation—six flying fortresses, fully loaded with bombs. My ship had eleven fifty calibre machine guns and two thirty's. When they opened up with all these guns, testing them of course, the huge fortress rocked. The noise was deafening.

EIGHT

Colonel Derby Takes Command

December 2–March 16, 1943

December 2, 1942

Dearest Dora,

The more I see of life and people, the happier I am to be an engineer, not a doctor or lawyer. We never have to decide whether nature is right or wrong. We don't "send her to jail for a year" because she causes heavy rains and washes out our bridge. Instead we build a better bridge.

December 19, 1942

Many cases of sodomy and other forms of sexual perversion becoming prevalent in the Regiment. It is a serious thing subject to trial by General Courts Martial. But in spite of the trials and convictions, the practice seems to be spreading.[1]

Surveying around Bomana today. Awfully muddy work.

December 20, 1942

Tired and irritable. Wish I could smile and mean it.

December 22, 1942, Port Moresby

It was eight months to the day that I landed at Port Moresby. It was a different place from what it is today. It looked like a tropical village which had been torn up a bit by Japanese bombs, but people went about lazily and in spite of the war's being so near at hand things did look peaceful. It was about two weeks later when the 96th arrived, the first American troops in New Guinea. In spite of our being a negro battalion, the Australians cheered our arrival with enthusiasm. The Americans had arrived to defend Moresby. Australia would be saved! Yes, we were heroes. The Aussies gaped at our equipment, inadequate as it was, and thought that the American Army was quite wonderful indeed.

When the Japanese started in this direction with a formidable fleet escorting a heavy convoy of troop ships, the 96th took up posts along the shores of Moresby to defend the place. Our Navy saved us the job by intercepting the Japanese Armada and turning it back in the Coral Sea Battle. We built Seven-Mile Airdrome: or at least, improved it so that it could be used by our modern fast-flying fighters and bombers. We built Bomana Drome and then Laloki Drome. Fighter planes drifted in, first a single squadron of Cobras, which remained but a few days. But there were replacements. More fighters arrived. The 101st Ack-Ack Regiment was the second American unit to land here; and helped by our fighter planes, they made it so hot for the Jap Zeros with their .50 calibre machine guns that it wasn't long before Nippo decided that it wasn't profitable to come down and strafe our dromes while our men were working. The bombing raids continued, at least two or three times a week; and much of our work was destroyed before it was completed. But we worked all the harder. We knew that as soon as we could get the dromes in good condition with adequate dispersal, we would have bombers based here along with our fighters. Then we could crack back at the dirty Jap! We were a good outfit in those days. In spite of the weaknesses of our Regimental Commander, we had been trained so carefully back in the 'States that his shortcomings did not affect the good work of our officers and men.

Then the Japs decided to take Moresby from the North. They landed at Buna and started their drive across the waist of New Guinea. Our Australian Infantry fell back time and time again until the Japanese were within forty miles of here. Then came reinforcements from the mainland, and the counter-offensive began. The Japs were driven back to Buna, where undoubtedly this very evening fighting is going on. But things are different now. We, the 96th as a regiment, have been beaten. Fresh engineer troops have arrived and are taking the lead in the work around here. We have been shoved into the background, maintaining three unimportant dromes while better engineer troops have taken over the more difficult task of getting the bigger dromes into all-weather condition.

Colonel Yoder has left the Regiment. He hated his job. It was a means of his getting eagles on his shoulders instead of the gold leaves that he was wearing when he joined the Regiment. And once he got his eagles, he did all that was within his power to get out of the Regiment. The only thing in his favor is the fact that he didn't deny the facts. You have to admire a man who admits that he is a scoundrel even if he is telling the truth. Major Martin is gone. As an engineer, he was a good insurance salesman. But the simultaneous loss of a Regiment's Commanding Officer and Executive Officer is a stiff blow to the general operation of the machine. Colonel Yoder has done more than any one individual to wreck the Regiment. Now that he has gone I fully expect to see officers and enlisted men lose heart, become sick and do whatever they can to get out of this place. Major Pickard is now commanding officer of the Regiment. I like him. He is quiet, seldom smiles, never laughs—a young pale-faced fellow with good engineering brains, a keen scrutiny of personalities, an open-minded thinker. But he is lacking in driving force. Give him Yoder's personality, and you would have a top-notch C.O. Behrens is Commanding Officer of the Second Battalion and is doing a good job. Thomas has been given the First Battalion. The officers in the Companies are entirely apathetic. Why should they work so hard, they say, when there is such an incompetent bunch at the head of the Regiment? And you can hardly blame them. The men are tired and need a break, but there is none in view. This general degradation of the Regiment has been coming on for some time. I fear that we are really sliding now! I hope I am wrong.

December [?], 1942

Colonel Yoder left for Australia before dawn. Pickard, acting C.O., Burkholer, Executive. King moved up here to work in motor pool. Nichols needs the help. Homesick as hell.

December [?], 1942

Made a complete report on the remaining work on Bomana Drome. It was interesting work figuring labor and plant distribution and quantities of material and trying to find the most advantageous combination of these factors. Yes, the planning was interesting but the work will not be done. The regiment is worn down and we just can't buck against real engineering any more.

December 25, 1942

Work as usual this morning. All work in the Regiment ceased this afternoon except necessary work, and naturally no one had work which was necessary. Most of the gang got dead drunk. I didn't touch a drop. They were drinking ethyl alcohol and that didn't appeal to me.

December 26, 1942

Survey work at Laloki. The damn place cannot be drained! Why don't we abandon the idea of draining it and use it as a dry weather drome only, concentrating our efforts on Bomana which *can* be made into an all weather drome?

December 30, 1942

Much rain has turned most of Laloki Dispersal area into a quagmire. Rats did a lot of damage to books and other property in old location.

Received some swell pictures of Dora and the baby. Dora looks beautiful on them, the baby cute but stupid.

December 31, 1942

The party which was planned for tonight was postponed until tomorrow, but that didn't stop most of the gang up here from getting drunk. There were arguments on every subject imaginable—a messy affair. Seeing these fellows plastered has made me want to remain sober always.

January 1, 1943

The party this evening was a fizzle. There was drinking, good food, and nurses; but everyone seemed tired, and we all sat around in isolated groups and talked. I could have enjoyed the sleep more.

January 2, 1943

Surveying at Laloki. Rains have dispersal area swamped but the runway is holding up nicely. It is a hard struggle against the rains from now on for awhile.

January 4, 1943

Captain John Farley cracked up today. Wanted to kill himself and other people. He is being evacuated as insane.[2] Stephens also went into the hospital today. He is anemic. Many enlisted men have also "cracked" under the long strain. Complete map of new dispersal area at Laloki. A fine piece of work if I must say so myself.

January 5, 1943

All day at Kila. Have established good "control" at all the dromes so that surveying is a pleasure. Dellavia took over job of personnel adjutant yesterday and is now my tent mate. Stephens has been assigned to B Company, but probably will not return to duty because of his physical condition. At supper this evening we checked up and found that of the 54 officers in the regiment only 39 are present for duty. My guess is that of the 39, no more than 25 are fit for duty. The Regiment is burned out. There's no sense in trying to deny it.

January 6, 1943

Willie Miller critically ill in hospital. It looks as if I'll get the S-4 [supply] job. Kalman is unhappy about my accepting the job. "I like my present job," I told him, "but there's a captaincy open in the S-4 job." I spoke exactly how I felt. All I have to do now is put in the six required months, get the recommendation which I feel sure I'll get and I'll be a captain. I wanted to go up to the hospital this evening to see Willie, but he is doped up with morphine. They believe it is kidney trouble.

January 7, 1943

Miller and Stephens leave for Australia. Road jammed with ambulances evacuating men onto hospital ships. Requisition! Requisition! Everybody crying for something! Don't know what end is up.

January 9, 1943

Exhausted! S-4 job is no snap. No light ahead.

January 10, 1943

Must be expecting Japs to use gas. We are drawing all kind of chemical warfare equipment and protective clothing. Still not much light ahead in the work.

January 11, 1943

Why does Engineer Headquarters cramp our style with supplies? I am tired of arguing with them. We ought to lay down and quit work. We can't even get nails!

January 14, 1943

Starting to see some light ahead. Thomas, my clerk, has gone to the hospital. Fourth attack of fever since he is in New Guinea. They will ship him out this time and I am having to do clerical work here too.

January 15, 1943

I am weary. No appetite. Smoking continuously. Dizzy and rundown. I must snap out of it. Can't read, eyes won't seem to focus on a printed page.

January 16, 1943

Sgt. Patterson away on leave. The supply section is really crippled now. Thank heavens for men like Sgt. Gadsden and Sgt. Ford. Otherwise we would fold up completely.

January 17, 1943

I am so weak and weary that I can hardly do my work. Can't hold anything in my hand steadily. I feel like folding up. Charlie Little back from leave, but Steele stayed in Australia—sick.

January 18, 1943

Lt. Col. Derby arrived today to take over command of the Regiment. Pickard moved to executive job.

January 19, 1943

Heavy rains have caused much damage to roads and many culverts have washed out. Place is in an awful mess. Supper this evening at new Officers' Club with Lt. Col. Derby and Regimental staff. I don't like Derby. Not much of a man. He has too much personal stuff up here with him. I like a person who can travel with one suitcase.

January 20, 1943

Working hard as hell. Getting results and that makes me happy. I have four trucks rumbling back and forth all day long, picking up and delivering supplies. It is all very interesting work, and I like it. Wish my aches would clear up. Back and knees giving me trouble. Quinine shortage acute. Remainder being taken up and sent to hospitals. We will take atebrine instead. See that 5% victory tax applies to men in service also. A good thing; will help keep down inflation.

January 21, 1943

Survey class becoming big success.[3] Eight fellows showed up this evening and they seem very much interest.

January 22, 1943

My supply section is really clicking now. I have two good men in Gadsden and Ford. I have coordinated the work well, and the system which Mills installed and which I am now following is indeed excellent.

January 23, 1943

We are playing poker nearly every evening. I could devote all that wasted time to studying and reading, but ambition along those lines has nearly left me. Anyway, I enjoy poker, and as long as I don't lose despite the heavy stakes we play for, I guess I'll keep on playing. I'd play more chess but I can't get much competition from any of the gang up here.

January 24, 1943

Of the 55 officers in the regiment, only 16, including Miller and Nichols, have been with the 96th longer than I have. So I guess I'm almost an "old" officer myself. An interesting observation is that of all the officers who were with the 96th when it was activated some 20 months ago, not a single one is higher than a captain.

January 25, 1943

The Japs have been bombing us every night. The raids are a nuisance, for although there is very little chance of being hit by a bomb—the nearest airdrome is half a mile away and a poor military objective for the Japs at that—there is considerable danger of being hit by shrapnel from the ack-ack fire. And whenever there is any firing overhead, you have to get up, put on your tin hat, and wait for the shower of falling steel to abate. It takes a full five minutes for it all to come down and is a dern nuisance in the middle of the night.

The first official thing that Colonel Derby did was to appoint a committee for planning a regimental dance. The second thing was to issue the first general order of the year placing himself in command. His third act was to establish a complete routine of bugle calls, including Retreat formations with prescribed uniform. Well, that was an excellent way to make himself very unpopular around here, for despite our weaknesses, we are trying to win the war. And apparently his idea was to make soldiers out of us. It was obvious that he had no idea about the existing situation. He did not know that we are a large labor force with a reasonable amount of heavy equipment and are capable of doing most types of engineering work with a reasonable degree of efficiency. We are not the kind that looks good on parades or even at a Retreat formation. So Colonel Derby was rather low in the opinion of most of the officers around here. But this afternoon he did something which tends to show that he is made of the right kind of stuff. There was a phone call for him and I called him to the phone. "This is Colonel Derby," he said. "Yes, that's right. . . . Yes. . . . Uh-huh. . . . Yes, I see. . . . Well I'll tell you so-and-so (I didn't catch the name) we are working for you, and whatever you want us to do, we will be glad to oblige. Yes, that's right. . . . If you think that we should put some of that heavy equipment on the roads in your area and take it off the drome, that is perfectly all right with us. But, er, just in order to keep the record straight, I'd like you to put that little order down in writing. . . . Yes. . . . But I'd like you to put it in writing to protect us. . . . Oh, I realize that no one will ever complain, but in case there should be a kick from higher headquarters about our removing heavy equipment off airdrome construction, I'd like to have the reason why we removed it down in writing. Just a sort of protection. . . . Yes . . . yes, we could. . . . No, not like that. You see, we are working for you. We follow your orders. You don't have to offer to lend us any jeeps or anything like that in order to get work out of us. All you have to do is tell us—in writing." I had to smile. It didn't seem that talk like that was coming out of the same man who ordered a regimental dance the first day he was here.

January 26, 1943

Bob Diddums dropped in today, back from the fighting around Sanananda.[4] The Japs are really tough, he claims, and victories like our recent one on the other side of the island are not the kind that will win the war for us. A bomb landed in camp last night. Knocked out six tents. No other damage and no casualties.

January 27, 1943

"You'd better get up, Sammy. They're just over Seven Mile and heading straight this way," I heard Del mumbling as I reached for my sandals.

"Damn those Japs! Every night! Why in the hell don't they stop these nuisance raids. They never hit anything, just wake us up." I grumbled, fought off a few mosquitoes as I went to the front of the tent. "Gosh that's a pretty sight." The moon was out brightly. The sky was clear. And about 20 powerful beams concentrated on the three Japanese planes moving ominously our way. "No ack-ack. I wonder why?"

"We've got a P-38 up there," answered Dellavia. "He ought to have a good crack at them."

"Look at those damn planes. They're going to pass right over our heads." We both got down into our slit trench. "No need to worry. I heard them drop their bombs on Seven Mile already."

Sw—w—i—i—s—s—s. "What were you saying, Del?" No answer. BAM! "That was close. That one must have hung up, huh, Del?"

"Look!" he shouted, "The P-38's among them." There were streams of tracers pouring into one of the bombers. It reeled over to the side, started to lose altitude. The other two broke formation. We heard the staccato of the machine guns above. The planes faded away in the distance.

"Well that one was worth while getting up for," I grudgingly admitted, "but now for some more sleep."

Bud Engle came to breakfast with a black eye. "How'd that happen?" we asked.

"Frank's head's harder'n mine. And he's faster'n me getting in a slit trench." We all laughed, all except Frank. We soon saw the reason why. His right arm was skinned and bruised from the wrist to the elbow. Sladon admitted that he tried to get out of bed without climbing under his mosquito net and that it took him ten minutes to untangle himself. This was all a lot of fun, but when we walked down to where the bomb had hit and saw how easily some of us might have been killed, it was no longer very funny. Sergeant Scott's bed had been pierced by shrapnel. Fortunately he was out of it at the time. Another man had his mosquito frame hit by a bomb fragment. He was still in bed. Three pyramidal tents were pierced by so many pieces that I had to issue new ones to replace them this morning. The bomb had missed the H & S Supply Tent by 30 or 40 yards. Hitting that tent would have made the Jap's raid worth while. Oh, well, nobody was hurt, and that is the main thing that counts.

January 29, 1943

If Bud Engle had asked me to get some salt tablets about six months ago, this is probably how I would have gone about it. I'd have gone up to one of the hospitals around here and simply told them I needed the tablets. They'd probably want to know how much I wanted, and I'd tell them twice as many as Doc Engle asked me to get. If I were lucky they'd have given me about one-fourth of what I asked for, and Bud would get half of what he asked for. But the whole thing would have taken less than two hours from the time he asked for the tablets up to the time he had them in his hands, and not a single piece of paper would have been used, not a pencil mark made. But that would have been the story six months ago. First Captain Engle prepares the requisition in triplicate. He keeps one copy, sends me two. I approve the requisition and send both of my copies down to regimental supply. Later one copy comes back, showing that no salt tablets were available in our supply. They kept the other copy of the requisition in Regimental Supply for their records. Now I have to prepare a requisition to the Medical Supply Officer for the salt tablets—in triplicate. I file one copy so that I can check on all unfilled requisitions. The other two copies of the requisition are taken down to Major Wolf, who approves the requisition. Next it has to be taken to the issuing depot. There a clerk checks the stock records to determine whether twenty boxes, total commercial value about one dollar, are available. He finds out that they are, and marks his O.K. on the requisition. He then hands it to another clerk who proceeds to type up a shipping ticket—in quadruplicate. One copy of this shipping ticket he will send to the warehouse authorizing them to issue me the salt tablets. Two copies he will send to me, one of which I will sign and return to him, the other of which I will retain in my already cluttered files. The fourth copy he will keep in his files until I return the signed copy to him. At the warehouse, the man in charge will issue me the salt tablets, and I will have to sign for them on a Tally-Out. This is also prepared in duplicate—the original for him and the duplicate for me. He keeps this as a hammer over my head until I send him a signed shipping ticket on the tablets. Then it is filed away in a dead file. At last the salt is in my hands. After I bring it to Regimental Supply and issue it to the Medical Department of our Regiment, they sign for it: two more sheets of paper, one copy for them, one for us. With the tablets, we return to them one copy of their original requisition marked FILLED. I then take the other copy of their original requisition out of my Incomplete—Medical file and put it into my Complete Medical file. And then the job is done. Fourteen sheets of paper were used, about four to six man hours of time consumed in typing, filing, and so on. I wonder how we win wars. God must be on our side. At least we do fight a good paper war. There's do doubt about that.

January 30, 1943

The pace is killing. Gadsden, my best man, has been shipped south with a buggered shoulder. That leaves me with only six men to carry on the furnishing of supplies to 200 times their number. They are a loyal crowd who are wiling to work as hard as they can as long as you tell them to. Perhaps there will be a break before long, but I see nothing in view.

February 1, 1943

Using Frank's expression I am living now on borrowed time. It happened this afternoon in the shower room. Someone discharged his rifle and the bullet tore through both walls of the shower house. Lining up the two holes we could see that the bullet had missed my neck by only four inches and would have hit me if I hadn't moved just ten seconds before the gun was fired. Frank was in the shower with me but I was between him and the bullet.

February 2, 1943

Survey school has dwindled to only five as I get deeper into the subject. Afraid that Boyd and Kicks will be unable to keep up with the work also, leaving just Hunter, Maxwell, and Gerald.

February 4, 1943

Colonel Harrison from Washington and Colonel Wright from Australia put me under pressure concerning supplies. Major Bard, Engineer Supply Officer of Moresby, was also in the conference, and so were Colonel Derby and Colonel Pickard. *What do you want?* That was the question they wanted answered. But it was understood that nothing was to be requested which was not essential to the war effort. Col. Harrison is making a tour of all the fighting fronts trying to ascertain the engineering needs. I never realized the world was so small. For instance I asked for two ½ ton dump trucks.

"Africa has first priority of them," he answered.

"We need transits."

"All frozen: Alaska, Panama, new Pacific bases."

I'd ask for something else.

"All of that is going to Russia."

"What about replacements on air compressor accessories?"

"We can furnish you with Ingersoll Rand parts. What kind are yours?"

"Thor."

"Will the Ingersoll Rand parts work?"

"I think so."

And on and on. It was the most enlightening conference I have ever been in.

February 5, 1943

"I'd like to speak to the supply officer."

I stood up. In spite of the laxness of certain military courtesies, I still show some respect to a full colonel.

"The supply officer isn't in, sir. I'm Lt. Samuelson, the assistant supply officer."

"How long have you been associated with supply functions in your regiment?"

"Over a year, off and on."

"Were you assistant supply officer when your regiment first came to Port Moresby?"

"Yes, sir. I was."

"Then perhaps you can help me now. Please stand up, lieutenant, raise your right hand. . . . Do you promise to tell the truth, the whole truth, and nothing but the truth in the case now being investigated?"

"I do."

His secretary took my name, rank, serial number, organization, etc.

"Tell me, lieutenant, when the 96th Engineers came to Port Moresby did they carry any reserve rations with them?"

"Yes sir, they did. A 60 day supply, theoretically."

"Are any of these rations still on hand?"

"A small quantity."

"Do you know why you took these rations? For what express purpose were they to be used?"

"Yes, sir. They were an emergency supply which we were to use if the normal supply of food was cut off."

"Were any of these rations consumed?"

"Yes, sir, they were."

"And did you have a regular source of rations aside from these emergency rations the whole time you have been here in New Guinea?"

"Yes, sir." I could see that he was directing his questions to the ruin of the Regimental Company funds, which would have to reimburse the Government for rations consumed without proper cause.

"Was there any written directive authorizing you to eat these reserve rations?"

"No sir, nothing written."

"Then under whose orders or direction were they taken?"

"By verbal order of the commanding officer, Col. Yoder."

"And why did he issue such an order?"

"Because our regular ration was inadequate."

"And how did you know that the ration was inadequate? Did a medical officer ever make an analysis of the food and determine that it did not contain enough nourishment?"

"No, sir; no report was ever made by a medical officer. But the men complained that they were hungry; and the officers ate the food and saw that it was inadequate—that is, inadequate for the kind of work we were doing."

"And what kind of work was that?"

"The men were working 12 hours a day. We had continuous shifts, 24 hours a day, in order to utilize as much as possible the small amount of engineering equipment we had here. Kitchens were running on a 24 hour schedule too."

"Was it that the quality of the food was not good enough?"

"No, the quality was good enough, but we needed more of it. There wasn't enough there to keep a hard-working man going."

"Then it was the quantity, not the quality?"

"Yes, sir."

"Hmrph—and so you supplemented the ration which you were receiving with your emergency rations?"

"Yes, sir."

"For how long? Until they were all gone?"

"Until we were able to obtain 1 and ½ rations from the Australians for each man instead of one ration."

"How did you manage to do that?"

"Verbal order of the Base Section Commander, Col. Mathews."

"And when did that start?"

"The first part of August, I believe." I called to Cheeks and told him to look up the date. It was August 3rd.

"And the organization arrived here on. . . ." He fumbled through his papers. "April 28th?"

"I believe that was the date."

"Then you were using the emergency rations for a little over three months?"

"Er . . . yes, sir. That's right."

"And during that time all the rations were consumed?"

"No, sir. Most of the B rations were, but the largest portion of the C and D rations are stored in our Regimental Supply now." I could feel the pressure of his questioning, and small beads of sweat popped out on my forehead. We lit cigarettes and went on with the investigation. The secretary took down every word in shorthand. The colonel was from the Inspector Generals Department and was used to asking the right questions. He knew how to pin me down to facts and figures, and I could see that I was losing the battle. Finally he asked this one: "Do you see any reason why the various companies of this organization should not pay the Government out of their company funds to reimburse it for the extra rations they have consumed?" I stood up.

"Do I! It's an outrage to even think of such a thing! Colonel, you can't come to Moresby now, now that it is a big Allied base and picture the conditions as they existed nine and 10 months ago."

"What were those conditions?"

"I don't want to be dramatic. And probably you don't want to put any of this down in your investigation, but do you realize we were the first Americans sent up here. The Japs had taken Rabaul and Lae and Salamau. The next blow was almost certain to come here. Our ship came in under the cover of darkness with specific orders to sail before dawn whether our supplies were unloaded or not. That meant getting the stuff off the ship in any manner we could and dumping it in haphazard piles."

I realized that I was nearly shouting and controlled myself. The secretary asked me to repeat the last sentence, and for the first time I realized that he was taking down what I was saying.

"You're probably not interested in this, colonel, and. . . ."

"Oh, no. I want to hear it." He leaned forward, showing real interest.

"Well, sir, the night we landed, there was the heaviest downpour of rain that any of us had ever seen. Trucks rumbled back and forth from the ship to the Sports Grounds all night long."

"What is the Sports Grounds?" he asked.

"That's a cricket field in Moresby about a third of a mile from the dock where in the early days all supplies were brought before being carried out to the camp sites. That was because of the transportation shortage and the necessity of unloading the ships as quickly as possible. Well, the Sports Grounds was covered with six inches of water and mud a foot deep. We had to push the trucks in—literally throw the supplies off of them into the mud, and then push the trucks out again. Thousands of dollars worth of supplies were ruined, including a large percent of our rations—things like cereals, flour, sugar; in fact, nearly everything that wasn't canned. Next day Moresby had three raids: the Japanese Emperor's birthday or something like that, and they decided to celebrate it by pounding the hell out of us. Our rations were among the least things we worried about. There were more important things to get out of the Sports Grounds and disperse in various camp sites: our 37mm guns, our ammunition, our gasoline. If a bomb had hit these things, all our supplies would have been wrecked." My answer had taken the proportions of a speech, and I was self conscious.

"I can understand the difficulties," said the colonel.

"Rations were stolen from the Sports Grounds by other troops. Some were eaten by the men who worked there, and around there. We tried to control it, but a guard was impossible since the Australians were helping us with the work. And that's another point. Remember that these supplies were carried to our camp sites by Australians in Australian trucks and. . . ."

"Why didn't you use your own?"

"We had none."

"I see."

"And on many occasions, these Australians undoubtedly lost their way to our camp sites and wound up in their own. Trucks were stuck in the roads. Often they threw off our supplies into the bush so that they could get out. There were no roads such as you see here today. It took nearly a week to get our supplies to our camps. We could have done it sooner perhaps but the men had to be put to work immediately."

"There was no time to settle down?"

"With our only drome torn up with bomb craters!? We had to work if we expected to get out of this thing alive. We needed planes, and we couldn't have planes unless we had a serviceable drome. Sir, the day my battalion arrived we were able to put one Kittyhawk in the air. It wasn't fun being strafed and bombed at every turn. We weren't worried about a little food. The war was near at hand then."

"Yes, I can appreciate your difficulties."

"And that's not all, sir. You should have seen the food we were getting. Every day the same thing! M and V, cornbeef, salmon. Oh yes, we were living on the Australian rations up here which looks adequate, but we never did get all the items called for. We were supposed to be getting fresh fruits and vegetables, eggs and fresh meat. I can count on the fingers of my hand the number of times we received these things. And, colonel, we got food like cabbage and potatoes which were rotten. The stuff had lain exposed to the weather and insects for a day or two before it was issued to the troops, and a large percentage of it wasn't fit to be eaten. We really did everything we could to keep from using the rations. We kept armed guards on the ration piles, issued written orders prohibiting the use of rations except under the direction of an officer. And something else. We furnished rations to other outfits. The 46th sent a company up here and we gave them rations. Company E of the 43rd sent a platoon to Rarona for a week or so and we gave them rations to take along with them."

"You'd better hold off, lieutenant, before the government will be owing *you* money."

I smiled at that, and for the moment the tension was broken.

"Well," he said, concluding the questioning, "you've given me a good argument, but words alone won't do the trick. I want facts and figures. I'd like you to prepare for. . . ."

The inspector is gone now, and Miller is getting out the information he asked for. It is fun being investigated when right is on your side.

February 10, 1943

Colonel Derby is carrying his ceremonial nonsense too far. He is now requiring that we set off charges of gelignite to take the place of reveille and retreat guns—a horrible waste of explosives if I have ever seen one. He has also published an *order* stating that we were not going home before the war was over and that all rumors to that effect must stop. Good Lord! That is the thing these men live for from day to day—that some day relief will arrive and we will go home. Derby has funny ideas about morale. It makes no difference whether the rumor is true or not. It keeps the men going just hoping that they are going home. Another thing which Derby complained about are the spirituals the Chaplain had the men singing. He wanted them to sing lively marching songs. Damn his ignorance! What does he know of the heart and soul of the negro?

February 15, 1943

The air activity over this place is amazing. All one has to do is stand somewhere between Ward Drome and Seven Mile Drome and look up. There is almost certain to be a squadron of flights buzzing or a formation of transports either heading for or returning from the other side of the island protected by swarms of fighters up above them. Or perhaps a majestic flight of bombers taking up positions for a raid on Rabaul or Lae. It is all such a common sight around here now that one hardly notices them. This office is almost in line with the Bomana Runway, our smallest drome in the area, and all day long cobras are whining overhead taking off or landing. Telephone conversation is almost impossible while this is going on.

February 16, 1943

Another man crushed to death under a tractor. It is a shame how many of our men have been killed through carelessness. The other day we lost another in an automobile wreck and a couple days ago one was shot in the chest during an argument. He is expected to live, however. Sickness is crippling us also. In our supply section alone, we have Sgt. Patterson, Sgt. Gadsden, and Sgt Westbrooke in the hospital, leaving us with two non-coms to carry on the work. Colonel Derby is a nuisance with all his foolish ideas. He insists on having an American flag in front of his door and the quartermaster won't issue us a flag for love or money. I wonder how we ever win wars.

February 19, 1943

"Samuelson?"

"Yes, sir?"

"Are you doing any work, or are you—? Would you like to play a game of chess?" Colonel Derby asked me.

"Very much, sir. Would you like to play in your room?"

"Yes, I think that would be nice."

"I'll go down and get the board."

Derby had watched Frank and me playing chess, had merely looked on for a few minutes without comment and then walked away. It was a surprise that he had invited me to play with him. I figured that it would be a dull evening with my beating him game after game and being unable to read a magazine between his moves as I could do with Frank. As I entered the officers' mess hut someone asked me to play poker.

"Duty calls," I answered as I held up the set of chess. They all laughed understanding without my saying another word. I had the whites and moved first. After three or four moves I could see that Derby knew the game all right. I had made a good opening, and it looked as if we were really going to tie up in a good game. Then I made a foolish move and lost a knight. I maneuvered my men into position for a kill, sacrificing a bishop so that on the next move I could take up a position that would lead to my winning the game. He made a brilliant recovery. I was rendered helpless. He gradually pushed me around the board and then mated me.

"Another game, sir?"

"Yes, I think so. You really had me worried there for awhile. My position was quite favorable to cover the space in front of my king."

"Yes, sir. It's just like war. It's fire power that counts." By this time the board was set up again and he moved. I tried a new opening from the sides. In four moves he had won the game. He chuckled merrily, and I blushed for letting myself fall sucker for the Fool's Mate. He turned the board around, still laughing, more nearly to himself than aloud, and I was determined now to beat him. Our third game was perhaps the best game of chess I have ever played, but it wasn't good enough to beat the Colonel. All I could do was to get a stalemate out of the game.

"I enjoyed that very much," the Colonel said. "Thank you."

"Thank you, sir." I started to pick up the pieces and put them in the box, conscious that he was watching me closely. I stood up.

"Sit down, Samuelson," he ordered, more as a request than an order however. "Why is it that so many officers in the Regiment have such long faces?" I was taken aback by his question.

"Er, I don't know what you mean, sir."

"Why do they feel so sorry for themselves?"

"I don't think they do."

"This matter of them being so quiet. It bothers me to see a group of men sitting around a table and hardly anyone speaking."

"That is not generally the case, sir. You might find some of that around our table because you are rather new to most of us and conversation is a little stiff. But you won't find that within the companies—and, sir, there is a lot more conversation, even if only to gripe about the food, at our table when you are not there. I think after awhile, you will see that there isn't too much of this quietness that you talk about." I knew that I had made a favorable impression on the Colonel the evening that Colonel Harrison from Washington and Colonel Wright from Sydney interviewed me on supply needs in this area. Colonel Derby had just taken command of the Regiment and simply sat back while I answered the questions which were fired at me. It was a golden opportunity to get into his good graces, and now was another opportunity to show whatever intelligence I had concerning the general morale and welfare of the Regiment. I was going to be diplomatic but at the same time I didn't intend to hold any punches. So far Derby hadn't asked anyone about anything, and this was a golden chance to put across some of the things which had been worrying the officers. "Colonel, there is some griping among the officers. There is no sense in trying to deny that, but there are good reasons for it."

"What reasons?"

"Promotions for one thing." I could feel my pulse step up a notch or two. It isn't often that a lieutenant has the opportunity to tell his Regimental Commander that promotions are not satisfactory. "You might not be familiar with the fact that of all the men who were with the 96th when it was activated nearly two years ago none of them are higher than a captain; and at that most of them were first lieutenants when they started."

"Well tell me," he interrupted, "Do you think that any of them with the exception of Thomas is qualified for a higher grade than captain?"

"I don't believe I'm qualified to answer whether any of our men are capable of holding down the grade of Major. Yes, sir—come to think of it, there are. Captain Miller for one. He has been supply officer for fourteen months. That's too long for any one man to hold that job."

"Yes, Miller is a fine officer. When did he receive his captaincy?"

"About a year ago."

"Too bad the S-4 isn't a major in the T/O [table of organization]. Each battalion should have a major executive officer too."

"Yes, sir. I realize—so do all the officers—that there are few openings. That helps break down the morale." I could see that my last remark wasn't very tactful. "And there's another thing, sir; almost all of our replacements have come in from the top. Take for instance Captain Hasemann. He came in and took over the S-3 job. He will probably be promoted to major before long. We have several officers in the Regiment who have tried to get that position for a long time. That hurts morale. Nearly all our replacement officers—Behrens, Williams, Farley, Kalman—have been captains. You can't expect the lieutenants not to feel that they are getting a raw deal." That was the blow I wanted to get across. I had often thought of telling that to him, and now it was out. His forehead was wrinkled and he looked at me with a frown. But he had definitely heard the words I had said, and they seemed to be food for thought that had never entered his mind before.

"But we have received a large number of second lieutenants also? They are a rather sorry lot, aren't they?"

"Some of them are poor officers, but there are a number of good ones among them—Layman, Sabastan, Heiston."

"Yes, I was very much impressed by Layman's speech the other night and immediately had Colonel Pickard send in his recommendation for promotion to first lieutenant."

"I'm glad to hear that."

"And Sabastan is a fine officer too. Heiston is that red-faced quiet chap?"

"Yes, sir—a good officer in spite of his dissipated appearance."

"Yes, very often a man is unable to impress you with his own good merits." Conversation lagged.

"And, colonel, remember we have been spoiled. For a long time we were *the* engineers of New Guinea. Now we are no more than another engineer regiment. The let-down isn't altogether easy to take. You see, sir, for a long time we were doing work which we could see was helping win the war—putting in new dromes, bridging the Laloki, constructing the new causeway. Now our work—it's just a lot of eyewash." He didn't like that at all. "For instance, we used to build dispersal roads and merely shove the planes off under trees to work on them. Now we build pretty circular hard-standings for them to park the planes on."

"The military situation has changed."

"Yes, sir. I appreciate that fact. I think most of the officers do. But some few don't. They are the ones with the long faces."

"I hope we will be able to move further on," he said.

"It would be like a tonic to the Regiment to move where we would be of more service."

"How were the men under fire around here?"

"They behaved all right under the strafing and bombings. Only a few had the opportunity of firing back."

"How did they make out?"

"I doubt whether they ever shot down a plane, but one group of men in B Company had the machine bags shot up around their machine gun, but it didn't stop them from continuing to fire at the Zero."

"I understand that some of the men have never fired a rifle."

"That's right, sir. It is a sad state of affairs."

"What I would like to do," he went on, speaking in full confidence, "is to bring the Regiment to the Mainland for about three months for a period of intensive training and then come back and start over."

"That might be the answer to the situation. Right now we are a drain on the government, and our consumption of food, clothing, and other material is not nearly offset by the small amount of work we are doing around here." There was hardly more to say on the subject. The Colonel broke in with, "I'm transferring you back to operations. We can't afford to keep a civil engineer in your present position." That wasn't exactly a compliment, but it was good to know that he knew I was a civil engineer. I felt happy when I walked out of the Colonel's room last night. I felt that I had done a lot of good for the welfare of myself, my Regiment, my Country.

February 21, 1943

Water one foot from Laloki Runway. Much of the dispersal areas is under water. Planes have been evacuated to other dromes. Part of the road across the river is washed out. The bridge is still O.K. All drainage systems are operating in reverse as the river continues to rise. Twenty Jap bombers were turned back last night. They just made a pass overhead about 10 minutes ago. Wonderful ack-ack barrage. Too cloudy to observe anything. They will probably be making passes all night long. That will mean very little sleep, because they seem to pass right over our camp every time and we get a terrific hail of ack-ack fragments. Wonderful letters from Dora today. It made me terribly homesick. Gee I wish she were here to go to sleep with me.

February 22, 1943

I am now conducting a carpenter school and a sign painting school in addition to other duties. I have a hunch we are to be on the move before long. Feverish air activity going on.

February 23, 1943

Completed lectures in surveying this evening. Will start a new series on electricity next Saturday evening.

February 25, 1943

Derby and Pickard are both away on reconnaissance near Wau, an old gold mining center. If we ever develop Wau's three airdromes, we will be able to hammer the Jap base at Salamau only 40 miles away.[5] Very recently the Japs made a determined drive against Wau and were turned back only after they had reached within a few hundred yards of the runway. There is a well-grounded rumor, really more than a rumor, that the Regiment or at least part of it is going to Wau. It is surprising how many of the officers do not want to go. About 50% of the men in the Regiment do not want to get any closer to Nippo than they are right now. About 10% would like the opportunity for new adventures, and about 40% are more or less apathetic about any movement. So for the past two days there has been a great deal of jabbering among everyone concerning who will go and who will not go, when we are leaving, how, and so on. The truth of the matter is that no one knows the details yet. That is why our two colonels went on the reconnaissance. Am anxious to go.

February 27, 1943

It seems that one company only will go to Wau. Derby is never around any more. We see him at breakfast, and then he is gone. I don't know what he is trying to cook up. Japs are landing many reinforcements on the other side. It is expected that we will be receiving *real* reinforcements by April. There should be a good show around here by June or July. The African situation looks glum, and the Russian drives have mired down. I'm afraid this is going to last for years.

March 3, 1943

The Japs are landing more troops on the north side of the island. Our bombers have been going after them all day long. They sank a couple of ships yesterday; and judging by the scale of today's operations, I'd guess they sent a few more down to Davie Jones' locker. Two good letters from Dora. I live with her all night long in my dreams.

March 4, 1943

Business is picking up. I have more orders for carpentry work than the carpenters are able to handle. I like it that way better than having idle men on my hands. The sign painting school is coming along satisfactorily, too. They are doing some nice work. We scored a major victory during the past two days on the other side. Our bombers sank 14 out of 20 Jap ships which were coming into Lae.

March 10, 1943

The medical officers of the Regiment are clamoring that it is murder to send men to Wau.

"Their health is shot to hell. They will have to be brought back out within a month," they say.

The health of the men is indeed poor. Exhausted from 10½ months of hard toil in New Guinea, they are going to the hospital at the rate of six a day. And they're not coming out nearly that fast. I have always advocated that such a change would do much good for both health and morale, but there is a lot in what the doctors say: "The men are willing to go, but they won't last any time under added physical and mental strain."

I disagree with that. Most of them, I am sure, would hold up. But perhaps our going to Wau is not such a good thing after all.

March 11, 1943

I wish I were assigned to some important job. I hate all this petty stuff. I feel like kicking Derby in the tail when he compliments me for putting up "such a good-looking flag pole" or for building a "nice latrine building." I'm sick of that. Why can't we build things which will help win the war: more airdromes, better roads, better harbor facilities. And if Moresby has reached the point where it no longer needs further development, then why don't we move on? Sometimes I wonder whether most Americans want this war to end very soon. It does have its advantages—even for me. I am sure that over half of the regular army officers do not want to see it end. For them it means high rank, prestige. It's their profession. Most workers back home don't want it to end very soon. What a hell of a mess!

March 12, 1943

There is all kind of commotion about tomorrow's review. Heavy equipment has been pulled off important engineering work to clear a field for the parade. My job is to fire the 11 gun salute for General Johns. I am doing this by setting off sticks of gelignite at two minute intervals.

March 13, 1943

The review was a huge success. I must give Derby credit for it. No one else believed it would go off so well. The band, drums and bugles, did a good job. The gun salute went off perfectly. The troops marched well. General Johns' extemporaneous speech was excellent. His talk was a wonderful morale booster.

March 14, 1943

The writeup of yesterday's review in the *Guinea Gold* was anything but complimentary. It sounded as if the editor was poking fun at us. You can hardly blame him. It does seem funny that we should bow our heads in remembrance of the two men in the regiment who have given their lives in New Guinea when whole companies have been wiped out on the other side of the island without any ceremony whatsoever. War is terrible stuff, really does make a man hard.

March 15, 1943

Among other duties, I have been keeping charts on all equipment of the regiment since the first of the month, showing hours that each piece has worked, been idle, and been unserviceable. They have shown how inefficiently it has all been used. We have an arsenal of engineering construction dynamite, but the charts show that only 50% of the equipment is serviceable and it is kept going no more than 60 to 70% of its maximum output. Colonel Pickard wanted to know: "What in the hell is the meaning of this chart?" For apparently

General Johns reviewing troops of the 96th Engineers, Port Moresby, March 1943.

Colonel Derby got on him about seeing that the equipment worked more. "What do you mean that this D-8 worked only ten hours yesterday?"

"That's all it worked, sir." This resulted in a big discussion with battalion commanders and all.

"The hell with the whole thing!" Pickard said when he left.

March 16, 1943

The doctors of the regiment believe we will be evacuated soon. The sick list increases in length daily. But who the hell wants to go to Australia for a rest? Especially with troops! That won't be a rest. I'd prefer staying up here where we can do some good, small as it is, than go to Australia where our troops would get in fights with white soldiers and in all kind of other trouble.[6]

NINE

The Hood Point Airdrome

March 17–April 22, 1943

March 17, 1943

I believe I am going to Hood Point to supervise the laying of some landing mat by the natives. Apparently another plane has made a forced landing around there.

March 18, 1943

I wish I didn't have this fever (up to 102.4 now) so I could write a complete account of today's activities. To sum them up briefly: flew to Hood Point in P-49 with Lt. Col. Shaw, 8th Service Squadron. Looked over the drome site. Staked out areas for mat. Contacted Major Austin, D.O., Moresby, and arranged for 140 native laborers. Saw W. O. Stephenson (Rigo) and outlined work I'd like him to start immediately. Told him to expect me back in four days. Damn! I'm sick. Can hardly see what I'm writing.

March 19, 1943

Colonel Pickard walked in yesterday morning, handed me a piece of paper, and said casually, "Here's the job you wanted." By the time I had glanced over the paper and looked up, the colonel had gone out. There was a note at the bottom of the sheet of instructions to make all arrangements with Colonel Shaw of the Eighth Service Group. I went out to see Colonel Shaw. He was very much in a hurry, and I had to chase his jeep with mine in order to catch him. "I am Lt. Samuelson— 96th Engineers." I said hurriedly.

"Yes, yes, so what?" He was annoyed with me, I could see. Rather than explain my position I handed him my instructions. "Oh, you're the kid who's going to take charge of this job. . . . Got everything arranged yet?"

"No, sir—I just got this notice this morning. It says to see you for details."

"Him-r-ph. Are you busy?"

"I'm trying to get some information on this job at Hood Point," I answered.

"Well, I'm going over the there now. Put this on," Shaw said as he handed me a life belt. I hadn't quite figured out how to put the thing on when he threw me a parachute. I climbed into the back cockpit of the plane. One of the sergeants around there fastened a safety belt around my legs. I was perfectly miserable with a dozen or more straps winding around my waist, over my shoulders, between my legs, around my legs. I noticed that Shaw didn't put on any of this stuff except his life belt. As soon as we taxied onto the runway, I slid out of my harness too.

"Hell, I didn't know you had a regular runway over here," I said as I climbed out the plane. "It's about 150 feet wide and a mile long."

"Forty-eight hundred feet."

"How was it graded?" Shaw wasn't anxious to make conversation but I wanted to know the facts.

"By the natives."

"With hand shovels?"

"Yes."

"A marvelous job. Have many planes landed on the field yet?"

"It's already saved three heavy bombers—all out of gas and forced down. They could have never made it to Moresby. The B-24 had two of its engines shot out of commission and the third one cut out just as she hit the runway. All the planes have made good landings and successful take-offs."

"Must be pretty muddy in rainy weather."

"Yep, pretty bad. That's why we want this mat put in."

We walked over to the operations building. It was just a tent where half a dozen enlisted men from the air corps stayed. There was a generator for lighting the field at night. A few drums of gasoline were on the sides of the runway. We got into a half-busted down jeep and drove to the southeast end of the runway, inspected the ground and decided where we would put the 150-foot square of landing mat. We also selected a spot for dispersing a big bomber off the runway. This is necessary because the 4800 feet is none too much for a heavy bomber, and if two would have to come in at the same time, there might be some trouble. Then we drove to the northwest end of the runway and selected similar areas there.

We went to see Stephenson, a warrant officer in the Australian Army who is in charge of the natives at Houla, the village on Hood Point. Steve told us about a couple of deaths in the village, one of them caused by some poison one of the medicine men had given to a native. "I've found out who this witch doctor—or whatever he calls himself—is, but I can't locate the drug he gave to this poor native. I'd like to send the body to Port to have the stomach analyzed. I'm sure they would find poison of some kind or other in it. The man's eyes had turned green—green as grass. I'm sure it's poison. The other natives want to get rid of this doctor, and I'd like to charge him with sorcery, but I have no proof."

Shaw volunteered to carry the body back to Port Moresby with us. "You don't mind a dead native riding in the back compartment with you, do you?" he asked.

"Oh, no; it's nothing to me." Nevertheless I was glad when they decided to bury the body in Hula. Colonel Shaw and I then drove up to the mission house. I was flattered that Mr. Short recognized me. I had spent a night in his home about four months ago on a voyage from Abau to Moresby. Shaw's abruptness broke down completely in front of the old missionary, and the three of us enjoyed an interesting conversation. I was mostly on the listening side, not that I was trying to be polite but because I was unfamiliar with many of the subjects they spoke of. Both had traveled widely, had read even more. Later Major Austin came in. He has, I believe, written about Papua in the *Encyclopedia Britannica* and several books. He was perhaps the most intelligent of the three. So at dinner time I just sat back and listened to these three men tell of their experiences. It was almost as enjoyable as the food. Major Austin said we would have approximately 140 natives available for the work. I went over the work with Steve, told him what I would like him to have done while in Port making arrangements for the landing mats and other supplies.

"You'll have to grade this up a bit better for the mat. And I'd like a path cut from that end of the 'drome to the water's edge so that the men can carry the mat without too much difficulty."

"I think we can cut a jeep trail without any trouble for that short distance," he volunteered.

"That's better. Now, I presume you have a pilot in the village who can take the boat and barge over the reefs? The boat we get for the job might not know its way into here."

"Oh, yes, we have several boys who know the waters around here the way you know your bedroom."

"Good. Then I'll have the boat report to Hula first for a pilot. Now the wind—does it usually blow like this?"

"She's a bit stronger than usual."

"I mean in direction."

"Hm—No, come to think of it, it doesn't. This time of the year she comes out the northwest."

"Well, this is the kind of wind we'll need in order to bring the barge in. I'm afraid we'll have to cut 'er loose a couple hundred feet off shore and drag 'er in, and we might lose it unless we have an on-shore breeze."

The trip back to Moresby was a treat. Shaw, either for his own amusement or mine, started to stunt the plane. He did some diving, enough to convince me that I don't want to be a dive-bomber pilot. He hedge-hopped all along the beaches, scaring natives who were fishing and nearly taking off the roofs of houses in their villages. The star above his silver wings assured me that he knew what he was doing; otherwise I would have fastened my safety belt. A parachute wouldn't have done any good at that elevation anyway; so there was no sense in sliding into it.

After supper my temperature went up to 102.4 and I felt so bad that I thought I was going to have to give in and tell Bud, but I knew that he would send me to the hospital and that my job would be finished. I cursed myself for getting fever, but I doped myself with quinine and aspirin, put heavy covers on my cot, and went to bed early. The fever was gone by this morning. I have worked all day, requisitioning supplies, trying to get a barge and a tug lined up. Frankly I had very little success. Tomorrow I'll use different tactics, the only kind that works around here: "God damn it! I need it!! And if I don't get it without any more of this red tape, I'm going right to Headquarters!" That kind of stuff usually gets results. Although very often the results are negative they're definite, and that's an achievement. But I just wasn't up to that today. This fever is slowly whipping me down in spite of the quinine I keep taking. I promise myself that I'll go to the hospital after this job is over, but I've got to finish it first. I hate myself for getting sick so easily! Milne Bay, Abau, and now again.

March 20, 1943

Shipping priorities might tie up this job at Hood Point for some time. I got the barge at the wharf all right but I cannot commence loading without permission from the commanding general. That will take three or four days. More red tape!

Red Tape

You endless bale of binding twine
That ties my hands and turns my dreams and plans
Into nightmares,
Where are your roots?
Where is the food on which you thrive?
Tell me where it grows,
And I vow I'll plow it under.
Why do men strive to keep you alive?
Is it worth the pain you cause a man who knows
And wants to do his task?
Who created such an infamous thing?
Who sews the seeds from which you spring?
Tell me these things!
Be fair Red Tape!
So the plans of my struggle might take shape;
For now when I slash you and cut you to shreds,
The little pieces that fall to the ground
Take new life, climb and wind around
My arms and legs and add to my strife.
But tell me the things I ask,
And I'll spend my life
In stamping you out,
In cutting you into tiny pieces
And scattering them far from sight
Of those who nourish you
So that if a man wants to work
Both day and night, *He can*
Unmolested by a serpent-like thing
A snake-like thing which used to be
A viper called Red Tape!

March 23, 1943

It's a comfortable grass hut that I'm living in. The mosquitoes are fierce, and I am forced to write under my net. The reason I am here can be explained briefly: We have lost many aircraft in the past because they have run out of gas and couldn't make it back to their base in Port Moresby. Hood Point is approximately sixty miles from Port and is on the course that many of the planes return along after completing a bombing raid on Rabaul or in the Solomons. Consequently the natives, under the direction of the Australian government, were directed to clear a strip of land for an emergency drome. They cleared a strip 150 feet wide and 4800 feet long in a marshy flat grassland. They selected such a spot because it would minimize grading, all of which had to be done by hand with no tools other than picks and shovels. The place is entirely satisfactory in dry weather. But when it rains, planes bog down, especially when they attempt to turn around. Since the strip has been cleared, three heavy bombers and several smaller aircraft have been saved from destruction. But each of these has torn up the ends of the runway while turning around, and one of the heavy bombers was delayed for several days when it got stuck. The Air Corps decided that the existence of the strip was desirable and that the ends must be prepared so that they could "take" the earth-churning action of big bombers while they turned. Landing mat spread over these areas was the answer. In addition to the two matted areas, one at each end of the strip, the Air Corps decided they wanted two parking areas of the runway, each large enough to hold a B-17 or B-24. I was given the job. There were 146 tons of steel mat to be transported from Moresby here. I made a reconnaissance with Colonel Shaw and attended to other details from this end. A seventy-year old two masted schooner which we loaded the night before last is on its way here with 25 tons of mat, a small part of the total amount needed for the job but a start nevertheless. Lt. McCluny and I flew over the *Lena Gladys* this morning as she was winding her way through the reefs. She was sailing with a fair wind which has grown stronger throughout the day; and if she doesn't founder under her heavy load, she should arrive today by dusk. The natives have cleared a path through a knoll which runs parallel to the beach on which we intend landing the mat. This is necessary so that our jeep can run down to the beach, pick up the mat and take it to the far end of the runway.

Later: This grass hut, built by the natives, is more like a small bungalow. It has three rooms.

The *Lena Gladys* has arrived and is spending the night at Houla. She will round the point and lay off shore opposite the southeast end of the runway the first thing in the morning. She pulled around to the point from which we had proposed to unload the mat, but the surf was so terrific that the small steel barge which was to be used to lighter the mat from the schooner to the beach would have been dashed to pieces. So it was necessary to bring her a mile down the coast where the beach was protected from the surf by a covering reef. She was able to get within a hundred yards of the shore. A tow-line was then passed to shore. The barge was loaded and pulled ashore along the tow-line by natives on the barge. About 50,000 pounds of mat was brought ashore yesterday in this manner.

March 26, 1943

All day long the natives carried mat down to the far end of the strip. I hope to finish this part of the job Monday. I wonder whether anyone will be reloading the *Lena Gladys* back at Port.

March 27, 1943

A day of complete rest and relaxation. Lt. McCluny flew in this morning and brought us 20 records for our victrola. We played a lot of cards. None of the fellows give me competition in casino or rummy, the only games we play; so I resort to solitaire. We now have a good native cook who does a dern good job in putting on a spread. I was so full this evening after supper that I could hardly walk down to the sea for a swim.

March 28, 1943

The *Lena Gladys* has arrived at Houla again. I understand that she was loaded by crane this time. I'll go down to see the skipper in the morning. The southeast traders have started to blow steadily. According to people who have lived here for years, their arrival means the end of the rains, but I fear something has gone amiss, for we have been having a minor deluge every evening. However the winds cause a beautiful surf on the beach not far from our hut and the swimming is great. It feels good to be with all these crazy fellows from the Air Corps. I didn't realize how grown-up I had become until this past week. Their conversations are about such foolish things. For example, which of them would be the bravest pilot if they were pilots. I can hardly take part in them. Their fear that the undertow is some mysterious force which will drag them to sea, their lack of mathematical calculation in cards, their foolish arguments, their meaningless profanity—so many things which I once did, and enjoyed, but which now seem foolishness to me all tends to prove that my *real* boyhood days are over, that I am a man and must accept my fate. I enjoyed their chatter last night after they all climbed under their mosquito nets. Each lit his flashlight and started searching for mosquitoes and other insects.

"Looks like a damn air raid around here with all those searchlights."

"Yep, I just got strafed by three mosquitoes."

"Look at dat beedle in here—a damn four engine bomber!"

"You stupid bastards—you ought to keep a few spiders in your net. They'll catch all the bugs and insects. See they ain't none in mine."

"These damn malaria jobs! They're hard as hell to catch."

"Yeah, they keep flying around."

"Got belly tanks; that's why." One fellow tore into all sides of his net swatting furiously.

"How d'you make out?" someone asked him.

"Aw, I was attacked by six of the sons of bitches. I got two for certain and three probables."

"Two just made a pass at me, but they pissed off. I couldn't get 'em."

"Only one left in my net. I'm sweating him out now. I'll—ah, there he is! Enemy sighted! Sank some." He flashed the light around the inside of his net awhile. "All clear," he declared and put out the light.

March 29, 1943

Second 25-ton load of mat taken from *Lena Gladys* today. Twenty natives laid 100-foot-square area at NW end of runway. My orders are to make these turn-around sections 150-feet square, but on my own accord I have cut the size down to 100-foot squares. It will be a saving of 12,000 sq. ft. of steel mat. No one will ever know the difference and it will be a big saving of time, labor, and material, not to mention shipping space. There is too damn much waste. If we would try to curb it, we could get this war over a lot sooner.

March 30, 1943

We are now out of native rations. So we could not work them today. Just another example of the kind of inefficiency which exists around here. If this war were being tackled with the kind of enthusiasm which should win a war quickly, we would work the natives anyway and pay them later. But it seems that ANGAU has its way of handling them and doesn't like to have its methods interfered with. Well, they have done a wonderful job with the natives and really have the natives' interest at heart. So I guess we army blokes ought to abide by their customs and methods without complaint.

These *boys* aren't such a happy-go-lucky lot after all. They shot and killed a dog this morning and wanted to do the same with another one this afternoon. I stopped the second murder. Furthermore they were very ugly toward three Australian soldiers who were doing some survey work in this area and who dropped in for supper last evening. We had three chickens for seven of us and they were angry cause the Aussies helped us eat the birds. And when the Aussies came in for breakfast this morning, the fellows told them, "Nothing doing—just got enough food for ourselves." That kind of behavior may be boyish, but I'm inclined to classify it as childish.

April 1, 1943

Over a dozen heavy bombers flew over around 4 o'clock going out on some mission. There's a heavy rain storm going on now and we are on the alert for any lost aircraft. Some have already returned from their mission and apparently had their bearings all right, for they were heading for Moresby. But all have not returned yet. Still no native rations. Stephenson turned over about 450 rations to us which he had been keeping for stranded airmen. The extra food will come in handy, for our rations were running low.

April 2, 1943

About 11 o'clock last night a flying fortress circled the field trying to land. He missed the top of our hut by less than ten feet: so Shucard, who was on duty, told us. I nearly wrenched my neck trying to push myself down into my cot when I was awakened by the roar of its four engines overhead. Although our field was water-soaked and soft from the heavy rains, we turned on the field lights to indicate the exact position of the field to the pilot. He circled widely in the downpouring rain and put on his landing lights. He was coming in. He hit the runway near its center. One wheel sank into the mire. Then out! He bounced and wiggled, side to side. And then he stuck fast! He was down in mud nearly to the wheels' hubs. It was a beautiful landing. The pilot, Lt. Kerby, got out the plane with his crew of ten. They were surprised when we told them where they were. "Thought it was Wards Drome," Kirby admitted, "That is until I hit the runway." We fixed up some chow for the hungry crew while they told us of their unsuccessful mission. "If we had reached the target fifteen minutes sooner, we could have hit 'er."

"Yep, and we were going faster'n I figured. Spaced the bombs too far apart," said the sergeant bombardier. We rigged up some beds and by midnight all were asleep. Kirby's take-off this afternoon was a marvelous feat. Only about 2000 feet of the runway was serviceable. To use 3000 feet would have meant the loss of eleven lives and $300,000 worth of airplane. It makes me angry when you hear of the

Air Corps refusing to land ships on a 4800-foot field, objecting that it isn't long enough.

Still no native rations. I hope some arrive by next Monday. The third boat load of mat should be in by then.

April 3, 1943

The *Lena Gladys* is in with the third load of mat. The skipper of the boat spotted the lugger with native rations off Round Point. I am going to try to get Stephenson to work the natives tomorrow so that we can get the boat unloaded and she can start back for Port Monday morning. I estimate the job will be completed on the 18th.

April 4, 1943

We unloaded the boat today. She will leave for Moresby in the morning. I wish I could sit down and have a talk with a particular native girl I see almost every day. I met her about eight or ten days ago while I was walking to the village. As I was walking through the tall grass I saw her about a hundred yards ahead. She saw me, then started running down the trail. She turned around and saw me laughing. Apparently she was embarrassed for behaving like so many of the little children who run at the sight of a white man for she immediately started walking. I noticed her slim figure and the rhythmic swaying of her hips, which were covered by her only piece of clothing — a grass skirt. And I quickened my pace. She was walking rapidly, but I gained on her. She didn't turn around but sensed that I was getting nearer. When I was about thirty feet behind her, she stepped off the trail and leaned backwards against a coconut tree. She was frightened. Her black eyes starred widely at me. She breathed heavily, her pretty breasts waving up and down.

"Good morning," I said in as harsh a voice as I could. It was the kind of good morning I would tell to any native.

"Good morning, taubada," she answered meekly as I walked by. I didn't turn around but I knew she must have watched me until I went out of sight, feeling foolish for fearing me. Frankly, if she read what was in the deep recesses of my mind, she had reason enough to fear me. When I passed back down the trail, she was working in her garden. This time she didn't run from me. Instead she smiled and said again "Good morning, taubada," I smiled and nodded; didn't answer, for it would be a breach of behavior for an officer of the American Army to take a pipe out of his mouth just to tell a native good morning. I have seen her half a dozen times since, but today was the first time we spoke. We were unloading the *Lena Gladys*. She and several other young women were watching the men unloading the boat. She started talking by asking me, "You build airdrome?"

I answered with a simple "Yes."

Immediately the natives started crowding around; and even though I would have liked to talk to this girl, it would have been wrong to chat with a whole bunch of them; for I still had to work these natives and I had to be somebody *above* them. To talk to them would wreck this relationship. It is horribly wrong, but it is the way of the native, and there is no changing it. I hope it rains this evening. If we don't get a heavy rain, it will be three full days without a bath—the longest I have gone without one since I came to New Guinea.

April 5, 1943

Hauled mat all day. Even with the aid of the jeep, it was a terribly slow practice. It is a 2¼ mile haul, and the natives gave all kind of trouble. It was the first day that W. O. Ryan was in charge and they tried to pull every trick imaginable, feigning illness and fatigue. One group didn't show up until late, and two boys deserted. Ryan has taken the bull by the horns and is doing a good job, but it will take several days before things run smoothly. This evening when we were almost sure that there would be no rain, we went down for a bath in the brine. We came back dirtier than we went in. The surf was excellent however, breakers well over six feet high, and we got a lot of exercise, but I feel miserable with all the sand and sea weed, tiny pieces, all over my body.

April 6, 1943

Started laying mat at NW dispersal area. The jeep was broken down all afternoon and got it to run only after we made some gaskets out of a carton of cigarettes to put under the gas bowl to stop the fuel pump from sucking in air. The generator gave trouble too and took an hour this evening before we could get it started. It makes me laugh how we eat food around here. Whenever we get some new treat, we eat it for the next meal. It makes no difference whether we have eggs for dinner and chicken for breakfast. It's a crazy philosophy, but it is an indication of the frame of mind a fellow gets into after he has been over here this length of time.

April 7, 1943

Hauled mat all day long. Jeep gave more trouble this morning, but finally got it to run. Plan to complete laying of mat at NW end of strip by tomorrow and might complete hauling mat from beach to SE end of strip by Friday evening. The *Lena Gladys* should be in by then with the fourth load. Rain this evening at last and a fresh-water bath! How absolutely wonderful.

April 9, 1943

NW end of strip is completed. Commenced laying mat at SE end. Finished hauling mat from beach to SE end of strip. *Lena Gladys* did not arrive this evening as I had anticipated, perhaps tomorrow. Natives claim to have seen some Jap planes overhead yesterday and today. Moresby has radioed for information about Jap planes over this area. None of us have definitely spotted any. Our field is buzzed no less than half a dozen times a day, and one of these times it will be by a Jap plane, and he will be meaning business. Our total weapons here consist of one rifle, two revolvers, and one tommy gun. We keep no guard at night so that two Japs could capture an airfield without any trouble if they could sneak into here some night. If they could capture this field, they could pour in several hundred troops by transport planes before anyone would suspect their having control of the strip. These troops could dig in and set up a defense which would take three times their number to dislodge. With a strip only sixty miles from Port Moresby, the Japs could send over dive bombers, concentrating on the runways, especially those covered with steel mat. Kila, Laloki, No 1. Strip, 7-Mile, Wards and Waaigani are all covered with this mat and could be turned into a heap of twisted steel wreckage with a few direct hits. Those planes on the ground could not get up. Those in the air would be forced to land on Bomana or on the No. 2 Strip of Wards. No 2 at 7-Mile is unserviceable. Large formations of high-level bombers could come in from Lae, Salamau, Rabaul, Gasmata and wreck our grounded aircraft. Simultaneously the Japs would have to hammer the airdromes at Milne Bay and on the other side of the island. Once the airdromes are out, Port Moresby would be doomed. The two six-inch guns at Paga and the two 155's at Bootless would make a poor show against a few Jap battlewagons. Port Moresby, swarmed with disorganized service troops, would become a mass of chaos. A force of thirty thousand men could do the job. *But* — can the Nips knock out all our airdromes simultaneously? I don't think they can.

There are thousands of Engineer troops scattered throughout Papua, thousands of natives who could help, thousands of other troops who could work on the dromes in an emergency. Yes, it could be done, but it would cost the Japs more than they care to pay at present.[1]

April 10, 1943

De Blaiso had the G.I.'s this morning and has been in bed all day. It is a wonder that we all haven't gone down with dysentery before this. I guess the spiders have been the biggest help in preventing it. They have lined the walls of our latrine with their webs so that flies, the evil spreaders of dysentery (or G.I.'s, as it is called over here), haven't much of a chance to get in and out alive.

Schuchart went fishing with the natives this morning and we enjoyed a big fish fry tonight for supper. They fish with rubber-gun spears which they "fire" at the fish from under the water. Koypy, the straw boss of Houla, says they stay under the water for five minutes and descend to a depth of from nine to twelve fathoms. Knowing how poor is the natives' estimate of distances, I doubt that they go down more than twenty-five feet. I'll try to arrange going with them next Saturday. Dionne and I drove into Kailo this morning to do some trading with the natives, but Sgt. White (AGUUA) was taking a census of the village, the first since 1939. Normally they are taken annually and our breaking in during the middle of the count would have thrown everything in disorder. So we agreed to come back Monday. Paula, the son of our cook, Jack, taught me how to throw his spear this morning. Paula is a thin chap of 16 or 17, not quite my height, fully 20 pounds less my weight. He threw his spear and stuck it up in an ant hill, 25 yards away.

"Let me try?" I asked him. He handed me the light spear. I tossed it and was surprised to see the point dip down and the spear fall short five yards in front of the target. Paula ran and got the spear for me, and I tossed it again, this time putting more force behind my heave. Again it fell short.

"You try again," I said. "You lucky first time." He ran after the spear, brought it back, balanced it carefully, something I had failed to do, leaned back, let it fly—jing, right into the center of the ant hill, penetrating six inches into the hard baked earth.

"I throw more far than you," I challenged.

"Okay," he said, still smiling over his success. I took his spear, handled it like a javelin, wrapped my hand carefully around it. Took a long run and with as nearly perfect balance as I could maintain, I let it fly. My heart went sick as I saw it quivering, wobbling in its flight, settling to earth tail end first not over 25 yards from where I had released it. Paula ran after the spear, marked the ground where my throw had hit, brought the spear back to the place from which I had tossed it. He reared back. I saw the spear fly like an arrow. Up! Up! Up! It leveled off—without a quiver—then sped toward the ground, and *stuck*, twice as far away as my toss had gone. Paula was whooping and shouting, and I had to admit defeat and ask him for instructions. By the time I quit, I could throw it over 40 yards consistently and hit the ant hill at 20 yards. The key to the whole thing was perfect balance and keeping the force of your throw in line with the spear.

Lt. McCluny and Lt. St. Pierre (8th Service Group) were up today and brought us a football, a bat, two softballs, some mosquito repellant, and mail for some of the fellows. Mac said that he would try to get around and pick up my mail and bring it to me the next time he comes this way. We had a game of touch football after they left. It was a bastard game if I have ever seen one. The natives didn't know any of the rules, which could be expected; and to teach them the rules was hopeless. But we needed the extra man power, so we had to let them play. It was a good work out even if it didn't resemble a game of football. We played soft ball awhile too. That was less strenuous. The swimming this evening was perfect. We found a good spot yesterday and a better one today. Our eyes are getting used to the brine, and the swimming is swell.

Right after supper we got a message from a native that the fever had hit Sgt. White and that we should come to see him. He had 104.2 temperature and we brought him back to Ryan's place in Houla, only to find Bill Ryan down with the fever too. The main reason that I mention this trip into Kailo is that it gave me the opportunity of seeing the loveliest creature I have laid eyes on in the Eastern Hemisphere so far. She was a girl of sixteen, I'd guess. She pushed aside the small children who were gathered around our jeep and walked up to where I was sitting. She had black curly hair which dropped all around her head and over her forehead. She had eyes, and a nose, and even lips, that any American girl would be proud to possess. Her face showed not a wrinkle, and an expression, if you could call it an expression at all, of arrogance. Firm, well-shaped breasts stood out from her small, slender frame. Her grass skirt hung low, revealing a pretty round belly. She was standing close to me and I eyed her hungrily. She didn't seem embarrassed. None of them do. She looked me full in the face. Some old man from the village told her to get away from the car but she shook his hand away. It was embarrassing having her stand so close to me, watching her breasts rise and fall as she breathed. She kept staring at me as I smoked my pipe. Schuchart, sitting in back of the jeep, chided me.

"Looks like you've made a hit with the village belle, lieutenant. She's all right too."

She leaned against the fender of the jeep, still watching me smoke. She reached down quite unconcerned whether anyone noticed, and scratched a bite on her rump. She did it gracefully, still watching me. I was amused and annoyed. All the little kids around the car jabbering and this black beauty standing in front of me, neither smiling, frowning, nor saying a word—just looking! I blew a mouthful of smoke into her face. Why, I don't know. The native girl coughed and backed away. All the children were delighted and shouted. I felt absurd. I climbed from the jeep. They all backed away, fearing I was angry. I started up to the house where White was lying and Dionne was giving him some pills. When I came back to the jeep with the rest of the gang, the same native girl was there. Without saying a word or showing any expression on her face, she handed me a necklace of snail shells, beautifully polished. I took them from her, held them up, tried to show my admiration and appreciation. I couldn't tell how she felt. I reached into my pockets, pulled out a shilling, and gave it to her. She took it, holding her hand well below mine so that I could let the coin drop into it.

"Let's go" I told Dionne.

"S' matter, lieutenant, that native gal getting you down?"

"Nope, I just don't understand women." I answered.

April 11, 1943

"Today's your birthday, isn't it, lieutenant?" Dionne asked me. He was 24 on April 7th; and when he mentioned the fact, I told him that he was but four days older than I. "It's not a very happy birthday, is it?" he continued.

"Nope, could be a lot better," I answered and went on with my game of solitaire. But it has been a happy birthday, a happy day, like most of the days I now spend. Here is a description of the day. I got up at dawn and washed. Sgt. White dropped in on his way to Kailo to finish taking the village's census. He was loaded with quinine, beating down an attack of fever which had hit him yesterday.

"I'm not doing anything. I'll drive you up to Kailo in the jeep," I offered. He gladly accepted. The ride through the two native villages between here and Kailo and across the countryside down the foot path on a beautiful Sunday morning is a treat indeed. By now the children have learned not to fear the jeep and run after it the same as dogs do. It is a lot of fun to wave at them and answer their shouts of "good-morning" and "okay." I don't know whether they understand the meaning of "okay" for they use it as a term of greeting, consent, and farewell. Breakfast consisted of a large assortment of tropical fruit. I doubt that one person in a thousand is as fortunate as I am in having such fruit available. We played a great nine inning game of pseudo baseball. Who wouldn't feel happy and thankful to see his muscles respond instantaneously to his wishes? The thrill of throwing a ball accurately, of jumping and catching a half-wild toss, of batting a ball for a couple hundred feet. Who doesn't find true happiness in that? And then the swim before dinner. Playing strip naked in the Coral Sea, as close to nature as a man can get; picking up pretty shells, tossing lumps of dead coral, browning in the tropical sun, running along the beaches. God, how wonderful is health! The entire fountain of happiness seems to find its source in health. And after a big dinner, what a grand feeling there is in scrubbing your teeth until they feel perfectly clean! And then to lie in bed and smoke. I have a splendid selection of pipes; and although my tobacco is running low, I still have enough, by smoking conservatively, to last me until I return to Port. To read *Macbeth* again and a few of Shelly's and Keats' poems for dessert: who could ask for a more restful and pleasant Sunday afternoon? And then sleep, how wonderful it is before a meal.

Just before dark a B-24 circled the field and landed. Back from an 11½ hour reconnaissance mission, nearly out of gas, and with a zero ceiling at Port, the pilot, Lt. Smith, decided to come down here. The field was in good condition. The plane made a perfect landing. In my small way, I felt that I had done a little toward the war effort; and that made me happy. After the crew had eaten and told us of their spotting a convoy off Wewak, of their unsuccessful bombing of two cargo ships, and of the other things they had seen, we all went outside where a hundred natives had gathered to look at the "big bird." The natives formed a ring and sang and danced for our amusement while we passed out cigarettes and hard tack as a token of our appreciation. It was a pleasant ceremony—natives of all ages jabbering, laughing, dancing and singing. Mothers with babies clinging to their breasts, old men leaning on crooked walking sticks, tots who could barely walk, all watched the show as the others joined in the merriment. After an hour or so we wished each other good night, and the natives went away. Back in the hut again, most of the crew, tired from their day's work, went to bed. De Blasio, Smith, another crew member and I finished the evening with two games of auction bridge.

And now all are in bed—all but Schuchart and I. He is staying on night duty and I want to finish up this bit before turning in. And going to bed at night is pleasant too—To think of Dora and home, to dream what our life will be like when we are together again, of Ian and our other children, of my teaching at a University, of the time when I can sleep with Dora—all of this is happiness. And then will come sleep with its mysterious dreams. Yes, I am 24. And it has been a happy birthday. Happiness is everywhere. The trouble with most people is that they look for it afar and never notice it lying beneath their feet.

April 12, 1943

The *Lena Gladys* has not appeared yet. The natives worked cleaning out the ditches alongside the runway. Coming back this evening from our round of trading with the inland villages, we ran into rain a quarter of a mile before reaching the hut. We managed to scramble in before getting very wet. Five girls ran up to the hut and stood under the eaves to avoid the rain. This was nearer than any female had ever come to the hut, except for Kela's wife Mary and some few others who were trading with us. The girls giggled and crowded around each other. They peered into the house and kept giggling. The wind shifted and drove the rain against them. They hesitated at first about accepting our invitation to come in out of the rain, but finally they all came in, looking at the strange hut with mosquito bars and other odd fixtures. It was supper time and we ate, the girls turning their backs to us while we ate the food. Actually we were more interested in the black, shiny, nearly-naked female bodies around us than the food.

"Just right," Schuchart suggested—"Five of them! Five of us."

"I got mine picked," I said. "The baker's daughter."

"That isn't fair," Dionne challenged. "That's the one I wanted."

"Well, you two fight over her," said Schuchart. "I'll take the one with her arms and legs around that post."

"Hmm—warming it up for you. She's not half bad."

"Well, I'll choose this one," Dionne agreed. "She's the cutest, even though she doesn't have the tits of your two girls."

"Yes, she is cute. Looks like Clara Bow, don't you think?"

The girls knew we were talking about them but I am sure they didn't know what we were saying; for if they had known, they wouldn't have merely giggled. "Only two left, De Blaiso. Which one do you want?"

"You can have my share."

"O.K., I'll take yours," I said. "This one—Hmm—Gosh, I got a nice pair there, don't you think?"

"Yep, lieutenant, you did all right for yourself. But what'll we do with the fifth girl? Gralin doesn't want her."

"Aw you two can split her," I answered, my mind reaching the very bottom of the gutter.

"You know, that would be dern nice," Schuchart said. "I hope the rain keeps up all night."

"Well, I'll let you in on a little secret. I've promised to drive them home in the jeep as soon as the rain slackens."

"I want to go with you lieutenant," Schuchart put in.

The baker's daughter sat on the hood of the car right in front of me. All the girls but one had taken off their skirts to keep them from getting wet. And the one remaining skirt, water soaked and thin, hid very little and left even less to the imagination. One girl, the one Schuchart had "picked," wore only a thin piece of red cloth wrapped around her waist.

"Dare you to slam on the brakes, lieutenant, and have all those tits fall on top of us?" Schuchart suggested.

We dropped them off in the village amid a lot of cheering and commotion. Boys and girls swarmed all over the car wanting a ride. The girls all said we were "good men" but we decided between ourselves that we were "God-damned fools."

April 13, 1943

We learn that Moresby had a 100-bomber raid yesterday. The escort was so heavy that even with all our fighters in the air, we were hopelessly outnumbered. The fighters claim to have shot down 29 bombers, and the ack-ack bagged eight. I'd like to have seen the show, especially the ack-ack hitting the planes. I think I'll go into Port as soon as I have the opportunity to check on the delay of the landing mat.

Tuesday night, April 13, 1943

Dearest little boy,

I got a letter from you today at last dated March 20, and in it you told me that you are going off somewhere again and that you won't be able to write until you get back.

April 14, 1943

I asked Lt. Feace for a lift to Moresby and he said it was all right
with him. God, what a ride! He climbed to about 800 feet right after
taking off, then went into a dive, right for water, pulling out not over
fifty feet above the waves. My stomach was in my mouth while we
were diving and in my feet while he pulled out of the dive. Less than a
hundred feet high, he followed the coast until he came to Kamp Welch
River. Then he dropped yet lower. He followed the winding stream
which was in flood, often dropping below the top of the trees along
the banks. I was "sweating it out" as the fellows around here say, until
he decided to stop his monkey shines. At last he came up, climbed up
and up, and went into another dive. He passed over a P-40 lying in
the marsh, which he pointed out. He then made another pass over the
wrecked plane and finally headed for Port. We landed at Jackson
Drome (formerly Seven Mile Drome). Right on our tails came the
pea-shooters—zoom!—zoom!—zoom! Feace taxied off to the side and
up into the dispersal area—ar-r-zoom—more fighters taking off. When
we reached the pen where the P-49 regularly parked, we saw two
enlisted men point to the sky and run like hell up the hill side. "Must
be an alert," I said as I scrambled from the plane.
    "Yep," Feace answered, totally unconcerned. He sat in the plane,
pulled out his log book, marked his flying time and so on. I watched
the sky nervously and looked around for a hole to jump in if—"What's
your serial number, Samuelson?" Feace asked. He was marking down
his records. "Reserve officer?" he went on. I didn't want to say that I
thought we ought to get off the hottest spot in Port Moresby during a
raid but the palms of my hands were wet with perspiration. We
climbed into his jeep. I gave another look up. No bombers in sight.
"Let's go up to engineering'" he suggested. "I got a few papers to clean
up. You don't mind coming with me?"
    "Oh, no. I have nowhere to go." The engineering section, located a
few hundred yards away from the runway, was completely deserted.
So was the drome. All the fighters had taken off. But the sky looked
like the outside of my mosquito net, planes by the score. Feace sat at
the desk meddling with papers while I searched the heavens for those
cruel-looking wedges. I pictured what the drome would be like when
the bombs hit. I wished I had a steel helmet instead of my thin sun
hat.
    "How 'bout a drink of water?" he asked.
    "Not thirsty," I answered even though my throat was dry. He
walked over to a lister bag and got a drink.[2] I followed him to the bag,

but I didn't drink. I kept on his heels, trying to get him to leave. I was a happy little boy when we drove off the drome. It was a false alarm. My nerves just weren't up to snuff.

I found out about the mat, that it had left this morning—a double load on a barge—so I decided to go back to Hood Point. I picked up some reading material, some papers and envelopes, a new coil for the jeep, and best of all, my *mail* which Mc Cluny had got from the 96th for me and had taken down to the 8th. McCluny flew me back to Hood Point after dinner. There I climbed into bed with all my letters and read and read—how wonderful—I was in a dream—32 letters from Dora, 5 from Papa, 4 from Dotsy. I am still in a semi-daze from it all. I guess this is the elated feeling that precedes the homesick feeling which always comes after a big batch of mail from home. They are all well; thank God for that. It is the most important thing.

April 15, 1943

A large boat, about 1000 tons, was spotted off Houla this morning. We then spotted a smaller launch and a large barge. I guessed that it was the remainder of the mat. Ryan and I got some Aussies to run us out in their boat. Mr. Williamson, the skipper of the small launch, told us that the large boat had towed the barge this far from Moresby and had now turned it over to him to bring in through the reefs. There were four or five American enlisted men aboard who were going down to Rodney. We went through the outer reefs without trouble. The native pilot understood exactly where we wanted the boat, so he said, and that we could go right in without any trouble.

"Look, you silly bugger," I told him, "Do you see those two cuts in the hill?" I pointed them out. "Just on the other side of that house?"

"Yes, taubada. I see."

"You say we can go right in there *now*. Water too shallow."

"No, him deep."

"All right, let's see you do it."

All went well. We went through the break in the reef. We headed for the same spot the *Lena Gladys* used to unload her cargo.

"Not here," Ryan told the pilot. "Down there—near hut."

"Can't go there, taubada."

"Why not?"

"Reef too bad."

"Just what I expected," I butted in. "When tide come in we go along shore."

"No, taubada. He no good. Water no deep there."

"When tide in, he deep."

"No." Ryan popped back into the picture.

"Can barge go along shore?"

"Oh, yes, barge he go all right."

"But big boat no go?"

"Yes."

"Well," Ryan said turning to Williamson and me, "I'll turn out all hands in the village with poles and we'll be able to push the barge on down."

"Good, God, Ryan, how will you do that? Look at the size of that barge. She's a hundred feet long, drawing three feet if she draws an inch, and the deck's six feet above the surface of the water. She'll run aground on you. You can't move a thing that large a mile down the coast unless you had the wind behind you. And the way the wind's blowing now, she'll wind up on the beach."

"You don't know what these natives can do, lieutenant. I'll turn them all out—men, women, and children—and you'll see that barge opposite the airdrome by dark."

"I wish you luck, Ryan. And I offer any assistance I can give. But you won't man handle that barge. But that's not getting us anywhere. Let's start rounding up the natives for the job."

Dusk came. The barge was in the same place. It was useless. "We might as well let the natives go home," Ryan said down-heartedly. A village councilor chimed in with: "Tide be no good tonight. He no come in far. Tomorrow morning he be good and come in far."

"Bull shit!" I shouted "You damn natives get the craziest notions. There won't be over six inches difference in your two tides."

"Well, it looks as if I'm going to have to bring 'er n 'ere," Captain Williamson said. "Seems we can't bring her in to the other place."

"Why can't you! Just because the natives claim there is a reef in front of you? If we can get that barge down there it will save us two weeks of carrying. There's gasoline aboard and all. We can bring it down here. Look, tomorrow at low tide I'll mark a channel along the shore. I guarantee I'll find four feet of water at the lowest ebb, which'll give you nine to ten feet at high tide. And your launch doesn't draw over six feet."

"That'll mean another twenty-four hour delay," Williamson answered.

"My orders are to expedite the unloading of this barge and proceed to Cape Rodney with it immediately to pick up some heavy signal equipment." I showed my orders to Mr. Ryan. "I can't keep mucking about around here."

"That's right, lieutenant."

"Yes, I guess it is a shame to waste twenty-four hours like that—Well, look if you won't agree to that scheme, how about going back through the passage, go down 'til you're opposite the drome and then go right over the reef?"

"I can't do that."

"At high tide you can."

"The native pilot said we couldn't."

"I'll ask Kila," said Ryan. "He knows all these waters. Kila, you savy this reef? Well, look. At the high tide, can launch go over reef?"

"Oh no, taubada. Too rough. Water too shallow."

"That's your answer."

"Damn him and all these natives. We can't go by their word. What in the hell do they know? I know that at low tide, you have several feet of water over that reef. At high tide, you get two fathoms. I go swimming out there nearly every day. I don't have to live a lifetime in a place to know whether the water is deep enough for your launch. You give these natives credit for knowing too much. Now look, you'll have a good high tide between seven and eight in the morning. And if tomorrow morning is like other mornings this past week you'll have smooth water. And damn it. You'll be able to go right over the reef. I'll accept full responsibility for your launch, the barge, the whole God damned show."

Williamson laughed at me. "All right, lieutenant, we'll give 'er a try the first thing in the morning."

"Now you're talking business." Little do Ryan and Williamson know how I feel right now. If that boat goes on the reef at high tide, she will be dashed to pieces when the tide runs out. Aw, but she will make it. I know! I'm not guessing. I hate these natives' feeling so certain that she won't clear the coral. But what do they know?

April 16, 1943

The launch and the barge cleared the reef easily. I was proud of it, but *acted* as if I knew all the time it would happen that way. Neither Ryan nor Williamson knew that I was up before dawn and had swum out to the reef at the first patch of light to make sure that its top was well done. It was a difficult job beaching the barge, and it was noon before we had it tied securely to the shore, the hatches opened, and mat pouring out. We moved about 400 strips up to the runway with some sixty-odd boys, not a half bad demonstration. There is a tremendous load on the barge. I estimate about 200 tons in all, about 5000 pieces of mat and 100 drums of gasoline. I believe I have another fortnight's work ahead of me before I'll return to Moresby.

Captain Wilson of Engineer Headquarters, Port Moresby, flew in today and wanted information on the status of the work and possibilities of developing this place into a regular fighter or bomber drome. We had a lengthy discussion, but I doubt that anything will come of it. Dionne down with fever and relieved today. Mosquitoes are fierce. We will all have it before long.

April 16, 1943

Dearest Dora,

What would you think if you saw me driving around with five native girls in a jeep? Good-looking gals too, with nothing on but a grass skirt. You should see the figures some of these girls have. They are really beautiful. I have seen so many pairs of naked breasts that it makes me laugh whenever I hear a fellow go 'wow' at something he imagines under a girl's sweater. You know, it isn't human nature for a woman to cover her breasts any more than her lips. The Arabs consider it immodest for a woman to show her lips in public. Wouldn't it seem strange if every male stared at your lips?

April 17, 1943

Unloading of barge proceeding satisfactorily. Houla natives had a holiday, but a score of natives from another village removed about fourteen hundred sheets from the hole to the beach. About 600 were unloaded yesterday; 400 carried to site of work on airdrome, east parking area. About 3000 sheets still remain in the hole with 100 drums of gasoline. The unloading, if we can get more natives on the job, should be completed by Monday night. The big task of carrying the 135 tons to the drome will remain ahead, but it should be done by the end of next week, by the 27th of the month at the latest. I took it easy today. Enjoyed a long morning swim, a couple of hours at the mission with Mr. Short, two rubbers of bridge with DeBlasio, and some letter writing.

April 17, 1943

Dearest Dora,

I have dreamed of you the past two nights but I don't remember the details. I also dreamed of Ian. It was an awful dream. I dreamed I was holding him in my arms, and he kept shrinking in size. Finally he was so small I held him in the palm of my hand. I was yelling for you to get a doctor while I kept my eye on him. He was no larger than an ant. He eventually disappeared completely. I was glad to wake up. Where do such dreams come from? Why do I have such awful dreams? Surely I have never thought of such a thing even unconsciously.

April 18, 1943

No work today. Enjoyed swimming and reading.

April 19, 1943

Today was one of the best day's work I have ever witnessed in my life. We unloaded about 100 tons of cargo in a regular working day entirely by hand (about 60 natives). I was in the hole of the barge most of the day directing the work and lending my hand when work slowed down. Even among the natives, a little leadership goes a long way. Ryan wasn't on the job with his swagger stick and neat uniform today. They seem to resent him for some reason. We removed the hundred drums of gasoline without a pulley: just with some rope and logs and manpower.

I'm getting brown as a berry from so much sun. I believe I have put on about five pounds. I'm feeling great.

April 20, 1943

The barge got away this morning, and with an enlarged crew of boys, about a hundred, we moved around two thousand sheets, perhaps a little less, up to the runway. We rigged a device for taking the gasoline drums over the dune utilizing the jeep for power, but Major Behren & Captain Feace came in and drove around in the jeep. We'll finish them in the morning.

We did some good trading in Kailo this morning. Beautiful paupaus, bananas, lemons, and oranges. We also got a chicken, but we have kept it in the hut all day and all of us have become so attached to it that we might not kill it. All kind of birds fly through our door and get "trapped" in our hut. A little while ago a beautiful baby something or other came in. We blinded it with the flashlight, caught it easily. Gosh, its little heart was pounding in the palm of my hand. Prettiest little bird I've ever seen. Some bats were in here too. We leave them alone.

April 20, 1943

Dearest Dora,

   The work around here is just about drawing to a close, and the end of the week should find me back at "civilization." Sometimes I wonder whether I'm not leaving civilization. The most I've seen since leaving the States. At least here there has been women and children and dogs. You know, it has taken a war to make me realize how important women are. You'd be surprised at the influence they have on a man, how differently he lives when they are around. They are good even if just to make you want to get away from them again.

   I had a real thrill yesterday. A native caught an octopus, not very big: about three feet across from tentacle tip to tentacle tip—the body not much bigger than my fist. But the native let him crawl all over his feet and arms. So I asked him to let me try. Gosh, little girl, you should feel how he clings to you. Hundreds of these little cups, sucking, releasing, sucking again gives the sensation of having your entire body being subjected to low-voltage electricity. It's a good feeling, honest, not slimy or repulsive as you'd expect. But I don't believe I'd like to tangle with this fellow's old man however.

   I've been trying to figure out how to say "I love you" in this native lingo for the past 20 minutes. This is the result of my efforts, fumbling through an ancient dictionary found in one of these plantation homes: *Na ura heniamumua lalodika.* That's a lot of stuff for saying "I love you," but they must think more of it than we do. I'll try to analyze it for you. *Na* means I (I know that's right). *Ura* means to will, to wish, or to desire. *Henia* means to give or to hand to. *Mu* means you. *Mua* (or *mu*) means that it keeps going on. *Lalo* means the mind or what one feels deeply inside. *Dika* means bad. So *lalodika* means strongly. Put that all together and you get "I love you."—I think. As complicated as that may seem, some of their speech is simplicity personified. In other words where we would say "to be struck by a stone rolling down a mountain side" they merely use *kei-atao*. Their language is full of words which can be translated only by a dozen English words. For instance, they have one word to describe sharpening a canoe pole time and time again until it is too short to be used and has to be thrown away. Such a thing is so common among them that they express it in one word, just as we use the word "ride" in a car. They would use several score of words to describe the act. It is all very interesting, much more so than studying French or German or Spanish which have nearly identical parallels in English.

April 21, 1943

It looks as if "Buck Buck" is to die of old age. We admired his beautiful feathers too long, became so attached to the fowl that we don't want to kill it. Last night when he came near our beds and crowed, walking from bed to bed, we cursed him, almost got up and decapitated him then and there. But by morning we thought that it had all been so cute that we decided to let it live another day.

Today, if my memory serves me right, a year ago I landed in New Guinea. A year of war and still in the same place. Tomorrow should see the end of the job over here. I plan to go to Port with Ryan by canoe Friday morning. We will take in about a hundred native "prisoners," the same boys who have done this job, for more work. It is a wonder that the natives don't rebel and help the Japs. I guess they would be treated worse by them. Here we *make* them work and help us, but at least we treat them reasonably well.

April 22, 1943

The job is done. Altogether 170 tons of mat was handled. In addition to the laying of the mat, a stockpile of 900 pieces of 10-foot sheets and 100 pieces of 5-foot sheets was established at the East End. Two planes in tonight: a Lockheed-Hudson with 18 passengers and a Dragon Fly (lone pilot—Lt. Montgomery). These fellows couldn't get in because of zero ceiling at Port and have worn me out asking questions about New Guinea. They are "fresh" from the States. Thought I'd enjoy talking to strangers about New Guinea but I didn't. Been trying to set up accommodations for all these "guests." Am worn out, but they are all turned in at last. I'm flying back to Port Moresby with Montgomery in morning.

TEN

Malaria

April 24–May 21, 1943

April 24, 1943, Port Moresby

Flew in yesterday morning with Montgomery in his Dragon Fly. The Laloki River was in flood and made a spectacular sight from the air. Recent heavy rains have done considerable damage to roads around here. The Engineers will be thankful for the coming of the dry season, which isn't more than a month away now. It really felt good to be "home" again. First there was a big pile of letters which I enjoyed a lot. A good triple-shower was wonderful. The Coral Sea and the rain don't exactly keep a fellow as clean as he would like to be. Then there were cigars, a real treat for anyone who has gone a month without smoking one. It was a treat to go to a latrine where you didn't have to fight every insect known to man for a seat. It felt good to eat a meal that resembled something back home: potatoes, meat. There was a package from Dora, and the herring (all gone now) was delicious. Even a haircut felt good. It surely felt good to see the old gang. A movie last night was good too. There were a lot of little things that made me happy to be back. Everybody commented on how well I looked and how fat I had gotten.

"Can hardly notice your ribs sticking out anymore," was one comment.

Lenny, tight as hell with his film, even took a picture of me "while I looked so good." He also offered to give me some pipe tobacco: for nothing too!

There have been a lot of changes in the Regiment too. The Second Battalion has moved out, companies D and E to Oro Bay and F to Milne Bay.[1] Also a few promotions: Thomas to major and Layman, Taylor, and Sabastan to first lieutenant: all wise choices. Thomas left tonight for Townsville, where he will meet General Steele and accompany him on a secret reconnaissance. I have an idea that it is somewhere in Dutch New Guinea, probably along the southern coast, and the First Battalion will go there soon. I am going to try to go along. Two days of Moresby and I want to get away. Haseman is also away with Engle and most of the men from operations on a reconnaissance on the islands between here and New Britain.[2] Mouron, who couldn't go with his company because he was in the hospital with malaria, is now acting S-2 of the Regiment.

April 25, 1943

There were Easter services this morning on the "parade grounds." Dubra gave a good sermon, but I hope it had more effect on the others than it did on me. Fortunately I am not in the depths of hopeless despair that he was trying to get us out of; for if I were, I fear I'd still be there. He would have had to give me a more concrete reason not to give up hope than the one he did: that the disciples of Christ had all become despondent when He was nailed to a cross (the same as we are now) but they kept hope alive, and He rose, and they were all happy.

April 26, 1943

I have heard today the best speech since I left the States. It was made by Lieutenant Colonel Willis, the instructor at a Chemical Warfare School being held this week in Port Moresby and which I am attending in the place of Ray Eardley, our unit gas officer. I could never write half the things the colonel said, never find the choice of words he used. And from him it flowed like liquid. Perhaps I can type some of his ideas:

Now the question is: Can the Japs gas this place? They can. The Japanese planes start spraying gas. What a panic our ground troops are thrown into. The men who are manning the 50 calibre machine guns and the bofors [antiaircraft guns] see the planes swooping down with streams of poisonous gas pouring out from under their wings. The men will drop their guns and rush for their masks. The bombers will roll on almost without any kind of opposition. They will pass over the dromes dropping gas mines, ordinary gallon tin caps filled with gas. Casualties will be high. There is no telling exactly what will happen.

But let us consider another more important question: Will the Japs use gas? In the immediate future I think not. Before the end of the war, absolutely. And I'll tell you why. Never in the history of the world has a nation considered to be inferior rose and captured so much wealth in so short a time and with such small losses as has Japan. Altogether, she has not lost over a thousand airplanes, a hundred ships, and perhaps four divisions of men. This is indeed a cheap price for Malaya, Thailand, Java, Sumatra, Burma, and all the islands, especially the Phillipines. Japan has won all these places with hard honest fighting, using the kind of ethics we teach in the United States. She is still powerful, more powerful than ever before, sucking the wealth out of the nations she has captured. Why should she use gas? Japan doesn't want any more land: not now. She doesn't want New Guinea. Yes, she would like to have it, but it is not worth the cost she would have to pay. The men she would lose in taking New Guinea she will use to fortify the bases she has already established. Then she will sit back and say "Come and take them away from me—if you can." So it seems that for some time we are going to be at a more or less stalemate.

But remember this: Japan is surrounded by enemies. China and India on the west, Australia on the south, the United States on the east, and Russia (we hope) on the north. Now, we can't starve out the Japs. She has as much of everything as she desires. And don't think for a minute that the United Nations are going to stand by and let Japan hold all that she has taken. They are going in and are going to try to take it away. Let's forget the things we learned as children about fighting wars for the four freedoms. Who in here believes that we are? Let's face the facts. We are fighting to enjoy the commerce, the natural resources, the wealth, the good earth itself. We are fighting now for the earth's crust. All wars have been fought for it. That is the way all empires have grown, no matter how the history books try to paint it. And we are not going to stand by and let Japan take from us the best part of the earth's crust. That means we are going to fight back like hell. And the first big blow is going to be at Rabaul. When and if we take Rabaul, we will be able to occupy the Admiralty Islands. And from them we can neutralize Truk. Then will come the blow for the recapture of the Phillipines. And once we control the Phillipines, we hold the solar plexus of the present Japanese Empire. Japan knows these facts as well as we do. She won't give up Rabaul without the bitterest fighting. And before she will let us recapture Rabaul, she will use gas.

What retaliation can we offer for the use of gas by the enemy? We hear all kind of proclamations by the Secretary of War, the Chief of Staff, even the President himself, stating that we'll gas the living hell out of those sons of bitches if they use gas first. I'll let you in on a secret: we have in Australia a scant thousand tons of mustard, and of the other gases we have practically none. Every third shell manufactured by the Japanese is filled with gas. We have one plane, our A-20's, that can carry tanks for spraying gas. Our supply of gas bombs in New Guinea is—well, a supply hardly exists. We have a good gas mask, not as good as the one the Japanese have, but it's a good one nevertheless and will do the job. We have a good gas mortar. Our 4.2 (I believe that was the size he mentioned) is damn good. It is now being mounted on the jeep and should prove a highly potent weapon. But we don't have enough of them. We don't know enough about our impregnated clothing to predict how effective they will be. All we know is that the dies we used in our shirts have caused them to rot so that they are useless. Our three-gallon decontaminating apparatus has turned out to be unsuccessful and can be used effectively only as an improvised shower or for spraying mosquitoes, not for decontaminating gased areas. The quart-and-a-half tank is no good too, for the decontaminating agent reacts chemically with the brass container, forming a copper residue which clogs the outlet of the sprayer.

The Japs are mixing mustard and lewisite. It is this mixture that we are expecting them to use. By mixing these gases, they have lowered the freezing point of the liquid down to zero degrees Fahrenheit, which is considerably lower than the freezing point of either of the gases by themselves. This adds a great advantage, because with a lowered freezing point, the gas can be carried higher in airplanes than they could where the gas would freeze at a relatively high temperature.

The President and the Prime Minister have both proclaimed that we will not use gas first. That is just so much rot. If the war should continue in favor of Japan, and if the use of gas would be our only means of winning, we'd use it. Of course the history books would never print the facts that way. Arrangements would be made where witnesses would testify to the use of gas by the Japanese first. How the diplomats would handle the situation is not our concern. The important thing is that we would use gas first if it became necessary. And naturally Japan would retaliate. And again we are faced with gas from the enemy. So you see, no matter what shape the war situation takes, gas will eventually be used, and we must prepare for it. It's too late to start preparing after the mustard has been sprayed.

April 27, 1943

For some reason I am terribly restless. Can't sit still to read, write, or think. God, how will I ever be able to continue with my graduate work at Tulane! I hope this restlessness passes by the end of the war.

April 27, 1943

Dearest Dora,

Little girl, you underestimate the natives' intelligence. And your doctor didn't know what he was talking about when he told you that Ian's chatter would sound like the natives' lingo. They have a *definite* language, a very pretty one indeed, and it doesn't sound like merely a babbling of tongues. Of course it does at first, but all foreign languages do. It might interest you to know that the average native child of five has a larger vocabulary than an American child of the same age. You see, where the American child will know the word "fish," the native child will know the names of several fish. The same is true of trees and many other things. However the vocabulary of the American child increases tremendously when he starts going to school.

April 28, 1943

Today marked the first anniversary of the arrival of the 96th in New Guinea. There was a parade this morning, and a holiday was proclaimed for the remainder of the day. They put us through the mill at gas school this morning. My throat and eyes were irritated. I sneezed and coughed and cried. So did we all. We had to smear mustard gas on our arm, then give ourselves first-aid treatment. Finally we put a tiny dab of the Japanese lewisite-mustard mixture on our arms. A speck the size of a pin head has caused a painful sore on my arm. It is really wicked stuff.

April 30, 1943

Gee, I'm down in the dumps. I have felt worse today than in an awfully long time. Don't know what's the matter. I'm not sick. Nobody has done me anything. I feel so useless and unimportant that I could cry. Aside from attending gas school in the mornings, I haven't done a thing around here since I came back from Hood Point. I find it difficult to read, don't seem able to get interested, not even magazines.

Writing is even more difficult. If I could write *everything* to Dora, I'd feel better, but I can't write. I hate war!

May 2, 1943

On the sixth of this month Company B will sail for Merauke in Dutch New Guinea followed by Company C on the 12th. Most of the motor pool personnel will also go.[3] A Company is to remain in Port Moresby and will represent the remnant of the Regiment here with a small headquarters detachment which will also remain for keeping up with certain paper work. Miller is going to Townsville to take care of the supply situation. Thomas will be in charge of the show at Merauke. He will have a staff consisting of Haseman (received his promotion to major today), MacDonald, and me. That places four of the five civil engineers of the Regiment on that staff which should be pretty powerful. We are taking a good selection of heavy equipment. It should be a swell job.

May 3, 1943

It seems that Engineer Headquarters is going to try to develop the Hood Point emergency strip into a regular operational airdrome. I am flying there in the morning with Major Butz and three enlisted men to make a survey for the practicability of making the conversion. More dromes are needed. Eight new groups are supposed to be on the way. That will just about double our air force in New Guinea.

May 4, 1943

The weather was so bad that we couldn't land at Hood Point. The ceiling was so low, in fact, that we never caught sight of the strip at all.

May 5, 1943

I received a recording of Dora's and Ian's voices today. It was wonderful to hear her voice, almost like a dream. I never knew that "I love you" could sound so sweet. Gee I'm homesick.

May 6, 1943

Dearest Dora,

Last night we had two courts martial cases. I was T.J.A. (Trial

Judge Advocate). It was the first case in which I was prosecuting attorney. I won both cases, but it made me sick. I hate to see people punished "six months hard labor—six months forfeiture of two-third of your pay." It is bad enough to have to be over here fighting not alone being in prison doing hard labor. But both of these fellows had done something which was definitely detrimental to good military order and discipline (placed an order for loaded dice and marked cards with some Chicago firm) and they deserved being punished. You see, one of the only uses of money over here is gambling, and among these colored boys the stakes are abnormally high. It is nothing for a man to win several hundred pounds in one evening. So you could see what would happen if a couple of the boys came in with marked cards and dice. Unfortunately gambling is a great diversion, something sorely needed in the evening, and we don't want to stamp it out. You see, there is no drinking, no women; and if we put a stop to gambling, the fellows would have a legitimate gripe.

May 8, 1943

I have malaria and am in the 166th Station Hospital for treatment. Last Thursday right after dinner I went to B Company to return a book I had borrowed and give "Swede" Johnson an approved requisition for some sheet metal to be picked up at an Australian dump. I got wet and felt rather weak as I drove over to the 46th Engineers where some of our boys were building water tanks. A chill ran through my body as I spoke to the noncom in charge and I hurried away so that he couldn't see me shiver. It was about two miles back to camp and I was going to drive back right away but I realized that I hadn't returned some photographs to the A-2 [intelligence officer] of the Fifth Air Force; so I decided to drive over there first.

While driving there I was hit by the chills. Every part of my body shivered. By the time I reached the sentry who guards the entrance to the Fifth Air Force, I could hardly speak and tell him my business. I walked up to the staff officer's desk and asked admission into Photo Intelligence. He looked at me peculiarly (I must have been ghost-like white), then said, "Go right in."

I returned the photographs but had to wait for my memorandum receipt. I tried to suppress my shivering and in so doing became terribly weak. I thought I was going to faint but I managed to make it out the doors again. There I let myself relax and shivered violently. It acted as a stimulant. The four-mile ride home was sheer physical torture. When I reached the 96th I walked into Levinson's office. I didn't have to tell him a thing. He stuck a thermometer in my mouth and started writing out a ticket.

"I don't want to go to the hospital," I said through chattering teeth. "Can't you fix me up here?"

"You're going to the hospital. This is the way I've wanted to catch you."

"But, Lenny, I want to go to Merauke, and they'll keep me in the hospital for—."

"You damn fool. You want to kill yourself? Malaria is nothing to fool around with. You want to be sterile? Hundreds have died of malaria up here already. You're going to the hospital. If you don't care about yourself, think of your wife and child."

It was the noblest thing Levinson had ever said and shortly afterwards I was bouncing along the road to the 166th Station Hospital. I was in bed at three. The chills ran out of my body as if someone had cut off my toes and let the cold liquid run out. Fever hit my forehead, ran down my face, into my neck and throat, and down my whole body. My temperature rose to 104. At last the medical technician came in to take a smear. Until he did that the nurse could not give me a thing to relieve me. Then she gave me a couple capsules, piled blankets on top of me and let Nature take its course. By seven o'clock I was perfectly normal again and have been feeling well ever since. But my smear was positive, and that means a two-week treatment. Berlinger is here, running fever also, but his smear was negative. In fact, of all the patients here in this ward, only two of us have positive smears. The other is Captain Wild (or something like that) and he doesn't budge from his bed. I can do everything. I am even going to eat at the mess hall.

May 9, 1943

We have a lot of fun in the ward. It feels good to be around nurses. We drive them all crazy with our fictitious back aches. "Back rub!" "Sleeping pills!"

May 10, 1943

It is a shame how many fellows are here who are here only with the hope of being evacuated. Jones, a platoon commander, is disgusted with his work and is trying to be evacuated. His smear is negative but he has spasmodic fever. Keyman, navigator in a B-25, overseas 14 months and in combat flying most of the time, says he is scared. Most of the fellows in his squadron have been killed, and he says the ace of spades is bound to turn up for him. Lean, pilot of a B-17, recently shot down, says he is scared too and wants to go home. In fact, most of the patients here are Air Corps chaps who are human beings and scared of being killed and not the reckless dare devils we read they are.

May 11, 1943

I have just finished a twelve-hour session of bridge and poker which cost me 15 pounds—nearly $50.00. It is a shame how we have no sense of value for money any longer. It is pretty useless stuff unless there are things to buy.

May 12, 1943

Jones was bragging about the money his wife and her father had. "My father-in-law wants me to work for him." "Same sort of set-up with me," Berlinger challenged. "My father-in-law wants me to work for him, but I'll be damned if I'll work behind a bar." Lean is down on all womankind. He received a drooling love letter from his sweetheart this morning. The catch to the whole thing is that a few days ago he received a letter from her posted a week *later* than the letter which arrived today, and in it she told him she was marrying another fellow.

May 13, 1943

I had the most sexy dream of my life last night. I don't know who the girl was, surely no one I know or have ever seen and probably none I have pictured in my imagination. She was blond with milk white skin, the loveliest creature anyone could conceive. We slept together naked and loved each other. The kissing was delicious, and the intercourse was as sensational as any reality. Best part of all was that I didn't wake up but slept through and enjoyed exhausted lying in her arms and having her pet me. I think there is a lot of truth in the theory that our dreams help us sleep as they fulfill desires which would otherwise keep us awake.

I read an excellent book today, *The Keys of the Kingdom* by A. J. Cronin. The story itself was only average but the religious philosophy which permeated the whole book was beautiful. After reading the book only a fool would declare any one religion superior to all the others. The older I become the more I believe all religions are a farce.

There are only two principles which they teach that are worthwhile: tolerance and consideration not to hurt others. These could be taught in school and all churches could be abolished. It would be wise perhaps to teach the existence of God but no man should be condemned for doubting His existence. It is only a coward, diplomatically selfish individual like myself who says "There is a God" without any plausible reason. Those of us who proclaim His existence say that because *maybe* there is a hereafter and we *might* have to face Him. I admire the man who can say, "There is no God. There is no heaven or hell. Death is oblivion. Life on earth is a great gift which we should use in any way we see fit without hurting our fellow man."

I hope that someday I'll be man enough to make such a statement *and mean it.* But as it is, every night when I crawl in bed I say a little prayer to God. It has become so routine however that only on rare occasions would anyone believe it sincere. I really try to ask God to grant life and health to Dora, Ian, Papa, Aunt Shanie, Dotsy, Beryl, Ethel, Herman, Razele, and Gwendy. I am afraid to miss my prayer. How foolishly superstitious I am, but I am too much of a coward to give up that precious faith and hope. It is all too complicated for me. I wish I could believe something definite, truly believe or disbelieve. As it is, I am a doubter on any subject relating to theology. The only thing I am sure of is that I can truly tolerate the beliefs of anyone regardless of what they are. That in itself is a religion.

May 14, 1943

The Axis has surrendered completely in North Africa. The unexpected flashing success has surprised the world. The campaign was brilliant. There is feverish talk of the defeat of Germany and Italy before the end of the year. It is too fantastic to believe, but perhaps the almost continuous bombings of her factories, the hunger and unrest within all the territory she holds: these might bring Germany to her knees sooner than we dare to dream.

Japan will be another proposition. I fear that Japan is going to come out of the war the winner. Of course our history books will be written with us as victors and we might "dictate" the terms of peace but these will include certain clauses which will give to Japan many things which she did not possess before, let us say, 1930.

Nieces "Gwendy" (Gwendolyn Midlo Hall), left, and Razele Midlo (now Lehmann) at Henderson's Point, Mississippi, summer 1944.

May 15, 1943

Dearest Dora,

I had an awful dream about you last night. I dreamed I had come home and everybody was greeting me—everybody but you. I wanted to break away from the crowd and go see you but they wouldn't let me go. "You ought to see the nice house Dora has rented," someone told me. "You'll find her there now." I stood in front of a big two-story house. It was old and shabby. It was the one you had rented. I walked in the front door and the whole lower floor was empty except for dirt and cobwebs. There was no furniture. I called out for you, but there was no answer. I ran upstairs and it was vacant also. Then I saw in the back room a cot with a mosquito net over it. I ran to it and found you lying on the cot. You were white as this paper. Your heart wasn't beating. It was awful, little girl. I slapped your face, trying to make you get up but you didn't respond. I started crying like a baby. Gee, it was awful, little girl. And then I woke up. Gee, it was wonderful to know that it had been only a dream. I didn't want to go back to sleep but lay in bed a long time smoking.

May 16, 1943

Dr. Waldron was just by and told me that tomorrow I will start another five-day treatment of quinine.

"You want to be really cured, don't you?" he asked. I didn't argue with him.

May 17, 1943

American troops have landed on Attu Island and have the Japs who occupied the barren island ten months ago out numbered. A blow at Kiska should be forthcoming.[4] Why are the Allies waiting to invade the Continent? Was this victory in North Africa such a surprise to them that they aren't ready to follow up their success? Do they believe they can make the Axis yield by bombings alone? If they do, they will be surprised. We will have to land an army on the continent, and the longer the delay the more difficult and costly will be the invasion.

May 17, 1943

Dearest Dora,

Guess where I am? In the hospital. Isn't that awful? I have malaria; and although I feel all right, I'll be here for at least two weeks taking the "treatment" which consists essentially of lying in bed and taking pills. I have been running fever off and on for the past four months, but yesterday I was hit with violent chills and I had to give in and come to the hospital. Those dern mosquitoes have been picking on me for over a year, you know; and I guess they're just a better man than I am. Well, it will be a good rest for me and I'll have a chance to read a lot. And if it kills me I'm going to do some studying. I have a few excellent engineering texts on hand and the only excuse I have for not studying is my own laziness. All of that highly technical stuff seems so useless over here that I find it hard to get interested. But if I expect to complete my graduate work and eventually teach, I had better do some review work.

Gosh, I have a nice nurse. I have had three rub-downs since I have been here: about 20 hours. And this morning she gave me a swell bath—much better than they do in any civilian hospital. Apparently I'm supposed to be pretty sick that I receive so much attention. Actually I could get up and take a shower without any inconvenience, but I like being washed and I might as well take advantage of the situation. Last night's nurse was swell, too. We got to talking and found out we came over on the same convoy. She sat on my bed and rubbed my back for fifteen minutes. It really felt good. You surely have a rotten husband, don't you? He doesn't care what it looks like; as long as it has a skirt on he thinks it's swell. But no joke, little girl, its awful to go for so long seeing nothing but men. Other fellows might not admit it to their wives, but I believe they feel the same way.

Berlinger, who belongs to another engineer outfit who was one of my five roommates on the boat, is here in this ward, too. Last night the doctor examined him carefully, making him say "Ah," and thumping on his chest, and all that sort of stuff. Then he looked at Berlinger very gravely and said, "You have a very rare disease for around here."

Berlinger turned a yellowish green and asked the doctor what it was.

"A common cold, the first case like it I've had to treat since I've been here."

May 18, 1943

I got a pass today and went to see the boys of the 96th. C Company was sailing for Merauke and I went down the dock with Pickard to get a case of whiskey aboard before one o'clock when they were sailing.

"We sure missed you around here during the rat race," he said. "It was the damnest job of loading a ship you've ever seen. The Colonel is surely pissed off at Hering and I'm on his shit list for recommending him for promotion. 'Why in the hell did you ever recommend that lazy scoundrel?' the Old Man said. He surely is mad at poor Willie. This bumping around isn't hurting you too much, is it?"

"Oh no, I'm all right."

"Strange to see you so pale. You always look so brown. Must have lost a lot of weight?"

"Not more than ten or twelve pounds."

"Looks like more. What's the trouble, no appetite?" His tone was kind. He seemed really interested in the way I feel.

"Oh, I eat all right. Only trouble is, everything I eat turns to shit."

We both laughed. I felt unhappy about seeing all the gang sailing away and with me having to return alone to the hospital.

"You seem to have shrunk a bit," Derby told me. "But you'll get your strength back in a little while."

As we were driving back to headquarters I asked Pickard, "Do I go up to Merauke as soon as I get out of the hospital?"

"No, the Colonel left instructions that you were *not* to go. The place is infested with mosquitoes."

"Well, so is Oro Bay. I can't sit around here and do nothing."

"Why not go to Sydney on leave? It'll do you good."

"This place has everything Sydney has with the exception of whiskey and women."

"Well?"

"Aw, I couldn't drink. I feel low enough without it. Some good clean loving would do me good, but I don't know any girls there, and any girl who would let me pick her up would—aw, I want mental loving as well as the physical stuff. I want to be in a woman's arms and sleep and have her pet me—not—"

"I know what you mean."

It was the first time I had ever spoken with Pickard about such a personal matter. Although he isn't much older than I am, he is a lieutenant-colonel, and I did respect him and didn't think it was right to speak so freely.

"Perhaps I can help out at A Company," I suggested. "They have only three officers."

"Yes, that's an idea. Henthorn is going on leave. Maybe you can pinch hit for him while he is gone and by the time he gets back you ought to be well enough to go to Merauke."

I felt like a little child. It all brought me back to my early childhood with Mama worrying over me. It made me feel so helpless when every time we'd hit a bump, Colonel Pickard would say, "Sorry, Sammy."

At dinner I realized that the others were just being polite when they pretended not to notice how my hands shook, especially when I passed a dish or lifted a cup to drink.

"Don't let it bother you," Al Mouron told me. "I use two hands. Embarrassed the hell out of me at first, but I got used to it," he said. My hands were considerably steadier than his.

"Won't it ever clear up? You're out of the hospital a month already."

"Gosh I hope so. I hate this nervousness."

"Mine isn't nervousness," I said. "It's damn physical weakness. You look pretty tired. Been working all night?"

"Yeah" he said. "I'm so disgusted I could—hell, Sammy you've never seen such a fucked-up mess in your life."

"Wish I'd been here to help with the loading."

He fumbled with a cigarette and his hands shook worse than mine ever had. He was worn out. Thirty-four hours without sleep, out of the hospital about a month, and working all night while a big lazy bloke like Willie sits around on his dead ass. Poor Al, the handsomest boy in the Regiment nearly a complete wreck.

"I'll be back with my company in another week. That'll do me good," he said.

I saw Tom Prindable, another malaria victim, and a shudder ran through me.

"I must never let myself waste away like that. I mustn't," I told myself.

They were all drinking when I left, some damn Coris (rat gut) whiskey. The immediate future looks black.

May 18, 1943

Dearest Hymie,

I got three more letters from you today. I'm all excited about the beads you said you sent me. I haven't gotten them yet, but I surely hope it will be soon.

These days almost every girl you meet will have a whole pack of her troubles to try to put on your shoulders and all she does is sit there and talk about herself until you are ready to fall asleep just listening. And they're so ready and willing to offer you their sympathy that you don't want, and that you know isn't sympathy. But not all of the girls are like that, thank goodness. There are still some who aren't.

May 19, 1943

I am resting, reading, and playing cards. I must get better.

May 20, 1943

Tomorrow will be my last day of treatment. Thank heavens I will soon be away from all these sick people and will be able to associate with healthy people again. I am tired of listening to the woes of frightened pilots, of men who are so disgusted that they don't care what happens to their health just so they can get away. I don't want to hear that fellow from the next ward shouting: "Germany's got to surrender! She can't stand it! She can't stand it! Those bombs! She can't go on!"

Some of the patients are deathly ill, like the young pilot they brought in a few days ago with dysentery. He will live, but it will require months for him to regain his lost weight and be normal again.

May 21, 1943

This is my last night here. I was a happy boy when I swallowed the last ten grains of quinine of the treatment this evening. And I didn't have to get under my net this evening. I get my first fogey today— three years in the army.[5]

ELEVEN

Taking Command of Company A

May 22–December 5, 1943

May 22, 1943, Port Moresby

It feels good to be back with the 9th. Dellavia went into the hospital yesterday with a foot infection. I am acting adjutant of the regiment. The temporary appointment rather rounds out my "education" of what makes a regiment tick. I have served in a line company, been supply officer, mess officer, training officer, and administrative officer in H & S Company. And as a staff officer I have worked at the S-2 post (intelligence), S-3 job (operations) and the S-4 task (supply). Now as S-1 (administration & personnel) I am completing the course. I doubt that any other officer with so short a length of active service has had the opportunity to serve in so many different jobs as I have. Our troops at Oro Bay had ten casualties during the last air raid and lost a substantial amount of supplies and equipment.

May 23, 1943

I made the rounds with Pickard today looking over the little engineering work going on around here. I sent Dora $300 in bonds bringing my total to 12 $100 bonds since the first of the year. Pickard assures me that I won't remain in the adjutant post for long. That is a relief, because all my work now consists of taking papers out of one box, marking the distribution of them, and shoving them into another box. With a lop-sided staff of clerks, I don't have a thing to do. I am feeling much better. Still a little weak but I should get my strength back before long.

May 24, 1943,

What a useless, lazy life I am leading! With a man like Sgt. Nash to do everything for me and to explain to me the few duties which I must do, such as signing papers, I don't have a bit of work. Well, this shouldn't last for long. An adjutant can make himself awfully busy for his desk is always covered with papers and he can be issuing orders to a half dozen people to type this or that, transfer so-and-so from Company A to Company B, tossing all kind of memoranda and regulations around. But putting it all together, the entire job can be done in one hour each day.

May 25, 1943,

I received a letter from Reese today. He writes that he is going back to the States. I am glad for his sake but I get tired, feel cheated at times hearing about boys going home after less than a year overseas. I believe that no troops should be permitted to go home unless they are casualties, but when I keep hearing about others returning to the States, I want to go too. Sometimes I wonder whether Uncle Sam knows we are still here. Actually we haven't been overseas very long, but there is no sign of relief anywhere. Our regiment has moved up into no man's land. The boys at Merauke could be wiped out in a few days by a moderate size Japanese landing force. Those at Milne Bay and Oro Bay are considerably safer, although the Japs can retake Oro Bay any time they think it worth the loss of two or three thousand men. The Nips are gradually getting air superiority again, and more and more of our transport planes are being shot down.

About ten months ago the Japs were but a few miles from here and we posted a heavier than usual guard around our camp area. I instructed the men that they must be particularly alert at night when some of the Nips might sneak in and kill our boys while they were sleeping. They all seemed to understand. During the night I went out to inspect the guard.

"Halt!" shouted one of the sentries. "Who's dere?"

"Officer of the Day," I answered. To check whether the sentry knew his duties, I asked him, "Now, Jones, if I hadn't stopped when you yelled 'halt,' what would you have done?"

"I'd a called the corp'ral of de guard, suh."

"A lot of protection you are to the men asleep. By the time you called the corporal of the guard all the damage could be done. Why in the hell would you call the corporal of the guard anyway?"

"To help me carry your dead body away, suh."

May 28, 1943

I received four wonderful letters from Dora today. She surely is a wonderful gal, never gloomy, her letters always spiked with humor and cheerfulness. For an outsider, her letters would seem childish and without feeling, but I can see through the thin camouflage. She hasn't had it exactly easy. Having a baby under any circumstances isn't pleasant, but she went through the whole mess without a whimper, always saying how wonderful it felt. And even now, she must feel empty when she sees George and Joy and Wolfie and Bellah happily together. But she never complains, always writes funny things; and although a bit sentimental at times, she never overdoes it. Gosh, it will be wonderful to be with her again.

May 29, 1943

Pickard, Hering, and Stine flew to Oro Bay this morning. That leaves me here in charge of the whole show. Although the adjutant's job by itself is rather useless, if he is given a few extra duties, such as C.O. of the regiment, executive officer, and command of a 70-man headquarters detachment, he can find enough to keep him busy. Engle and Paulson came in today. Paulson is going on leave and wants me to go with him. I could get away as soon as Derby came back and Dellavia got out of the hospital. But I can't make up my mind whether I want to go. Sydney, I hear, is nearly void of soldiers; and the women, having received so much attention for a long time and now without it very nearly rape everything in uniform. It is an exaggeration, I know; but when I hear of the tales (and tails) Sladon and Lake have to tell about, I cannot help but feel that I am missing an awfully good time. It would be wonderful to lie with a woman. But hell—why should I go! Unless the woman were a young lady, clean and pretty, I couldn't have anything to do with her. And if she did come up to my specifications she would not have anything to do with me. What I want is real loving, not mere intercourse. And for that I'll have to wait until I am with Dora again. Furthermore the trip would be expensive and with these present pains in my chest, back, and stomach, I am not altogether sure I would enjoy myself.

Hymie after siege of malaria,
May 1943.

May 30, 1943

Colonel Derby came in today, and I really made a big hit with him.
"Have you enough to keep you busy?" he asked me.
"No sir."
He didn't like that reply at all. "Where is Dellavia?" he asked.
"He's in the hospital — a foot infection."
"Who has been doing his work."
"I have, sir," I answered.
"Hmph — and where is Colonel Pickard?"
"He went to Oro Bay yesterday."
"And Hering?"
"He went too. I've been taking charge of the headquarters detachment."
"And you still don't have enough to keep you busy?"
"Not the way I like to be kept busy."
"You're probably doing none of the jobs properly."
There was no "gun" at Retreat this evening and he called my attention to the fact.
"Who has authorized its discontinuance?"
"No one as far as I know. We have no blasting equipment. It has all been sent up to Merauke."

"Then get some new equipment," he snorted back. I like that man when I don't see him. Engle says that the pains around my diaphragm are caused probably by an enlarged spleen.

June 3, 1943

It seems that Moresby is past the peak of its boom. Although there is constant air activity and a steady stream of shipping in and out of the base, the feverish tempo which reached a crescendo around two or three months ago has definitely started to fade away. More troops are leaving the base than are arriving. Camp sites which consisted of pup tents have grown into small villages, equipped with electricity, running water, wooden or concrete floors for tents, and so on. There is even a sign on the road leading up from Moresby which states that civilians will not proceed beyond this point without permission of the military authorities.

It has been wonderful to watch Moresby grow from a wrecked little town to our most powerful base in the Southwest Pacific. and now to see it wane away, giving out its strength to other bases such as Milne Bay and Oro Bay, makes me feel awfully old. Or at least, it makes me feel like a real "old timer" around here. The Engineer Amphibious Brigade is assembling boats at the rate of six a day in Australia. It will be months yet before the armada will be completed; but when it is, we can be sure of seeing some real action. I understand that it is capable of carrying a whole division at one time. I have a premonition that I'll be home next April. Everybody here laughs at me for being so optimistic, but I really believe it.

June 4, 1943

Pickard has his heart set on going to Oro Bay, but Derby says "no." So I guess Pickard will stay here. He seems to be rather unhappy about the set-up. I surely like him. He is a regular fellow.

June 5, 1943

Derby off to Oro Bay again. The old man really gets around. Burkholder came in today, will spend several days around here before proceeding to Sydney. He is a swell fellow too. Ninty per cent of the men you meet over here seem to be better than average—a mathematical impossibility but an apparent truth nevertheless.

June 13, 1943

An air raid this evening was welcome for it broke up our dull class. It was an awful sight to see the officers scramble all over the place when the alarm was sounded. Some of them had never seen an air raid before and after getting out the hut kept asking, "Where are they? Where are they? Where do we go?"

"You've got about a fifteen minute wait yet," I told one of the fellows. "And it's best to stay where you are. Unless they take a crack at *Seven Mile Drome* we'll be safe here. And even then they've got to miss by a mile and a half and they got to miss in this direction. Little chance of getting to even hear the bombs where we are."

The two flying boats came over. The ack-ack cut loose. The planes must have been two miles away and the ack-ack wasn't bursting overhead. The planes flew off.

"Glad that's over," one of the new second lieutenants said. "Where'd the bombs hit?"

"They didn't" I told him. "I don't believe they dropped them yet."

"The hell they didn't. What were all those explosions over there?"

"Nothing but our own guns. They crack. When bombs hit near you, you'll be able to tell the difference. They *grunt* —H Ru—o—n—p—h—H—R—u—m—p—h—You didn't hear any of them."

"I still say they were bombs," said another officer. He was from the 91st Engineers, a real veteran, not one of these green 857th or 842nd boys.

"Well, we'll see. If they come back again, you'll know they didn't drop their eggs."

"Look—look—a flare!" It was Crafton. I looked at the "flare" then up at the moon to be sure that my suspicion was true.

"That's not a flare. It's Venus. Just came out from behind a cloud."

"I've seen stars before, and that isn't a star," said Crafton. I laughed.

"It's going to take an awfully long time for that flare to reach the ground." I listened to the officers arguing whether it was a "star" or a "flare" and enjoyed hearing them gradually change their minds until they all agreed that it was a "star." The Japs tried to come in a second time, but the ack-ack beat them off.

I had just arrived at Headquarters when the Nips made their third run. They flew over the heart of our military installations. We heard no bombs. The ack-ack put up a beautiful barrage but did no good. The planes passed a half-mile south of us, looking as if they were almost overhead from the ground. We got a nice shower of ack-ack fragments but no one was hit around here. Funny how the stuff whizzes all around you but seldom hits you.

June 17, 1943

There was an air raid. Our ack-ack stinks. A thousand shells must have been thrown up but not a plane was hit. We had a hail of ack-ack fragments after the raid. Nips flew around us; no wonder we had such a shower.

June 18, 1943

Derby left for the mainland today, will probably be gone for three weeks. He says he is going to Sydney, told nobody exactly his business, said it was something in regard to "Colored troops."

June 23, 1943

Was up to see Dellavia this evening. The infection has spread onto his hands so that he cannot use them. I am handling his personnel job.

There was an Australian officer shot about ten days ago up the road. The nurse with him wasn't hurt but claims the officer was attacked by two or three negroes. The officer died several days ago, and now the MP's are not letting our boys go up the road. There were three guards halting all cars when I went up to see Del this evening. This one affair—the hysterical screeching of a frightened woman—may be the cause of a lot of friction between the Aussies and our colored boys. Why in the hell don't people realize that negroes are the same as Whites? We don't segregate blonds from brunettes or blue-eyed people from brown-eyed people. Why should we draw a social barrier between dark-skinned and light-skinned people? I hope this affair blows over. It would if the matter were dropped—except, of course, the search for the murderers. But if they start restricting our boys in their movements around here they are only looking for trouble.

June 25, 1943

Nichols is back from O.C.S. [officers' candidate school]. He was kicked out because of a fight in a saloon. He says there must be at least 15,000 marines in Townsville—part of the First Marine Division I presume. They are filtering into Milne Bay now and I hope it won't be very long before they will be landing on New Britain. The whole trouble is that an operation of this nature requires long preparations and the Japs are undoubtedly wise to them. So we might expect a Jap blow to come a week or two before our scheduled attack. Their intelligence—especially around here—has always been weak. Their failure at Milne Bay was due to faulty intelligence. But assembling barges by the hundreds cannot go unobserved. The political situation in Australia is reaching a sad state of affairs. I guess they will have a new election immediately.

June 26, 1943

From the heavy air activity around here this morning, I thought the Japs were landing reinforcements on the other side, especially when 19 B-25's went out at one time. But the activity died down during the day, unlike the Bismarck Sea Battle; so I guess there wasn't a Jap convoy on the other side after all. The Nips are pressing us hard at Bena Bena and these planes may have gone out to help our men.

Roosevelt vetoed the Anti-Strike bill and both Houses passed it over his veto. The general comment around here is that Roosevelt is through because of this blunder. I don't think it was a blunder at all. Roosevelt, if he had signed the bill, would be called a tyrant. He wanted the bill to be passed as much as anyone else, and if he wasn't sure that two-thirds of Congress wanted it too, he would have signed it. But he knew that it would become a law without his signature; so why should he be the *one* who would go down in history as the tyrant who suppressed the poor working class, who made them work against their will? No, it would be better if history books spoke of him as the great leader who, despite the trials and hardships of the times, honored the rights and privileges of the laborer and who would do nothing to shake any of our democratic principles. A shrewd man—a genius!

June 27, 1943

There were some fellows over here this evening who left the States 26 days ago. Captain Barker, Infantry, said he got the surprise of his life when he sailed into the harbor with everything lighted up.

"I had cautioned the men," he said, "that they were going into territory which was subjected to heavy bombing and that they couldn't even smoke a cigarette without being under cover. I felt like a damn fool when we arrived and saw Moresby lit up like a Christmas tree with big flood lights all over the ships and barges."

"Yes," I told him, "we seem to do everything just the opposite of what you are taught. It seems effective however. I believe the Japs must have a complete library of all our military texts and are fools enough to believe that we do what the good books say."

"I noticed that. Why, when I asked Colonel Eads if he would check our camp site to see whether it fitted in with the all around defense of the area, he merely laughed at me."

"I guess you were worried about camouflage too?"

"Well, I can see that nothing over here is camouflaged. Whole squadrons of heavy bombers parked in the open. You must lose a hell of lot of them during a raid."

"Seldom lose any. Occasionally one or two are hit. We believe dispersal is more effective than camouflage. Camouflage is costly in time and material and really offers no protection. You see the Japs have used high-altitude pattern bombing. When they go after an airdrome, they really plaster it: not only the runway but all adjacent areas. Camouflaged planes aren't protected; but if the planes are parked in blast pens well dispersed they won't get more than a couple.

"Well surely you had a defense plan when the Japs were a few miles away."

"You might call it a defense plan if you want. Take for example our mission in the plan: occupy that little hill adjacent to the road leading to Moresby with a two-weeks supply of food and ammunition. Dig in and kill as many Japs as you can. I imagine every other outfit around here had a similar mission."

"Guerrila tactics?"

"Yes. Well, the best tactics at any rate. You won't find it described in a book. You see, here there would have been no escaping, not even a Dunkirk. It would have been another Bataan. We knew it. But that's history, mustn't dwell on it. What's new back home?"

June 29, 1943

Pickard has gone to Oro Bay and I am here in charge of the show again.

Really busy now. Not only do I hold the jobs of adjutant, personnel adjutant, intelligence officer, operations officer, and headquarters detachment commander, but without a C.O. and executive officer around, I have to make a few decisions myself. I like all of this but it does keep me on the go. With the first of the month coming up, I know I'm going to be snowed under.

June 30, 1943

Some wonderful pictures of Dora and the baby. Gosh they both look delicious on the pictures. I think I could spend a solid week with time out only for eating with the two of them.

July 1, 1943

Derby is probably working down South. A wire came in today stating that Pickard is to go to Sydney on detached service. I imagine there will be many more changes before the month is over. Derby is all right. Hope Dellavia gets out the hospital before long. This job of personal adjutant isn't a bit of fun.

July 2, 1943

Well, it looks as if we have started a little action around here. American troops have landed on New Georgia and are pressing on toward Hunda. Actually the papers are making a big stink over some minor moves. For instance, they announce the occupation of the Trobriand Islands by U.S. Forces. Actually the 46th Engineers have been on the islands a month preparing docks etc. After they have everything all set, boom! The marines and infantry move in and "take" the island without enemy opposition. Hurrah for them. All the engineers get out of it is the knowledge that they will be able to get something besides hard tack and bully beef to eat. Similarly all the troops around here have been cited for their work in this area between July and December of last year. They don't mention the nine weeks before July when we were up here and this place was a real hell hole. Gosh, if the true story is never printed while an event is occurring, how can anyone dare to believe what history books tell us?[1]

July 8, 1943

The world seems to be blazing up again. The Germans are attacking between Orel and Bylegorod apparently trying to recapture Kurak, and, according to the Russians, are meeting with a lot of casualties but very little success. It is hard to figure out Hitler's motive. Perhaps he wants the Allies to land on the continent and try to invade Germany. Perhaps his food and oil supplies are getting dangerously low and he wants the Allies to give their blow while he can still "take" it. His people are undoubtedly tired of the war and restless. He might feel that if he starts an offensive on the Russian front he will "suck in" the Allies. And that is what he wants. Then again, he may want it to have just the opposite effect. He may feel that the Allies will feel that he is trying to suck them in and become skeptical and not attack. And that may be what he wants. In other words the smartest man or the biggest fool has an equal chance of guessing, or predicting what Hitler wants. And the flip of a coin would be as good a way as any in finding out.

July 10, 1943

The Allies landed on Sicily this morning. There isn't any definite news yet but it is safe to assume that the Italian Navy and Air Force are out in strength to crush the invasion force. Italy's top-heavy navy is going to get a bad beating when subjected to the dive bombers and torpedo planes which we have based nearby. We will have substantial losses in the landing operation, but we should be able to bring in many troops without too much opposition. A lot is going to depend on how well the Italians can fight to hold Sicily. If it surrenders within the next two weeks, we can expect the Italian Peninsula to do the same when our forces land there. That they will land in Italy is inevitable, except of course if Italy surrenders first. Even then our troops will use Italy as a place to land troops to get them into the heart of the Continent. I hate to feel so optimistic but I can't help feeling that Italy's unconditional surrender is but a matter of months.

July 11, 1943

Operations in Sicily are proceeding according to plan, is the report we get. Apparently our troops are heading up the east coast of the island toward Messina. I don't believe they are more than sixty or seventy miles from Messina now, but it is going to be a long sixty miles.

July 13, 1943

I didn't realize before how much the men of the Regiment hated the officers. I received two reports from operators today which opened my eyes.[2] This is one of the things circulating among the men: "One of the high officials at Base Hq. ask (sic) Colonel Derby how long it would it (sic) take for him to get the 96th Engineers together so they could send the regiment back to the States and that Colonel Derby said that he wanted the Regiment to do some more work. Colonel Derby went to Australia for the purpose of seeing the Commanding General for the purpose of retaining the 96th Engineers in New Guinea." Another report from one of my operators gave this information: "There is an undercurrent movement at the opportune moment to 'get' certain officers."

In regard to that, Chaplain Dubra said something last evening at supper which was startling. He had just come back from leave and was very bitter about the way the negroes were being treated in Australia, especially by white American soldiers. Anyway we got on the subject of mob psychology and he said, "I bet I could go out there," pointing where some sixty colored soldiers were sitting down waiting for a show to begin, "and in ten minutes I could have those boys storming this place—just by talking to them."

I doubt that he could myself but it was a strange thing for him to say. It didn't take much in Townsville to make the men revolt against Captain Williams after he took over C Company. Well, getting back to some of the things the operators reported, there was this statement: "Two-thirds officers (in all branches) want the war to last indefinitely." I realize now that a similar statement by the reserve officers about the regular army officers must have been as false as the one handed me by this operative. And I imagine the regular army officers say the same thing about politicians back home. Then there was this startling statement: "Our (96) C.O. is to be courts martialled for splitting the organization and sending the men to various points knowing they were physically unfit. We (96) are to be sacrificed to a man. Reason: We are to do combat duty without the proper training." There were other annoying lies that the men apparently believe. "Furloughs are to be canceled for all colored troops. Anyone can get a rating if enough money is put in the right places" (I didn't know that any of the men felt that way). "Censors (like me, I guess) and mail handlers appropriate money and packages for themselves. Doctors say Natives are diseased to keep a man from having a woman, still officers use them for intercourse. We (96) are awaiting orders daily to embark and rejoin the rest of the companies and other units and start an invasion of Rabaul. The Doctors say everybody in New Guinea has malaria. Various personnel are teaching the Colored personnel that they are to be the losers regardless of the outcome of the war. A certain element are determined to voluntarily surrender to the Jap." And that is part of the rumors which are circulating among the men. It is a shock to find out that such stuff is true.

July 14, 1943

I spent the afternoon at the dock which A Company is building at Tatana Island. It is a rather interesting project. The work is interesting in as much as they have to build the new dock without interrupting operation of the floating dock.

A squadron of 25 P-47's arrived today. They roared over the top of our car like a score of locomotives. I thought I didn't recognize the sound of their engines and when I looked up—there they were—P-47's. We have been expecting them here for over fourteen months.

July 16, 1943

Poor Del surely was an awful sight this morning. His bed was a mess of oozy yellow stuff that had flowed out of the open ulcers which had spread over his whole body. Every part of him was swollen. His eyes were nearly closed. I had to dress him so that he could go to the hospital. He was still pulling on his pipe when he went however.

July 17, 1943

There is plenty work again for me now that Del is in the hospital. I like to be busy like this. I wish Derby would come back.

July 21, 1943

Colonel Derby arrived on the 18th. I thought he had flopped a lot of work on my lap that day but the next morning he sat down with me and for three hours gave me jobs to do. I have worked on them ever since and still can see no light. He seemed well pleased with the way I had run things during his absence and told me to put in my recommendation for captain.

"I don't like to do it," he said. "I don't like to recommend anybody to the position of captain until he has demonstrated he can command a company." I said nothing. He then added. "But you have more than demonstrated it for you have run this detachment here which is the size of a company and has many more complications."

The Tatana Island Causeway, Port Moresby, July 1943. Company A, 96th Engineers built the causeway in both directions and the road leading to it, greatly expanding Moresby's port facilities. The land jutting out is to allow trucks the space to turn around. The causeway was still there when Captain Samuelson visited Papua during the early 1970s.

On guard at the power shovel. The soldier carries the 96th's basic weapon, an old, bolt-action Springfield. It was an accurate weapon but no match for the automatic rifles issued to combat troops.

July 22, 1943

Dearest Hymie,

I'm glad to hear you all are eating so good. I know us "poor" people back home surely don't mind eating less as long as the boys at the front eat more. And don't worry about us eating so little. Even with food rationed as it is there are still a lot of people who are getting fatter by the day and other people who have to watch what they eat or else they will grow fat, too—for instance, me.

And so you're writing a book. I knew you would start writing books someday, only I didn't expect it so soon. I wouldn't be surprised if it turns out to be a best seller, too. I wish you would tell me what it's about. Curiosity is getting the better part of me and don't think I didn't have the sad-eyes 'cause I can't sort of be there while you're writing it—you know—sort of help you along, and all.

Don't think I don't get the sad-eyes when I see how happy some couples are and have such beautiful little apartments with babies and all. But don't think there are too many happy couples these days. Most people around here are separated too, and more husbands go off to war by the day.

July 23, 1943

Bishop Gregg, A.M.E. Church, was out to visit the regiment today. He is a personal representative of the President checking into the spiritual and moral welfare of negro troops overseas. It is a big political show his being over here.[3]

Derby seems well pleased with my work. I have been getting a score or more jobs done for him daily with almost uninterrupted success. It feels funny to be anyone's servant the way I have to be with him, to "yes, sir" all his requests and orders even when I think they are foolish or out of place. I am learning a lot from him: diplomacy in particular. I am learning to express my views quietly and without becoming angry. I have Joseph Scott acting first sergeant now and he seems to be doing a good job. Sgt. Nash reported to me drunk this morning.

"Sir," he said as he saluted "I am unfit for duty."

I almost chewed his ass out for not reporting to me last night on air transport then changed my mind.

"Sergeant," I said "what did you accomplish yesterday on that job I sent you out to do?" He told me.

"You'll go back to your tent and remain until you can report to me for duty sober!" He started jabbering.

Bishop John Gregg, African Methodist Episcopal church, with the 96th Engineers Band, Port Moresby, July 23, 1943.

"That's all, sergeant. You can go."

I saluted. He saluted and staggered out the office. I don't know what I'll do with him. He was a good soldier even when he was drunk.

August 1, 1943

A damn wave of psycho-neurosis has swept the outfit. There has been a certain amount of mental disorders from time to time, but there has been a marked increase in the past few days. First of all, Sgt. Nash, the Regimental Sergeant Major, went on the blink. Then Ridly, our mail orderly, cracked up. Engle came back and said they are sending Captain Marcuson home for the same thing. And I received a letter today stating that Floyd Jones, motor pool dispatcher, is being shipped to the states for the same ailment. The Colonel made me write a letter to Mouron making him go on leave before the strain at Oro Bay beat him down. Al came in today and excluding his nervousness which he has had ever since his second attack of malaria seems altogether all right. Then Scott left me. He was second in command (enlisted) of the administrative section; but I had promised to send him to Haseman; and when Nash cracked up, I didn't want to go back on my word. So the Personnel Section is also crippled, although the work continues to roll in and I have to try to keep it rolling into the proper places. Then in addition to all this 74 casuals arrived from the Mainland yesterday.[4] We were up all hours of the night last night putting up tents and cots and trying to make the men comfortable. Sixty of the men were brand new, had been inducted in the Service January of this year, fresh into the combat zone, green soldiers and as ugly and mean and mentally unbalanced as new negro recruits can be. It was a rough job keeping them in order and I couldn't help wishing for another officer to lend a hand or at least a good top sergeant. But my acting top kick, who isn't very good anyway, is in the hospital, still suffering from the shock he received some time ago when a bomb caved a slit trench in on him. Right now there are over 150 men here—a terrible mixture of motor pool personnel, clerks, casuals, and what have you. And I am the only officer for duty. When I signed the morning report this morning, I noticed that there are 13 officers at Headquarters, either assigned and attached, but I was the only one who came under the present-of-duty column. I have worked all day like a bastard, first interviewing these sixty new men, then getting them assigned to various companies, then trying (in vain, I must admit) to make arrangements for air transportation for them to the various bases to which they are assigned. Then there was their service records to check, clothing and equipment forms to mail to their future company commanders, and so on. Then too this is the first of the month and there are a dozen or more reports due. One doesn't realize just how many reports are submitted to Regimental Headquarters until he has a list of them in front of him. I also asked the Colonel to let Cass go on leave in my place, and the Colonel agreed provided that I could hold down his job in supply while he was away. He also stipulated that Cass couldn't go until Holmes returned. That might seem like additional work to me, but actually it isn't, because I am familiar with supply routine, and the supply work around here has been greatly simplified with the creation of these numerous sub-bases which have their own supply systems. And now I will be free from Cass's constant nagging about his going on leave. He offered me ten pounds if I could convince the Colonel to let him and me trade places on the leave roster. I should have taken the ten pounds from him after I swung the deal, but I was afraid that it might be prohibited by Army Regulations; so I told him to regard it as a favor, and a mighty big one too, for I never do anything in the way of a favor for anyone. He has an Aussie gal down there that he wants to marry, and would sell his soul to get away and marry her.

August 3, 1943

About 4:30 yesterday afternoon we got a phone call that Major Farrar had just come in from the Mainland and was waiting to be picked up at Ward's Drome.

August 7, 1943

Gosh, I've missed Dora all day today. I thought my going out with Flake [a nurse] would tend to ease the pain of being away from Dora, but I guess Flake is like any other female and her shortcomings only make me miss Dora more. I miss her bodily and sexually as well as any other way. Damn, but I'm restless. I want a woman I guess. There is no other way to explain it. And I want Dora in particular. I don't believe any other could quite do the trick.

August 13, 1943

I went into town with Major Farrar this evening and listened to a long bull session with him, Colonel Teal, Colonel Dies, and later in the evening with Colonel Mott. So listening to these men who are really in the key supply posts in this Theatre, I learned a lot about their problems. I was surprised when Mott said that Class I supplies at Oro Bay have diminished to eight days. Our men fighting around Salamau are pitifully undernourished.

"How in the hell will we supply the Ninth Division when they make their push?" he asked. He spoke of the failure of our amphibious engineers and the miserable handling of their boats. Apparently they tried to shove off all their boats onto the Navy, and the Navy doesn't want them. The engineers at Woodlark[5] are not getting the docks completed there in time, and it looks as if any future offensive, unless there is time to bring up more supplies, will go haywire. Well, I don't know all of their problems, but I think they are bungling the supply situation pretty awful. Listening to those brass hats talk about their problems this evening has sort of knocked the starch out of me. I thought they had everything under control. I guess they are only human beings like the rest of us and are as capable of making mistakes as anyone else.

The President made a speech this evening in which he promised "as there is a God in Heaven" that he would give the Filipinos their independence the day their enemy Japan has been crushed. Undoubtedly the Japs are about to grant the Phillipines its independence, and the President doesn't want to let the Japs be the "good guy." He wants the United States to be the great liberator. I predicted earlier that the one nation who is really coming out on top in this war is going to be Japan, and as time goes on the more firmly am I convinced of my earlier beliefs.

August 14, 1943

Spent the afternoon watching A Company working on the Tatana Docks. I'm hungry to get my teeth into some real engineering work for a change.

The old man is leaving for Oro Bay in the morning with Farrar. Farrar will stay over there. It surely is going to make Haseman unhappy to have someone who ranks him move in on top of him. Well, there's no work here at Headquarters for Farrar to do, and we have to put him somewhere. It's a damn shame how the army has to support these high rankers who are no earthly good to anyone but themselves.

August 15, 1943

I gave the men a complete holiday today. It was the first holiday they have had because it was Sunday since they have been overseas. I don't know how the Old Man will feel about it, but if the work around here doesn't suffer from it, and I don't see why it should, I plan to give them all Sundays off in the future. I took the day off for the most part myself. Came up to the office for about an hour and a half cleaning out the "In" basket, censoring the mail, attending to a few odds and ends. Sgt. Nash was alone in the next office; so I called him in to talk to him.

"Sergeant Nash," I said. "How do you feel about going on leave?"

"I don't want to go, sir."

"I think you ought to go, sergeant. You've been working pretty hard, and I think it will do you some good."

"I know what you're thinking, Lieutenant," he said, "but I'm going to behave myself from now on. I promise you that I won't be drunk on duty again. I'll even promise not to drink any more."

"I don't want you to promise me anything," I said. "I'm concerned mostly with your last request for transfer. I want to know why you put it in. Are the reasons you stated in your request the real reasons?"

"No, sir. You know, Lt. Samuelson that the officers of the 96th have always been good to me."

"I know they have, and that's the reason why I want to know why you wrote such a thing."

"Sir," he said, "I'll tell you the truth. I wanted to see how I stood around here. I wanted to make the colonel mad and I wanted to make you mad."

"You succeeded pretty well," I said. "Do you mean that you wrote all that stuff and didn't mean a word of it?"

"Yes, sir."

"Well, then you look here, Sergeant Nash. I'll forget about this incident this time; but so help me if you put in for transfer again, I won't rest until you are out of the Regiment. And you can rest assured that you won't be transferred in grade. There isn't a unit over here that will want you in the grade of master sergeant. And that means you will leave here as a buck private. You know damn well how you stand among the officers of the Regiment. You wouldn't be Sergeant Major if we didn't think you were pretty good. When a man asks me for a transfer, I like to believe that he is sincere and really wants the transfer, not that he wants to see how he stands with his superior."

And I rambled on, really raking him over the coals. I don't know what effect it will have on him. I think it will straighten him out for a little while. It came as a surprise to him I know. I don't believe that another officer in the 96th has ever told him off that way, because of his sixteen years' service and his splendid knowledge of army regulations and administrative procedure.

August 21, 1943

I am now commanding A Company. Last Monday morning the old man called me in and handed me two lists of emergency supplies that were needed at Oro Bay and instructed me to see what I could do about it. Apparently he didn't expect me to do very much, for that evening when I told him that I was able to procure most of the supplies, he looked surprised. There were a half dozen other things that the Colonel wanted me to do, and I succeeded in all of them. He seemed pleased. Tuesday and Wednesday were the same—work from reveille until the wee hours of the next morning—loading trucks, trailers, etc. at Tatana for shipment to Oro Bay. In this connection I was able to fill their request for seventeen vehicles to the exact piece and was able to sneak aboard an air compressor which they hadn't asked for but which I thought they would be able to use to good advantage. Derby was so pleased that I was able to handle all these things in addition to running headquarters that he couldn't hide it.

About 4:30 Wednesday evening the old man called me into his office.

"Sit down, Samuelson," he said. "The situation at A Company is getting worse by the hour. I have just been considering sending you down there immediately instead of waiting until Mouron came back."

"Yes, sir."

"Now what do you think about Holmes's taking over your job here? Do you think he can hold it down?"

"I think so, sir. But that's a question that you ought to ask him. I'm not qualified to answer for him."

"Then I think you had better call in Holmes." I sent the charge of quarters[6] for Holmes but he came back and said that Holmes was taking a shower but that he would be up in about ten minutes.

"What do you think about Martin's holding down the personnel section?" Derby asked me.

"Personnel work requires no brains. It's just routine checking of papers. Any officer who can sit down for five or six hours a day can handle the job. A lot of the work is new and different, but once a man checks an application for insurance, he knows how to do it. If he checks one machine record roster, he can check any of them. It does require patience though."

"If I send you to A Company, I expect you to shake the place from top to bottom. There is over 15,000 yards of dirt to move. I expect you to get out about a thousand yards a day. I understand that all the equipment is down. You've got to get it running. You've got to get those junior officers straightened out. All I see whenever I go down there is turmoil. Nobody seems to know what is going on. I want you to get the company reorganized and back on its feet. You had better call Kalman and tell him to come out to see me this evening," he said. I made the call, got in touch with Kipp and told him to deliver the message to Jack. I went back into the Colonel's office and sat down again. Darby said, "I want to get the best running team that is possible, and I'm not interested in Martin's or anyone else's feelings."

When I reached the job, it seemed to be at a standstill. There was a shovel (a half-yard Bucyrus Erie) sitting idle near a bank of almost solid rock. About eight men were sitting around with some cable apparently doing nothing. I saw two dump trucks, but there wasn't a driver in either one of them. Up on the hill a dozen men were drilling into solid rock, placing gelignite for blasting. I caught site of Vanden-Boom and he saw me. He didn't walk over to me; so I walked over to him.

"Morning, boss," he said in a surly manner. Jack had obviously told him that I had taken over the company; so there was no point in my telling Van that I had.

"Why isn't that shovel operating, Van?"

"Hell, I don't know—one of those tracks is off it or something."

"What do you mean, one of the tracks?" We walked over to the shovel, and we looked it over. "She looks all right to me. Where's your motor sergeant? Get hold of him, and tell him to get this shovel going." I then walked around the job, puffing on my pipe and feeling shaky and nervous about finding VandenBoom so uncooperative. When I got back, the shovel engine was running.

"How many dump trucks do you have out here, Sergeant Thomas?" I said.

"I think there are three, sir."

"All right, then. Get this shovel moved away from that rock wall and start walking it down the bend in the road. Just keep it walking. I'll be around there in about ten minutes and show you where I want it spotted. Get those truck drivers in their trucks and have them follow the shovel. Is that straight?"

"Yes, sir."

"Then move out," I said. I then turned to VandenBoom. "What platoon is out here now?"

"We don't have platoons in A Company."

"What sergeant is in charge of those men sitting on their dead asses over there? Find out what they're supposed to be doing over there."

When he came back, he said, "They're fixing a cable on to a dead man, but they don't have any cable clamps."[7] I heard what he said, but I made no comment. "What's wrong with the D-8?" Actually I knew that the power control unit was broken and had been taken to Ordnance for repairs, but I asked him anyway, just to see whether he knew. "That D-2 running?" I said.

"Yeah, I think so."

"Then you'd better get it started up cause I have a job in mind for it. And when you finish that, give A Company a phone call and tell them to send out every damn dump truck that is around. I want them all sent out here. I'm going over to spot that shovel. Come around the bend in the road when you finish your call."

"Okay, boss," he said more scornfully than he had the first time.

It was a little after dinner when Colonel Derby drove up. By then six dump trucks were shuttling back and forth from the shovel to the fill. The shovel was operating in loose earth bank, and was really putting out the dirt. I had had the men blast the nineteen charges which they had placed in the rock and then took them off that job. I sent in all the air compressors with the exception of one, and I gave VandenBoom instructions that there would be no more blasting until I thought it would be necessary. I had sent out the supply sergeant after cable clamps, staples, and a few other supplies which were holding up operations, and I was using the D-2 and as much hand labor as I could find clearing the scattered lumber, tips of piles, etc. By this time VandenBoom had taken an interest in the work, and when the old man drove up, he was very happy with what he saw. At four o'clock Henthorn came out with his relief. I told him about the changes I had made and told him that I wanted him to continue the work the way it was going. He made some sulking remarks, which I ignored. The crucial point came when he asked me, "What time will I be able to knock off to come in for tonight's party?"

"Your shift is over at midnight. You can come in any time after then."

"The party will be over too," he said. I didn't reply.

August 29, 1943, Port Moresby

Things have been going pretty good in the company. I have been a man of stone, acting firmer and harder than I am, but the results are showing up. Last week we moved over 8300 cubic yards of rock and dirt, considerably more than Colonel Derby expected me to accomplish. But it still isn't as good as I hope to do. I'd like to move 10,000 yards this week, but I fear that it will be hard to even meet last week's performance.

Sunday morning I had a meeting of all the NCO's and told them that I was out scouting to bust a bunch of them.

"There are only 51 NCO ratings in the company," I told them, "and there are a lot more men than that in the company who deserve these ratings. Consequently it is going to be a struggle among yourselves, the survival of the fittest, as to who gets the ratings and who remains privates and PFC's. Remember, those stripes on your arms are not only a reward for good work. They symbolize that you are superior as a soldier to the men under you. You are drawing more money, getting more respect. Therefore you have to produce more than the privates. And as soon as a private demonstrates that he is better than you, you can rest assured that he is going to get the rating which you now hold and you are going to lose your stripes. Now you don't have to do anything wrong in order to be busted. You are going to have to prove time and time again that you are the best man in the company for the job you are doing. A Company has a lot of good material in it, and the competition is going to be keen. In all fairness to you noncommissioned officers, I want to warn you that I and the other officers of the company are looking for NCO material among the privates and PFC's and we are looking among you to see which of you are not doing the work commensurate with his rank. So be on your toes. Don't let us catch you napping. One offence is all that you will need to be busted. There is one thing that I want to make clear before I leave and that is if any of you are reduced, don't feel licked. All that it will mean is that another man is showing that he can do the job better than you. If afterwards you can show that you are better qualified for the job than he is, you can get your rating back. I hope to keep the ratings in the company flexible so that a man who is really working hard and putting out his best can get one of the ratings and not have to remain a private or a PFC because there is not a single vacancy in the company, and the only way we can get some is going to be to bust some of you present NCO's. So be on your toes."

The other officers have come around swell. The main drawback that they had before was lack of the opportunity to assume full charge of the job. Now that they are really running the job for eight hours a day on their own hook they have become interested in the work and are getting good results. Henthorn, for example, got out 1019 cubic yards on his shift last night. That is really going. That amount of yardage may not seem very large for an eight hour shift, but when you consider that the eight hours include time-out for servicing, a half hour break for something to eat, etc., it is a fine showing whether it be army or civilian engineering. Taylor is doing better too. He has always cooperated and tried and now he seems to be coming across all right. VandenBoom is keeping up his good work. I hope to have the dock, the Causeway, and the island road all completed by the end of the month. I have started a company diary giving an accurate account of the engineering work we do and a sketch of other activities. The original is being kept in the Orderly Room, available to any man in the company who may desire to read it. I am keeping a duplicate copy of my own which I shall attach to my own personal diary when I leave Company A.[8] A twenty-four hour break begins at eight o'clock tomorrow morning. And I feel sure that I need the break as much as any other man in the company. I am going to sleep, read, and write, and then sleep some more, eat, and then sleep some more—sleep and sleep.

September 2, 1943

Dear Hymie,

I got you two pairs of captain's bars. They were the last sterling silver bars in town. For a while I thought I'd like to wear one of them myself. Everyone seems to be wearing their sweethearts' bars these days. But you're not my sweetheart. But then I might pretend you are 'cause these bars do look awfully pretty on anything I wear almost.

I might as well get to tell you some good things about me, or you're liable to think you made a mistake marrying me. And I wouldn't want that to happen 'cause then you might want to get rid of me and that would really be sad 'cause you'll never get rid of me, stinky, even if you hide in the deepest jungle in the deepest island in the deepest sea—I'll track you down.

September 5, 1943

We know that the offensive against Lae has started, but there has been no public mention of any action yet. The huge formations of transports carrying paratroops to the other side of the island made a beautiful spectacle this morning. The transports got into formation over the harbor while Kipp and I were driving back to camp this morning. We don't know exactly where they landed, but I imagine they dropped in the Markham River Valley behind Lae. A strong force will land (actually they must have landed by now, although we haven't heard for certain) north of Lae and come down the coast. I imagine we will see some tightening up on the part of our troops at Salamau also. Those damn Japs! If they would only surrender when they know they are hopelessly outnumbered, it would make the situation a lot easier, but they insist on fighting to the end. Japan will be fighting against us long after Germany and Italy have surrendered. I wonder how the Italians will react to a landing on their soil. I bet we have a surprise in store for us there too. They'll really put up some resistance, I bet, when they see their homes and property threatened. I played a set of tennis and a little basketball at Headquarters this afternoon. It was most enjoyable.

September 10, 1943

Since I have last written my diary, Italy has surrendered. The news was received over here with utter complacency. Either no one realizes the importance of this development or else they just don't give a damn. The Russian offensive is continuing and actually growing in intensity. They are overrunning the Ukraine like a brush fire, and are only eighty miles from Kiev now. Their offensive against Smolensk has somewhat petered out, but they are really moving forward on their entire front. Our offensive in the Lae-Salamau sector is coming along in good shape also. Latest reports place the bulk of our attacking force within four miles of the center of Lae. My promotion has come through also. The promotion was dated September 4th. Everything in the company has come along swell. Colonel Derby is leaving in the morning for the Woodlarks to help in the preparation of an offensive from there. He will be gone for about two months. Farrar will be in command of the Regiment during the Old Man's absence. I don't think I like Farrar.

September 14, 1943

Sunday night I posted the reorganization of the company, including the reduction of about half a dozen of my NCO's. I could sense the general resentment of the men in the air. Consequently, in order to show them who was boss, I had the entire company turn out this morning in khaki uniforms, helmet liners, etc. and form up into the organization which I had set up on paper. This was followed by a strict rifle inspection. I looked over the 150 men lined up in front of me. Real soldiers they were. Seasoned by nearly 18 months in New Guinea, they were hardened. They had been through a lot of hell and didn't give a damn about a new company commander who had just stepped in and was messing up their organization. Soldiers standing in ranks are always at a disadvantage, and their commanding officer can bring home almost any point by talking to them while they are lined up. Theirs is not to reason why, but to stand at attention and listen to what they are told. I was going to give them a speech, but I prepared nothing. I knew what I wanted to tell them, but I couldn't find the exact words. So after a few moments' hesitation, I called for the First Sergeant and told him to dismiss the company. The entire formation had been carried out in such a military manner and the entire company had responded so well to the few necessary commands that I had given that I felt they had all come around to my way of thinking and that anything I would say would be superfluous. I walked over to the Orderly Room, sat down at the desk, and worked over some papers for five or ten minutes. I then got up to leave.

"Sir," Sergeant [Lloyd H.] Smith (the first sergeant) said, "there are a number of men who would like to speak to you." I saw a large group standing outside the orderly room—an unhappy looking lot.

"All right, sergeant. Send them right in—one at a time." I knew that it would be easy to tackle them one at a time.

"Sir, they would like to see you as a group," Smith said. I hesitated a moment, lit a cigarette, then said, "All right, send them in as a group. As forty-some-odd non-com's and ex non-coms filed into the orderly room, I turned to some papers on my desk and pretended to be working. When they were all in, Sergeant Smith called them to attention. I took a long drag on my cigarette, then pushed it out on a shell ash tray.

"At ease," I told them. I looked them over from my chair. I started to stand up, but I realized that my 5 foot-9 inches would make me look like a dwarf among all these six footers. When the 96th was first organized, all the tallest men were placed in A Company. I knew that I would be at a disadvantage sitting down, but standing up would be worse. I waited until the shuffle of feet subsided and there was absolute silence.

"Very well," I said. "Who among you is acting as spokesman for the group?" There was no reply at first. I could feel a horrible frown on my face and the muscles in my arms and legs tight as knots. I kept looking over the group. Finally Staff Sergeant Eggleson stepped forward.

"I'll speak for them," he said. I was amused that he had said "for them" and not "for us." I realized immediately that it was a weak group. "We would like to know, sir," he said "what have all these men done to be busted." There was a pause.

"Is that all you want to know?" I asked.

"Not exactly, sir. We want to know just what is happening. Why all these changes? And why so all of a sudden like this?"

"Why were all the sergeants reduced without doing anything wrong," Staff Sergeant Donnely said.

"And without consulting anyone," came another voice. There was in a moment a babble of voices, angry voices. I sat back, trying to hear as many of them as I could. I didn't answer. I waited until there was complete silence again. I kept fumbling with words in my mind. Here before me were the key men in the company. I wanted them to know that I was boss but I wanted to enlist their confidence and cooperation too. And they were angry, a mean lot to handle.

"I am glad that you men came to me like this," I said, "to find out what is going on. I would much rather you do it this way than go back to your tents and sulk. For the past three weeks, ever since I came to A Company, I have been thinking of ways to increase the efficiency of the unit. Two days ago, after many attempts, I finally drafted up a chart showing what type of organization I felt would bring as many men in the company doing the most good. This entire organization is shown in detail on the plywood board that I had posted in front of this building yesterday. You men ought to study it. After having completed this chart, I allocated all the ratings in the company to these various sections. This table is located on the plywood board outside this building also. And I'd appreciate it if all of you men took a look at that table too. You will find that every rating in the company is shown on that board. I'm not holding back any ratings. I am not keeping any secrets from you men. Everything is out there in black and white.

"After this was completed, I had a meeting of the company officers and told them what ratings were available to them in their platoons and that they should select those non-coms who they thought were best. And that is what they did. I discussed with sergeant Donnely the men in the kitchen. I went over the whole scheme with sergeant Smith and got his recommendations. These 'busts' and reductions and promotions were a result of lengthy discussions. Nothing was done suddenly on the spur of the moment." I had run out of words and there was a pause. "Does that answer your question?" I asked. "But, sir, why was I busted?" Irby asked. "I was a sergeant, and then they put me on driving a truck. I was doing a good job as a truck driver. It wasn't my fault because I was put on the truck. And then I was busted. I can't figure out why."

"You were reduced because of your job of driving a truck did not call for a sergeant's rating and none of the platoon officers thought you were better than the men they had selected to hold the sergeant's ratings in their platoons." My reply was short, but it had hit the nail right on the head. I had said exactly what I wanted to. "Any other questions?"

"Yes, sir; my name is Atkinson. I was driving that dump truck which was side-swiped on the Eli Beach Road. I was reduced from a sergeant to a private. Was it because of the accident?"

"It was."

"But there was no investigation. How do you know that it was my fault?"

"A preliminary investigation showed that you were at least partially to blame. A formal investigation is being conducted by Lt. Kipp right now. As I told you men the first time I spoke to you three weeks ago, a man who is instrumental in the wrecking of any piece of equipment will lose any rating that he might hold. And I repeat, as I told you then, the driver does not have to be completely at fault. If he had anything to do with the accident at all, he will be busted. A dump truck is capable of carrying as much material as a whole platoon of men. And if we can keep our dump trucks running we are helping win the war. One of you men wrecking a truck does as much harm to the war effort as a zero pouncing down and shooting up that truck and destroying it. And I won't have any men in Company A destroying trucks and holding stripes at the same time. Are there any more questions?" There were many more, but for all of them I had a good answer. After I had answered all of their questions, I stood up and gave them a speech on our part in the war, about our primary mission over here—to assist combat troops by engineering works to destroy the enemy. "And in reaching that goal, if I have to hurt a few men, I will do it. But if you men are made of the right material, you who were reduced will work harder than you ever did before and show that you are a better man than the one who now holds these higher ratings. And you can rest assured that as soon as you demonstrate that you are the better man, you will earn back your stripes and he will lose his."

September 17, 1943

Things are running along pretty smoothly now. The American Dock job has been completed, two weeks ahead of schedule. That high priority housing project which Major Liles threw at us toward the end of last week was completed before the deadline that he set. We have been given four more jobs, and I feel sure that we can complete them before the anticipated completion dates set by the Base Engineer. The men in the company are coming around all right. I am still driving, making them pay for all the clothing and equipment which they lost, and so on; but at the same time I am getting them paid off, putting a stop to these illegal "donations to the slush fund" that Jack had. It is a difficult task to make these men realize they are soldiers again after the way Jack had spoiled them. For example, a grader operator by the name of Steele refused to go to work one morning. I told Kipp to send the man to me, and I asked Steele why he hadn't gone to work. He answered that he didn't have a rating and didn't see why he should run a grader and still be a private. There is no point in repeating what I told him, but he has been operating a grader ever since. Then there are all kind of squawks from men that they can't work because they don't have shoes, etc. But they are getting shoes now—paying for them too. The way some of these men lose and throw away equipment, it is nothing short of sabotage.

September 19, 1943

Right after dinner yesterday I started feeling rather punk, and by 4:30 my temperature had gone up to 104. I called Bud (Captain Roland B. Engle, regimental surgeon) and told him what the situation was. He says its that damn malaria again, but I talked him into letting me take the unauthorized four day cure on my own instead of sending me to the hospital where I would be tied up for over two weeks. Holmes went down with malaria; and once he got to the hospital, they wouldn't let him out, and now they are shorthanded at Headquarters. With Taylor gone, this company would be short of officers too if I went into the hospital. It surely makes me mad to have these attacks of fever, because although they don't last very long, they leave me so washed out that it takes two weeks to get my strength back. For example, my temperature yesterday went from 104 to 97 in two hours' time. That sort of stuff really knocks the starch out of a man. I'm taking 30 grains of quinine a day now, and that will keep the fever away, and if I don't have to do too much running around for the next day or so I ought to be all right shortly.

Lae and Salamau have both been captured.[9] The Fifth and Eighth armies have joined in Italy, and the Salerno beachhead has been firmly established. The damn Russians have gone hog wild with their drive through the Ukraine. They are only 45 miles from Kiev. If the British Ninth would only come across the Channel, the Allies might be able to get the European mess cleaned up in another few months. No telling when these damn Japs will be beaten though.

October 3, 1943

Things are more or less routine now. We are still getting numerous job orders, involving hut erection, road construction, bridges and culverts, utilities; but the pressure is off, and things are going along smoothly. Colonel Derby came in from the Woodlarks last Wednesday and visited the company Thursday. I drove him around in the sedan to the various job sites, and he seemed very much pleased with all the work we had accomplished during his short absence. After the subject of conversation got off work, he asked me, "What do you think about the Regiment's needing a rest? Do you think it ought to go South for a rest?"

"No, sir. I have always argued against the idea of our going South for a rest, mainly because it wouldn't be a rest."

"I am beginning to feel the same way," he said.

"I am sure that 95% of the men in the regiment feel the same way. What we want is to go home, and we know that by going down to Australia for a rest we aren't bringing any nearer the day we do go home. I think what we need is a good variety of useful work," I said.

"I think you're right," he said. "I do believe however that last January or February the regiment did need a rest. They had been through a nine-month period of real strain, and the rest would have been beneficial. But I am gradually changing my mind. I believe that what we need is to get the regiment together again."

"That would be a big factor, sir."

"What do you think about our going to New Britain?" he asked after a pause. I looked at him and smiled.

"That would be fine. The Japs might take a pretty pale view of our landing on their island though."

October 11, 1943

Sergeant Smith came up and said that the dissatisfaction in the Company had risen to a dangerous pitch, that there was almost universal grumbling, that the men were tired of being shoved around, busted without reason, and so on. "Just a little while ago, sir," he said, "almost all the non-coms had gotten together and were going to come up here and give you their chevrons. They said they all wanted to be privates, that they might as well give up their stripes voluntarily rather than have you take them away from them." "Sergeant, if ever that sort of thing comes up again," I said to Smith, "you tell them to come on right up the hill, to line up and come through the door in single file. I'll take their names and have Headquarters publish a Special Order immediately reducing them all to private—just the way they requested it. But you had better tell them also that if they ever do it, they can rest assured that they'll never wear a stripe on their sleeve again."

We talked for nearly an hour and a half. I know that the company has improved greatly since I have taken over. I haven't made the men suffer unduly. I have managed to get them a holiday on Sundays, and that required plenty of fighting. I have gotten them all kind of new clothing and equipment—without having to make them pay for them, and that required nearly signing my life away. I have gotten the men living together in better tents than they ever had before—nearly all with wooden floors. We are working on the motor pool, supply, and the kitchen, making them all better than they were before. So I know that I am doing a good job. And I believe, in spite of what the First Sergeant tells me, that the men do appreciate these things.

But what they do resent is the fact that they think I am shoving them around. They resent my dictating the whole show. They feel that because I am white and they are colored that I am taking advantage of them. That is one thing that I won't be able to knock out of their heads. Before I die I must help stamp out this crazy idea that the white man has about his superiority over the colored man. In no concrete way has he ever demonstrated it. Here we fight the Germans because they declare themselves a superior race. Individually they have demonstrated their boast. Their medicine, science, manufactures, are or at least were superior to that of any other nation. Yet this did not give them the right to declare that they were superior to all other men and to be able to dictate to others. Yet we Americans, the ones who are trying to thrash out Germany's idiotic ideas, feel the same way about the negroes. It's wrong—damn wrong! The negro is our equal physically. He is superior to us spiritually. He has the same intelligence as a white man. What he lacks is opportunity, opportunity to get an education, a decent job, decent living conditions. And these are the things which we white men deprive him of. And they are smart enough to know that we are wrong, but being in the minority they can do nothing about it.

Sometimes I would like to be able to tell them just how I feel, but it would do more harm than a thousand bomber raids in our camp area. And they are inclined to believe that I am just the opposite of what I am. I am harsh and firm and tell a subordinate to do things, not ask him, and expect him to do it—and do it right. And if he doesn't, he catches hell. But I'm that way because I accomplish more—for myself and my country. But the men think I treat them that way because my color is different from theirs. That hurts, really hurts. I wish there were something I could do about it. I will—some day. Yes, some day I will. But now is not the time. I must keep doing what I think is right, even if it means a knife in my back some night.

November 6, 1943

Things have greatly improved. There are still some of the men who think I am a son-of-a-bitch and who would stick a knife in my ribs if they knew they could get away with it. But on the whole most of the men are beginning to like me.

November 11, 1943

Dearest Dora,

You have probably been reading a lot of stuff in magazines about the hell the men in this place have been going through. And to a certain extent that is true, but that doesn't go for me. Now I am working a normal day with Sundays off and evenings to myself. I have made lots of friends, men and women, American and Aussie, more friends in fact than ever before in my life. And I know that they really like me. For instance last night we had six AAMWS [Australian nurses] over for supper and a little dancing, and it felt good to have them come in just like a bunch of old friends. They all think that "Cap'n Sammy" is a pretty good bloke, and that makes me feel good. I like them too. Honey, I can't explain this sort of thing to you. I am just getting all the pleasure I can out of life regardless of how fate tries to twist things; and it seems that I am succeeding. You can take all the fellows who have cracked up over here—physically, emotionally, or otherwise—all of them have been introverts who have sat around moaning for a wife back home or just griped themselves to death about all the money the people back home have made and how cruel life is and what a raw deal they have gotten. Now, these fellows are no good to anybody. They surely aren't good to themselves. They are no good to the country, not man enough to fight for the things that they think everyone is cheating them out of. Little girl, you wouldn't want me to act any way but the way I am acting, and I know that you realize how hard it is for me not to have seen Ian, especially the way I wanted to have a child of my own. And can't you realize how hard it is being away from you like this. But, little girl, there is nothing I can do about it, and there is nothing that you can do so the best thing for us to do is make the most of the situation and gather whatever pleasure and happiness we can. If there has been any one single factor which has kept me happy over here, contented with my work—it has been knowing that you are home and that we will be together when this thing is over. And knowing that Ian will be home too waiting for me. Gosh, little girl, if that little boy doesn't run up to me and throw his arms around me and kiss me the very first time he sees me, I'll beat the daylights out of him right on the spot. So you had better make him practice.

November 18, 1943

Around 8:30 Major Farrar came in. He barked out his usual good morning, which is enough to deafen anybody within ten feet of him. I believe I was more sullen than a company commander should act toward a regimental executive officer, but I was rather peeved.

"What was this message that Holmes delivered to me all about, Major?" I asked.

"Didn't he tell you?"

"He gave me some orders in your name which have been complied with months ago. I didn't need any orders about keeping my officers on the job. They always have been on the job."

"This is a special occasion," he said. "We are going to be visited by the Chief of Engineers, General Reybold."

"He is the top kick of all the engineers in the whole army, isn't he?" I said.

"Yes, that's right—no lesser man the Chief of Engineers himself is visiting us. There will also be General _____ and General _____ two of the side kicks of Reybold, and General Casey; you know Pat Casey, don't you?"

"I had the pleasure of working with General Casey," I said.

"And there will be Brigadier Main, GRE of all Australian forces in New Guinea and General" this-and-that who was the commanding general of something else other. "And then there will be some lesser men such as Colonel Robinson, Advanced Section USASOS, who (blah blah, blah)." It took ten minutes for him to give me the whole list of "distinguished visitors.

"And I want you to put on a good show for these distinguished gentlemen."

"I think we can do that, sir," I said.

I drove up to headquarters with the Major where he held an officers' call and bored everybody with his constant line of bull shit for half an hour. Then we drove out to the jobsite, where he wanted to talk to the men. When we got there, I told Don and Dick to knock their men off and assemble them in the vicinity of the tool shed. Some of the men had been working on the reservoir and several other isolated spots so that it took about fifteen minutes to get them all together. I had Sergeant Nettles give the company fall-in, and then he turned them over to me. I then gave them at ease and told them to pay attention to Major Farrar who had a few words to tell them. Now I can't quote his speech, but I do remember enough of it to put over the general idea.

"Now the next time I see you men assemble, I don't want it to take so *God-Damn* long. You're a bunch of soldiers. Not a *God-Damned* pack of bums. You men are going to have the honor of being visited by some very distinguished gentlemen, and General so-and-so will be here, who is the chief director of . . . and General . . . who is in charge of all the. . . ." This ran on for ten minutes, all a lot of tripe that no one was interested in. "Now I don't care if you men don't do any work for the rest of the day, when these distinguished officers come out to look over the job, every *God-damned* one of you had better be working as hard as he can."

Every time he said "God-Damned" with his damn emphasis on it, I could have punched him in the nose. Then he went on to tell the men what a wonderful Regimental Commander they had and what a wonderful company commander they had, how he had taken a company which wasn't worth a good *God-damned* and made it into the best in the regiment. Then he praised the men a little, told them of their heroic work under enemy action in the "early days" of New Guinea, of their heroic fight against the Japs at Milne Bay, how they drove the Japs back into the sea while the commanding general sat in a Lockhead Hudson Plane on the only serviceable airstrip, ready to pull out in case the going got too rough. Where he got these crazy ideas I don't know, because the 96th did not get into any action at Milne Bay. Then he proceeded to call numerous white engineer outfits sissy outfits because they were going to the Mainland. He called them by name: the 808 Engineers, the 43rd and 46th Engineers. He wound up by telling the men that he wanted to see them be the best *God-damned* colored outfit in the world. He said a lot more stuff, all of which irritated me to the point of popping.

When he left, I called the men together, had them sit down in a circle around me. I waited until the mumbling stopped; they were griping about what the Major had had to say.

"Give me your attention, men, for a few minutes. I would like to clear up a few points that the Major was trying to put over to you. Now Major Farrar has been with the 96th for only three months. Before then he had a desk job in Brisbane. As far as I know, he has had no experience with troops (I was careful not to say *colored* troops, although that is what I meant to say). He had a message to bring you today, but I don't believe he put it over. Now first of all, I hope none of you took his cursing to heart. It wasn't meant personally. When he said 'the best God-damned colored outfit in the world,' he meant to say the 'best colored outfit in the world', and in that regard I want to see A Company just the best outfit in the world." I noticed looks of approval on the faces of some of the men. "Now, he spoke about some of these outfits being sissy outfits. You men know that that isn't true. You men know what kind of work the 808th did here in Moresby. You have probably heard what they are going through on the other side of the island right now, fighting like infantry and all. What the Major was trying to tell you is this: The 96th and the 91st Engineers are not going to the Mainland for a break. The 43rd and the 46th Engineers, two white general service regiments—the exact same kind of organization as our own—are going to be relieved for a rest in Australia. And the reason that we aren't going to be relieved is because we (I kept saying *we*) are a colored outfit. The problem isn't a simple one. There are no colored women in Australia, and unfortunately whenever a large colored unit gets in Australia there are fights and other trouble. Now I know that this isn't your fault. I know that you men want to go down there and enjoy yourselves like men, that 99 out of a 100 would stay in line and not cause any trouble. But there are white soldiers down there who don't understand you, who have some funny ideas, and these are the ones who cause the trouble. But there are plenty of white soldiers in Australia—and they can't clean them out just to give you boys a break. It's a mean set-up. But it is one that I can't do anything about, and I don't think you can do anything about it either. So it looks as if the 96th is going to move ahead, and all I can tell you men is to keep a stiff upper lip and be real men.

"I'm sorry that I got off the subject. What I really wanted to talk to you about was this visit this afternoon by these various generals and brasshats. Your work since I have been in A Company has been real good, good enough for any general. Now when you go back to work this afternoon, you are not to follow the instructions that the Major gave you. You are to go to work as usual. You are not to sit around and do nothing until the generals arrive and then put on a good show. You are to go back to work straight on through. And when the generals get around here you are to continue whatever you are doing, the same as if they weren't around at all. You men always do good work, and you don't have to put on any show for a general or anybody else. That's all I have to say, men."

When I turned and walked away, they all stood up and clapped. It made me feel so good to hear them clap at what I had had to tell them that it nearly brought tears to my eyes.

November 19, 1943

Farrar called me on the phone this morning and notified me that the ceremony scheduled for 6:30 would be held at 5:30 instead.

"What ceremony?" I asked.

"What? Do you mean that you don't know anything about it? Well, I want the company out for a parade this evening for me and some of my guests. There will be Colonel Balisario, Commanding Officer of the Second-Fifth Australian General Hospital, and my friend Major Fitzsimons, who, as you know, is a member of the Australian Parliament, and Major Christie, who is in charge of all the beautiful AAWMS on the island. Of course you know her. And perhaps there will be my Royal Australian Navy friend, so-and-so."

"You want the company formed for 5:30? I'll probably have to knock them off from work a little early if you want them dressed properly."

"That's all right," he said. "Knock them off a couple hours early. It isn't often that we have a celebration like this."

He mentioned nothing about the details of the affair; and when I asked him about them, he told me not to worry that I would receive written instructions in ample time for me to make all necessary arrangements. Five-fifteen arrived. No instructions had arrived. The bugler blew first call. The company lined up—all in good-looking khakis, leggins, helmets, rifles; they really looked good. A photographer took some pictures. There was a special service representative present who had been sent out to cover the story. He asked me what it was all about, and I assured him that I didn't know. At 5:20 Sergeant Egleson, who is acting First Sergeant while Smith is on furlough, gave the command "Fall In," and the company lined up. He then turned the company over to the officers. At 5:25 I gave the Company "Right Face" and then for the first time since I left the States I gave the order "Forward March" to an entire company. It felt good to see them step off the way they did. Then I moved up to the head of the column and got that old awkward feeling of marching out in front of everybody. My marching is poor. For some reason I cannot relax the way I should and get into the swing of things. I formed the company in line, and after having them do "Center Dress" gave them "Rest." We were facing the half track, the pulpit from which Farrar was to deliver his sermon. The Major arrived a few minutes after five with his distinguished party. I called the company to attention and reported to him that the company was present.

"Carry On!" he bellowed back.

Company A, 96th Engineers standing in formation before formal review, Port Moresby, November 19, 1943.

I thought to myself, "Carry on with what?" I hesitated a moment, then looked at him for some kind of signal or gesture or order or something. I didn't know what was supposed to be done. He was looking straight ahead. I about faced, gave the company "Parade Rest," then faced the bugler who was standing at the end of the column and nodded to him to sound "Retreat." He hesitated. I made the motions with my lips, "Retreat." He didn't understand. "Sound Retreat!" I ordered.

"Hold it! Hold it a minute," the Major said. "A march is the first thing on the program." I turned around and faced him while he fumbled with a paper on which he had the program written.

"May I have a written copy of the program, sir?" I asked. This was an embarrassing thing. I had to walk up to him and get the program, looked it over, then gave the orders to carry out all the wild ideas that he had devised. After a few selections from the band came his speech.

"We are gathered here today to celebrate several things. First we are to celebrate the second anniversary of the departure from the United States of your beloved Regimental Company, Colonel Derby, and myself. Just two years ago at this time the skyline of San Francisco had slipped beneath the horizon." What a thing to celebrate! His entire speech was devoted to "me, myself, and I." When it was over,

we had Retreat. Then the band played the Star Spangled Banner. I
was so angry that I could have screamed.

"Form the Company in a close column of platoons and bring them
up on line!" he ordered me. I hesitated a moment, tried to figure out
what he wanted. If I had been a good officer, a well disciplined officer,
I would have given an order which would have accomplished what I
thought he wanted, but instead I acted mean, and I sounded back.

"There is no such movement Sir. Would you like me to mass the
company to the front?"

"Yes, that's what I want." Then in a lower voice he told me, "Don't
embarrass me." I believe nearly everyone heard him say that. Then he
gave another speech which was full of tommy rot, and then he read
from the bible, and then he recited poetry. We stood and we stood,
and we heard nothing that we wanted to hear. Then it was over, and
we all said "Thank God." He had all his distinguished guests up for
supper, after which he asked me, "How do you think the men reacted
to my talk?"

"I don't know sir."

"Who censors your mail?"

"I censor it myself."

"What I want you to do is to make an accurate check on the total
number of letters written, the total number of times it is referred to
favorably and the number of times it is referred to unfavorably. I
want you to write down what they have to say — actually copy their
words. And then I want you to turn in to me a report on your
findings."

"That cannot be done, sir. First of all, it is prohibited by Army
Regulations. Secondly it is prohibited by postal regulations. And, sir,
if it weren't prohibited by any regulations, I still wouldn't do it. That
mail is censored for only one purpose — for its military value, to catch
anything that someone might say which he shouldn't say. Those
letters are read by one individual who tries his best not to notice the
name of the writer and who tries to form no opinion of the individual
by what he writes."

"Wow, don't I say the wrong things at times!" he bellowed midst
one of his roaring outbursts of laughter. "I'm learning a lot from you,
Sammy."

"That information, Major, can be gotten another way — through
our monthly intelligence reports. You will find a copy of these reports
at Headquarters. They're under lock and key. In these reports you will
find out pretty well what the men think. I'm sure that some of the
operatives in my company will report on the way the men responded

to your speech, and that will go into the monthly intelligence report. You'll be able to find out all you want to from that report. This system of getting information how the men react toward different things is authorized by the Army and is a vital branch of the Intelligence System of the Army."

November 21, 1943

Farrar's interruptions at Chaplain's Dubra's services today were the last straw. He is going to see some things in next month's intelligence reports that are going to stand his hair on end.

November 26, 1943

I have received some bad news about Dora. She writes that she hasn't menstruated since the baby was born, and that she has been suffering from pains in her right side and has been in the hospital off and on since last April. I still haven't recovered from the shock. I suspected that she wasn't feeling well because she kept nagging me about my being sick, afraid that I was keeping something from her. This was a result of her not telling me the truth about herself. I never knew before how much I loved that little girl. Bud tells me that she probably won't be able to have any more babies. If that is all, it will be all right. I just hope that it isn't anything more serious than that.

December 2, 1943

Farrar is dead. He shot himself through the heart a few minutes after I spoke to him late this afternoon. I went into his office a little past 4 o'clock at his invitation to read a report. I read the report and we discussed it. While I was reading the report he had told Sergeant Cheeks to bring him a pistol cleaning rod, that he wanted to clean his pistol. Cheeks told him that the rods had all been crated but that he would try to find one. The Major told him not to bother. We talked about our forthcoming move, and I told him how Colonel Bruce was trying to gyp us out of one of our graders. Farrar said that he would check into it. He told me that I ought to start crating. He asked me to stay up for supper, and I thanked him but told him that I had a little discipling to do this evening in the company. "I'll be back this evening, Major," I told him "to listen to some of those records you have."

"Sure, come on up," he said. "We're glad to have you any time. And bring some of the other officers along." I got a few papers out the

main office, got in my jeep, and started for camp. By the time I got
back to A Company Farrar was dead on the floor in his office.

December 5, 1943

The irony of the Farrar affair is that I have been appointed investigating officer to determine whether his death occured in line of duty
or not and whether or not it was a result of his own misconduct. I
have gone to the Base Adjutant and tried to shake the responsibility
but I had no luck.

TWELVE

Moving Forward

December 14, 1943–August 19, 1944

December 14, 1943, Port Moresby

Approximately 100 men of the company will sail for Milne Bay on Thursday. I am trying to get a plane ride over there tomorrow so that I can make arrangements at the other end for unloading supplies and setting up a camp. Last night I had my last date with Myrt, and it was swell.

"When are you going home?" she asked. "I've been hearing rumors that they are going to relieve the 96th."

"Naw, they're just rumors. If we move at all, we'll move forward. They can't send engineers home, not with all the work that has to be done over here," I said.

"I don't think I'd want to go home," she said, "not if I had to come back again after a few months. Would you?"

"Would I! I'd take that trip on the worst boat afloat just to be home for 24 hours."

"Yes, I know," she said. "it would be wonderful for you to see your little boy and to see your wife again."

"Myrt, I'd give anything to be holding my wife now the way I'm holding you." When I said that she pulled away a little then relaxed and slid back into my arms.

"Do you love her very much?" she asked.

"I did love her more than anything else I knew. And I know I'll love her that way again when we are together."

"But now?"

"I don't know, Myrt. Sometimes I think I love her only because it is proper for me to continue loving her even though we're separated — more of an obligation than real love. Then there are other times when

I'll lie awake thinking about her in spite of myself until it hurts. She seems more like a person I know in another world. Sometimes she is hard to picture as my wife at all. Other times she is everything in my life. I guess I do love her pretty much after all."

December 16, 1943, Milne Bay

About three weeks ago a memorandum came out stating that certain personnel would be returned to the United States sometime during the month of March of this year. I had to select 18 enlisted men of the company. It wasn't easy. I worked a long time over service records, getting recommendations from the other officers of the company, from the Chaplain, the Regimental Surgeon, and from Sergeant Smith. A few days ago I published the list of recommendations that I sent in. It was like cutting off my hands and legs to recommend the men whom I did. They included my first sergeant and my motor sergeant, the two key enlisted men of the company; and as far as I know they are irreplacable.

December 28, 1943

Dearest Hymie,

You all seem to think that we're going to beat Japan island by island. But you all are wrong. It won't take all that time to beat her. You all have the sad eyes mostly because you can't come home on a leave the way thousands of others are doing and the more you think about it the gloomier your mind gets. But if you ever expect to get anything done, and with good results and still keep sort of happy, you can't possibly be going around thinking the war is going to go on for years. I know I don't know about the real things of war the way you do, but I'm sure that if we're taking years and years to beat Japan, we will have to be the losers. And we won't lose this war, no matter what. I know you hear about all the strikes here at home and about the mess in Washington. But that is the way Americans have always been. And it's a good thing, too. They don't want to be pushed around and taken advantage of like the puppets in Germany and Japan and I know what I'm talking about. It will be over soon sweetheart. Maybe not in 1944, but I bet in 1945 it will. There is no telling what people will do—because this is a peoples' war. And even puppets collapse sometimes. I don't mean to sound as though I'm always hoping something will happen like a miracle or anything but there is no telling what time will bring.

February 2, 1944

Dearest Dora,

Well, little girl, I won't be home as soon as I had hoped for. We received a list of the Colonel's selections the other day. It was a real disappointment. He selected men who were "beaten down." Nobody who was and has been "on the ball" was selected. I was really disappointed in the way Colonel Derby selected the four men, not so much that I wasn't one of them but because he is sending home, not the ones who have done the best work, but those who are no longer — well, let us say — up to par. I guess officers are supposed to be able to take things like this realizing that the "has beens" are the only ones who are to go home and all those who still have a lot of "fight" in them should stay on to the end. But I'm afraid we are human and react the same as enlisted men. We sort of look at going home as a reward for good work. I'm sorry, little girl, that I won't be leaving in March. There will be only one officer in April and I know I won't be that one. And then there won't be any in May. But there still remains seven months in 1944 after that; so there is still plenty of hope of our being together some time this year. I love you, little stinker. Take care of yourself and the baby. As long as you two are all right I won't mind staying over here for another five years.

February 7, 1944

Colonel Derby came in yesterday, and today when I drove him around the various projects we were working on and those which we have already completed, he was amazed at all the work we had accomplished in so short a time. There really was a lot to show him: Two warehouses, 90 feet wide and 400 feet long, both with concrete floors; an oxygen generating building over two hundred feet long; an acetylene generating plant, about half the size of the oxygen plant; a generator building housing a 102 KVA generator; large open storage areas within the depot cleared by our equipment; a third warehouse under construction; another 400 feet x 90 feet concrete slab completed and the forms set for still another 300 feet x 90 feet; pipe lines which served the docks; and a dozen or more little odds and ends. Some of the men were working on a thirty-ton bridge across the Bauli River when we drove up. Everything was clicking fine.

Later on in the day he blurted out with, "What do you think of the rotation policy, Sammy?"

"What do you mean, sir?"

"About going home. What do you think about that?"

"Well, sir, as an army policy, I think it is as good as any other scheme that can be devised. It is vague and indefinite, can be interpreted almost any way a man cares to see it. And I think that is the kind of policy we need, something flexible which can be changed as the situation changes. Anything more specific in its text would be a backward step and soon get us involved in the kind of problems our military leaders had to face in the Civil War and in the Mexican War when soldiers could just quit in the middle of a battle because their time was up."

We talked about this for a while, agreeing with each other in very dull conversation. I knew that he had meant for me to tell him how I felt about the rotation policy personally, but I had avoided committing myself without a direct question from him. Finally he asked me how did I feel about going home.

"I want to be rotated right on back to New Orleans," I told him.

"You mean you want to go home?" he said.

"Of course, sir. Don't you get a unanimous answer from all the officers of the regiment on that question?"

"Not exactly. Avery doesn't want to go home."

"Avery has spent his overseas tour in the big cities of Australia where he is right now. He is living in a civilized part of the world and is probably in line for a promotion. I can think of a lot of reasons why he might want to stay overseas, but none of them—well, let's say the main reason anyway—isn't devotion to the 96th or even devotion to his country."

"I'm a little surprised that you are so anxious to go home," he said.

"Just because I don't lie around and moan about my being home-sick doesn't mean that I don't want to go home. It's just about two years since I have seen my wife and a little over two years since I've seen my folks, and I never have seen my little boy. I've got a lot of reasons to want to go home, sir."

"Yes, I know you have. But we need leaders over here."

"I know that too sir. And don't think for a minute that I would like the idea of leaving the 96th. The 96th means a lot to me. I think I know as much about the men in the regiment as any other officer—if not more. I've been through everything with them—the hard way too, not just paying visits. I've worked with the men when we were under fire. I came ahead of the rest when we moved to New Guinea and took charge of the unloading of our boat. I've seen—well, sir, the 96th does mean a lot to me. And I don't mean a lot of flag waving and parades. But, colonel, my home means more to me. I wish we could get the regiment to go home as a unit."

February 20, 1944

Pete Bojinoff got his foot crushed today loading an air compressor into an LCM [transport ship]. His leg was crushed just above the ankle. At first they thought that he would lose his leg, but this evening while I was at the hospital the nurse pinched his toe, and he said that he could feel it. Circulation has also started in the foot. However, the poor guy will be partially crippled for the rest of his life. It's hell to see these guys get hurt. Just the other day a crew putting up a steel building let the thing fall over and a couple of fellows were killed. The whole trouble is that we are doing real engineering work, and most of these guys are not engineers.

The whole trouble is that the old man isn't going to send me home. He is now sending Nichols, and has suggested that VandenBoom will go next. Willie tells me that I'll never get to go home. "Colonel Derby likes you too much. He wants to make you a major."

Well, I want to be a major, but the price is altogether too high.

February 23, 1944

Dearest Dora,

I just received your letter written on January 31st. You told me about your forthcoming operation. Little girl, I bet I'll be chasing my mail orderly to the post office a dozen times a day until I get a letter from you saying that everything is all right again. I know that worrying over such things will do no good, but I can't help but feel a little anxious. How come the doctors didn't find anything before? Cramps! Constipation! And you with a cyst the size of a grapefruit. It makes me mad. Little girl, I just got to get back home now. I'm tired of—oh it seems that my life just ended in one world and started again in another about two years ago, and I want to get back.

Simms just brought in some more mail. One of the letters was the best I have ever received. Your operation was over and you are all right. I surely hope they found out what the cause of your trouble has been and removed it. Gee, little girl, it's hard to realize that you are going through all these things. I got to talk the old man into sending me home. He wants me to stay. It's my duty, he says. But I'm tired. Sure, it's my duty. I've always given my best, but I'm human. I want my reward. I feel like the fellow who was awarded a great big pie as a prize for winning a pie-eating contest. The old man wants to reward me for good work by promoting me and making me stay on. It's a rough situation, little girl. He is a regular army man. The army is his career. And he thinks he is bestowing a great honor on me. But—oh, I can't tell him: "To hell with it all. I want to go home." Because if I do, I'll destroy his faith in me. And if I don't, I'll stay here. I'm licked either way.

February 24, 1944

The orders came out today on those men who are to return to the states in March. There surely were lots of happy faces.

February 25, 1944

I wrote Dora a letter this evening which was one of the most difficult tasks of my life. I had to tell her that I am not coming home in the near future as I had anticipated when the rotation policy first came out. Now that I have told her, I feel greatly relieved and ready to go back to work in full swing. For the past few weeks I have been torn between duty (and it is my duty to stay over here longer) and my own selfishness to go home. Poor Dora is the one who is really being punished. She has been through all kind of hell since I left her, and she needs me. But tonight I made up my mind. I keep on giving my best: all I've got until Derby decides to let me go. I'm enough of a realist to realize that won't be before 1945. God, take care of Dora and the baby. The rest will be easy for me.

February 25, 1944

Dearest Dora,

This business of going home has upset me, I guess. I have tried to be philosophical about it, to take what comes along, to trust the Colonel in his decisions. But that isn't easy when I hear of your being sick and of Ian's being sick. Now I'm not the kind to worry about such things to the point that they affect my work, but such things do increase my desires to go home. I am torn between what Colonel Derby calls duty and what lies foremost in my heart. Derby doesn't want me to go home—not just yet. He hasn't committed himself, because he is smart enough to know that in this changeable war the situation varies so much that a man's plans today will be impracticable tomorrow. But it is rather obvious that he wants me to be operations officer of the regiment. I am acting operations officer now in addition to my usual duties as company commander. The job calls for a majority, and there is every reason to believe that I will get the promotion—let us say—four or five months after I take over operations as a full time job. You see, honey, it is a little different with an officer and an enlisted man. An officer when he accepts his commission swears that he will defend his nation against all enemies in any manner as directed by his superiors. It is not for us to question why, but for us to do what those over us think is best for the welfare of us all. I admit that many of our officers are no more than glorified corporals and do not have as much leadership as some of my sergeants, but I don't like to classify myself in that group. Now, I could probably approach the Colonel something like this: "Sir, when am I going home? My wife and child aren't well. I have served overseas for two years—faithfully, day after day. I'm tired and I want to go home."

I have thought time and time again of going up to him and putting the question just that way. But I wonder whether it is the right thing to do. I wonder if I were the colonel how I would react to someone approaching me in that manner. I think I would size up the man physically. Then I would ask myself whether or not that man has given his country the best he has in him. I would ask myself whether that man was capable of holding a higher, more responsible position, a position which it is difficult to find men to fill. I would ask myself whether that man was just being selfish and looking out for his own happiness and disregarding our common cause. And I think Colonel Derby would ask himself those same questions. And I think that in me he would see a man whose duty is to stay on, to help keep the 96th the kind of unit it has become or better still, to improve it. And I think that he would feel that I was a coward and a quitter. I'm not sure that it is right to pop the question to him. It is contrary to all the discipline which I have taught my men. For instance, not a single man in my company has approached me on the subject—not a single one! And when I published the list of those who were to return to the 'States, there were seventeen very happy boys, but there were nearly 200 others who, after congratulating the lucky ones, merely shrugged their shoulders and said, "Well, I can sweat it out a little longer," and went back to their routine daily grind.

Don't misunderstand me, little girl. I haven't become a stone-hearted individual, swept off his feet by patriotic ideals. It is a matter of self-pride. Oh, little girl, I can't put these things into words. All I want is to get home and hold you in my arms, and I don't give a damn if the whole world comes to an end. But when I stand out in front of my company, I get a different feeling. I know that every one of those men feels the same as I do. I know that to even admit that I'm tired and want to go home would mean that their work would suffer, that the efficiency of the whole company would decrease. Do you think it is easy to have a man cry to you like a baby about his wife and three children and merely forget himself when the sergeant keeps driving him to work harder? All of that goes on day after day. And I have to be hard—harder than you can imagine. Do you think it is easy to tell a man like that: "Get on your feet and quit squabbling like a child. You're under arrest and will not leave that tent until I tell you to do so."

And then at night I have to prepare papers for a court-martial against him. It isn't easy, little girl, to act that way, especially when I'd like to kneel down beside him and put my arm around his shoulders and help him to his feet. But that policy wouldn't work. Our jobs call for the maximum output of every man in the company, and we cannot tolerate foolishness from several emotionally unbalanced individuals, because we are more or less all in the same boat; and a few spoiled apples will soon spoil the whole barrel.

I know that what I have told you shatters a lot of your dreams of our being together very soon. And I know that hurts you. And nothing hurts me more than hurting you. We will be together soon— maybe not this year but surely next year. But, sweetheart, not even for you would I do anything which I knew was wrong or which would destroy faith and confidence in myself. For if I did, I couldn't love you, for you are too wonderful a person to be loved by a husband who is not at all times striving to reach the perfection which is inherently yours.

February 27, 1944

The men going home in March will leave the company tomorrow morning.

March 5, 1944

Derby got away without my getting to see him. He placed me in command of all 96 Engr. troops here at Milne Bay. Normally that would pep me up, but I'm tired. I don't feel that I want to be over anybody anymore. I wish they would send me home. Frank Eddy is going in June. Bud Engle will probably be transferred South. The old gang of officers is dwindling down to nothing.

March 5, 1944

Dearest Dora,

The boys are having church services in the mess hall now. I surely like to hear them sing. There is so little for them to do around here in the evenings that they hold services almost every night. At our last base we had all kind of recreational facilities, including a ball diamond, volleyball court, and basketball court, but we have been too busy around here to work on anything like that. I haven't been able to even put up a little hut for them to write letters in. About all they can do is sit around and talk or go to movies. That becomes terribly tiresome after awhile, because the films are always breaking, and the sound is no good, and there is too much noise in the audience. Or they can shoot dice—or they can go to church—their own church. That isn't much variety, is it? But they seem to keep reasonably well occupied. I keep their minds off of home by making them work hard, shifting them as soon as their jobs become monotonous. The trouble with shifting men around too much is the fact that one can become pretty damn tired and bored with being shifted around. No joke, every man is an individual case. The cut in our quota of those going home has been a pretty big blow. For April, May, and June together, I'll be able to send only five men. That would mean approximately 20 men in a year. And it would take ten years at that rate to get all the men over here back home. It's kind of rough on these boys who are now starting their third year overseas. Yep, it's hard to believe it, but we're in our third year now. This damn place is becoming a second home to most of us. We reckon that we'll take out our naturalization papers before long. Keep smiling, gal. We'll be together someday—maybe someday, maybe Tuesday. Who knows?

March 7, 1944

I am now Commanding Officer of the Regiment. Special orders are all published "By order of Captain Samuelson." All I need now is to act as Regimental Executive Officer and I will have made the rounds completely. The best part of the whole deal is the fact that I have acted in all these capacities officially: that is, by published order. I think I would like to be a real regimental commander. Hope the war doesn't last that long though.

March 12, 1944

Today was the roughest day I've had in the company ever since the first month I was in it. Sgt. Newton was just in—on the verge of a nervous breakdown. Talked to him a long time. Hope he comes out of it.

March 13, 1944

Sgt. Newton is gone—cracked up completely. I have been with him most of the day. I finally got him into the 17th Station Hospital; but when I left him, they couldn't hold him and he ran away. I picked him up and got him into a cell at the 124th Station Hospital after going through one of the roughest ordeals of my life. I am cracking the whip in the company now, trying to get things running smoothly again, but I am tired. I musn't let myself get tired. I must keep reminding myself that I am these men's leader. I must keep going. Going right!

March 14, 1944

Poor Newton. He is a complete loss now. I am the only one he wants to see and he remains reasonably quiet when I talk to him, but as soon as I leave, he goes wild again. Right now they have the poor boy strapped down in bed—took six huskies to get him down. I'd like to spend more time with him; went to see him twice today, but I can't let the company go to hell because of him.

The first group going home sailed on the *West Point* today, and the rest of the men are just a grand mixture of conflicting moods. I'll keep them straight though.

March 15, 1944

Dear Hymie,

I never for one minute thought of your doing anything but your best, of your throwing up your arms and telling everything to go to blazes because you want to come home. Of course I know it's hard for you being away from home with the hells of war all around you. And of course I know you and I know how wonderful you are. And I know you would never do anything but the right thing—always. And I'm awfully proud of you. It hurts, yes, it hurts so much to know I won't see you for another hundred years, but Hymie, I'm so happy that you are well, and that they aren't sending you home because you're inefficient—in fact as far as your work there is concerned, sweetheart, I know that they will keep you there as long as they can, and even though I know that means that it will be so much longer that we are apart, I only hope that you will always be well and strong as you are now, if not stronger. If you can stand New Guinea and if you can give them your very best always, I can stand it here at home where I am safe with my parents and our baby.

Please don't worry about me, little boy. I'm fine. I'm over the diarrhea and food poisoning I had and in another week or so I should be as strong and as well as I ever was. And we'll always be here waiting for you, Ian and I, all two both of us.

I must take my hat off to your Colonel. I thought at first that he was "touched." (Not that my opinion mattered.) But now I see that it's a good thing there are men like him in the army. And of course I know this is no picnic but a war. And that we must fight it with the best we have in us—especially our best men. And I know that deep down in my heart I'm happy that you are one of them. And I'm awfully proud, too. Of course there is a price we must pay, but you are right, little boy, we will reap our reward in the end. Just take good care of yourself always, and I'll do the same on this side. I guess now I will send you a pair of major's insignia. You will need them by the time you get them. I'll be downtown sometime next week and I'll get them for you. It's funny, but I always knew you would be a major pretty soon and whenever Bluma and I would pass the counter where they lay, I would always stop and say that I ought to get them while they had them because you would be needing them soon, and Bluma would laugh and drag me away and keep telling me to stop bragging so much.

About my operation, Hymie. I'm going to tell you what the doctor told me. He told it to me straight from the shoulder and he didn't spare any punches. My organs were terribly inflamed from the cyst that I had and they had to remove my right ovary. They managed to save my other one. But my tubes have closed and it will be a while yet before they open. If they open: not *they*, I mean *it*, the only tube that will open will be my left one leading to my left ovary. If it opens, then I will menstruate, and if it doesn't then I won't. It may take a while and it might not. You never can tell about those things. And of course I lost a lot of blood during the operation so it will be another two or three months before I menstruate—if I menstruate. But he did tell me that I am young and strong and I have everything in my favor, but that there is a possibility that my tube may never open. And you know what that will mean, little boy. I will never be able to have any more babies. And even the doctor said that I have it all in my favor, and I know he wouldn't tell me that if he didn't mean it, because one thing you can always be sure about is that he will tell you everything and he doesn't mince words.

March 18, 1944

Dearest Dora,

Willie Hering promised me that he would call you up when he got back to the States; so you can expect a phone call from him. My ex-first sergeant promised that he would give you a ring when he got in New Orleans. His name is Lloyd Smith; so don't be surprised when a colored man by the name of Smith calls you up. Smith will be able to tell you a lot about me, and I think you'll enjoy talking to him. You can tell him that I miss his services around here a lot and that most of the men in the company miss him too. Tell him that everything is running along smoothly and that Sergeant Thompson is doing a pretty good job in filling his shoes but that they aren't completely filled yet. I am going to a party tonight at one of the hospitals. My newest flame is Chris. She is 36 years old, one of the other nurses tells me, but Chris hasn't told me her age, and I haven't asked her; so I don't know. She comes from Massachusetts; and although she is a "little" older than I am, we have had some pretty good times together. Well, little girl, I can't think of anything else to write about. I love you. I don't know how I can prove it. I've often thought of a way that I can demonstrate it, but I reckon you'll just have to take my word for it until I get back home. Once I get back home to you, it will be an easy matter to prove.

March 21, 1944

Dearest Dora,

I never knew that I could learn to love a bunch of negroes the way I do the boys in my company. I guess the word love isn't the right word. But I've got to stick by them. I've got to see that some of them get to go home. I've got to keep them from breaking up. Every time one of them cracks mentally (and they do every now and then) I feel guilty that I haven't done all I should have. Perhaps I am flattering myself when I think my presence among the men is a big factor, but when I look over the facts since I have taken over the company I cannot help feeling that my egotism is unjustified. Not one life has been lost. There has been only special courts martial cases. Our engineering work has been something of which we are all proud. The men are reasonably cheerful; and although there have been a few psycho cases, their health and morale has remained high. The men like me. I know they do. And they do what I tell them without a moment's hesitation more because they respect me as a man than as an army officer. These aren't just my ideas. They are things which others have told me. They are the reasons Colonel Derby told me, which means that I cannot go home just yet. Honey, I just can't junk them. Yes, sometimes I feel like telling them that two years of New Guinea is enough for any man, and I'm tired, and I want to go home; but little girl, this is all bigger than you and I. I know it's hard to take this attitude. I have to keep repeating it to myself over and over again to be sure that I believe it. It is a lot harder for you than it is for me. But it isn't easy for me either. I love you. I need you. But if we can't be together for some time yet, I also need your telling me that you understand and that eventually everything will be all right again.

March 22, 1944

A swell party at our place this evening. We really had fun. Unless Chris was bluffing, she had one of the best times of her life. On the way home she told me: "Oh, Sam, you're precious. I wouldn't want to give you up for anything in the world." When I took her down a few notches and told her to cut out the jive, she said, "No joke, Sam, you are priceless. I didn't know there were people like you."

March 25, 1944

I wish our conversion into a construction battalion would happen already. This business of running a company when you know that you will lose it soon is rough.

March 26, 1944

What a drunken brawl we had tonight in celebration of Don's departure to the 857th Engineers. I started drinking around three and didn't quit until around 10:30. I must have put away over a quart by myself; and Chris wasn't far behind me. We are supposed to have another party Tuesday night, but I am going to break my date for that one. Too much is too much.

April 3, 1944

Dearest Hymie,

I had a good conversation with Ethel this past week—you know I really like her. I surely enjoyed talking to her. She told me she wrote you that she didn't think you should write me about all the nurses you go out with, and that if she were me she would resent it. And she asked me how I really felt about it. I told her that it did feel sort of "funny" to hear you tell me about your "new flames" but that I didn't say anything because I understand and that I'd rather have you tell me about them than not. And she let me see the letter you wrote her telling her how good and understanding I was and all. You made me sound pretty wonderful. I hardly recognized myself. You are awfully sweet. It's not often that I hear you praise me these days. One reason is because you're not here—or didn't you know?

April 3, 1944

We can't keep the nurses away. I was all comfortable this evening with a book and a pipe when Mike and Tony drop in with dates, and along with them came Minnie. Well, I had to talk to her and take her home. This place is getting too many women.

April 7, 1944

The first good date Chris and I had together was one evening about six weeks ago when she invited me to a party that the nurses were giving at the Staging Area. It was terribly warm that evening, and the small "dance hall" was packed. I had brought a quart of gin along with me, and Bud Engle had brought some G.I. [ethyl] alcohol. We left the crowded hut before we had even tried to dance or to get a drink. One drink led to another. We never did go back to the hut. When the gin was gone, we drank the alcohol; and when the alcohol was gone, we drank some black looking stuff which Chris called "enbalming fluid."

April 8, 1944

We had a nice retreat ceremony this evening. The men looked good. They have been doing good work lately too.

Ian at Audubon Park, New Orleans, winter 1943.

Ian with his Aunt Ethel (Samuelson Midlo) at Henderson's Point, Mississippi, summer 1944.

April 9, 1944

Dearest Dora,

This morning we had Easter services in our new recreation building. We had just completed the building yesterday morning, and I had a squad of men install benches and decorate the interior with palm leaves yesterday afternoon. It looked very beautiful this morning. Chaplain Dubra dedicated the new building to all the men just before his sermon this morning. When I looked around at them all, I couldn't help feeling happy. The men sat in orderly rows inside a comfortable building. The benches were nothing fancy — just some planks resting on the top of some half-sections of corrugated culvert pipe. But they had on clean clothes. Nearly the whole company was present. They sang the hymns beautifully and, little girl, you have never heard hymns sung right until you hear these boys sing. They put real meaning in it.

The Base Engineers Office called just before dinner with an emergency job, but I went out to look at it and convinced them that it could wait until tomorrow; so I didn't have to break up the holiday for even a single man. The boys brought some negro Red Cross girls up for dinner, and we had a delicious meal: fresh pork, potato salad, pie. Some of them were out playing baseball, others out playing volleyball. Our new recreation hall was full of laughter.

But then came the best part of the whole day. When I walked into my office about an hour ago, I saw on my desk two letters from you. One was an answer to the letter I had written you in which I tried to explain why I had to stay overseas longer. How can you understand? I don't believe another woman could! To get a letter from you in which you tell me that you do understand and that I'm doing right — thanks, darling. There isn't much more than I can tell you but thanks. It would drive me mad to hear you cry about the situation. Little girl, do you know what such words as "give them your best always" and "I can stand it here at home where I am safe with my parents and our baby" mean to me? All the sermons on hope given by all the priests and ministers in the world today could not equal your words in giving me inspiration. I'll always remember those words.

And little girl, about your operation — don't feel disappointed if you can't have any more children. I've never seen our boy, but he must be wonderful. He will take the place of all six that we had hoped to have. And you will have more babies too. I know you will. Oh, but little girl, right now that doesn't matter to me. You are the important thing. Take care of yourself. And take care of Ian. And don't cut his hair 'til I get home. I won't tell you that I love you, because anybody can say that; and man has never invented the words which would express the way I feel about you.

April 10, 1944

We have been alerted to move again, probably to Oro Bay for a rendezvous with other elements of the regiment before our being converted into a construction battalion.

April 13, 1944

Looks like we'll move sooner than I thought.

April 14, 1944

We're continuing our engineering work and crating up a bit on the side.

April 16, 1944

Jimmy King assigned F Company and takes command.

April 16, 1944

Dearest Dora,

Hey, I haven't even told you about the birthday party I had last Tuesday. No joke, little girl, it was beautiful. It was all pretty much of a surprise. I invited Chris over for supper, and I knew that Kipp and Mike would have dates for supper too. But I didn't know that there would be a regular banquet. Kipp had gone out and got fresh pork, and Pepper (our cook) made some delicious salads. The mess sergeant cooked some extras for the occasion. There was enough food to feed a crowd of forty. And there was almost that many people in all. Some Negro Red Cross girls presented me with a great big pink-icing birthday cake—candles and all. And nearly everybody brought me some kind of present. They were silly little things, but they made me feel happy. I really felt happy at the party. It seemed that everybody had nice things to say to me. The Chaplain made a nice little talk about me, and everybody drank a toast to me. It surely made me feel funny—sort of embarrassed, but sort of good too. We had plenty to drink afterwards, and everybody got tight. And me especially.

I had a stinky dream about you and the baby the night before last. I dreamed that I came home (It seems that I always dream that) and when I saw Ian I was so happy that I started to cry. You got mad. You asked me what was I crying about.

"Don't you like him?" you said. I tried to tell you of course I like him, but you wouldn't listen.

"If you don't like him, then I'll make him go away," you said. And with that you threw a glass of what looked like water on him, and he started to shrink. I grabbed him in my arms, but he kept on shrinking until I could hold him in the palm of my hand.

"Do something!" I kept shouting at you, but you just looked on as if you didn't care. And then he vanished altogether, and I started crying like a baby.

"What are you crying about now?" you asked, "He's gone now. I thought you didn't like him." I was so choked-up that I couldn't talk, and you got mad and told me that I ought to go back to New Guinea, that all I was was a big cry-baby. And then you walked out the room. Gosh, did I feel empty. And was it good when I woke up and found out that it was all a dream. Don't think I like to have dreams like that too much, even though it does feel good when I wake up.

I would like to command the 96th myself someday. It is a good outfit. Most of the men are wonderful. But right now I have my hands full running a company, and shouldn't be worrying about how a regiment should be run.

April 18, 1944

A peculiar wire from General Frank today. He wants to know how many men will be eligible to go on furlough between 1st May and 15th July. Can't understand significance of the wire.

April 19, 1944

Spent the day with F Company. King seems to be in pretty good spirits. Had a date with Chris this evening.

April 20, 1944

For the first time last night Chris talked about herself. She was supposed to have sailed yesterday morning for Finchaven [Finschafen], but there was a delay.[1]

April 21, 1944

Chris told me a lot more stuff this evening. She was a Catholic, now has no religion, speaks Jewish, likes the religion. Gave me two St. Christopher medals, said they were her *mazoozie*. She used to go with a Jewish Doctor in New York.

April 22, 1944

I have given up job as C.O. of A Company. I have appointed Kipp as C.O. even though Paulson ranks him. F Company should start loading tomorrow or Monday. They quit work at noon today. King is doing a good job over there.

April 23, 1944

Chaplain Scott, our new regimental Chaplain gave a wonderful sermon this morning. We're going to miss Dubra however when he leaves. He has done a wonderful job as chaplain.

Had an all day date with Chris. I think we're getting too involved. The whole situation is in my hands and it's hard to resist.

April 24, 1944

F Company starts loading at one o'clock. Still no ship assigned for troops on this side. Got a letter from Myrt Mellon from Moresby. She surely is a good old gal. I'd like to see her again. But I've been missing Dora. This incomplete satisfaction I get from these women makes me miss Dora more.

April 25, 1944

Chris and I still going out. I ought to break this up. It's going to lead to something I don't want to do. She seems so appreciative though that—oh, I don't know. I wish she would fight against me. It would be easier.

April 27, 1944

A crazy wire today. 96th has first priority over all troops for leaves. As many men as want to can go. I don't like that. It means little chance of real relief. It's raining again.

April 28, 1944

F Company leaves for Oro Bay. Heavy rains all day long. A frantic wire from General Frank cancels all furloughs, all leaves for 96th. That has some significance—but what? B & C Companies are in Brisbane.

May 1, 1944

Chris wants me to go to Australia with her on leave in August. I told her that it would be too cold then. She said she would wait until November or December, when it would be warm. I told her that I don't plan that far in advance.

May 2, 1944

It started raining Thursday. It rained all day long. And all that night. Friday morning it was still raining—a steady monotonous downpour. The earth became saturated with water. It could absorb no more. Every drop of water that fell from the heavens flowed over the surface of the ground. Friday night came the first guba [typhoon]! Wind and rain! Tons and tons of water on every acre. Thousands of tons of water came pouring down the rivers and creeks that no longer could confine within their channels all the runoff. And along with the water came trees and logs, crated supplies. Trucks were washed off the road. Telephone lines were swept away. Bridges were torn from their anchorages. In a few hours nature had caused more damage than the Japanese were able to cause in two years' bombings. Cut off from other engineer units and headquarters by wide rivers where bridges were the day before, we set to work Saturday morning "opening" up the road. It rained all that day. Saturday night another guba struck. This time there was less rain, but the wind was terrific. The 17th and 18th Station Hospitals were laid level with the ground. Trees snapped like tooth picks. There were broken legs and broken backs. People drowned. Communications were still down. But communications were not necessary. The engineers knew what their jobs were. We started out from our camp and worked on the main road in both directions, clearing the debris, keeping the road open to light vehicles.

When Colonel Wallander, the Base Commander, came out the first thing Sunday morning he found that he could cross the Gadia Rani, which we had bridged through the town. He was pleased. The main road was open for two miles on both sides of our camp. The bridging of the Gadia Rani was an accomplishment worth while writing about in detail. This river had been bridged by a pile-trestle bridge, sixty feet long. The guba had caused a solid log jam on the upstream side. The water, unable to flow under the bridge because of the log-jam, broke around the ends of the bridge and started washing away the approaches. The water was widening rapidly both gaps. The jam was solid against the bridge.

May 3, 1944

Kipp and I had dates with Terry and Chris Saturday night, but because of the storm that had hit the night before and because we worked all that night repairing bridges which had been washed out, we didn't keep those dates. We didn't even attempt to call them, but we knew that they would understand the situation. The next evening things were pretty much under control. Although all the bridges had not been repaired, the flood waters had subsided sufficiently that those streams which could not be crossed on bridges could be forded. Chris and I wandered up to my tent, took off our muddy shoes and lay down on my cot. We took out cigarettes and smoked.

It was still raining. Everything was wet, even the bed. I unbuttoned her shirt, then my own, rolled over on top of her, kissed her. I coughed.

"What's the matter, honey? Catching a cold?" she said.

"Nah, just smoking too much."

We kissed and held each other tight and rolled and rocked. I found myself worked up pretty much. Then I rolled over off of her.

"Chris?"

"Yes, Sam?" There was a pause while I took a deep drag on the cigarette.

"Do you want to?" I asked. She didn't answer. I said no more. We smoked lying on the cot side by side holding hands.

"Sam?"

"Yeah?"

"You know I'd love to, but do you, Sammy?"

There was a slight hesitation. "Yes, Chris, I do."

We both sounded strangely calm.

"Whenever you want to, Sammy. I want to. We've fought this long enough. I don't think it's wrong. I—oh, I can't resist any more."

"Chris, we ain't done nothing yet. And I won't do a thing unless you want me to. I've gone over two years without it, and I can keep going."

She threw her arms around me and kissed me. She was trembling.

"I've gone over three years. I don't want to. But I want you to. I want to be with you. Sam, how could this happen—all in such a short time?"

"There ain't nothing happened, Chris," I said.

"I mean how could I want so much to happen in such a short time." A long pause, "Will you hate me if we—"

"I'm no child, Chris. I know what to expect."

"Believe me, Sammy, I've never let this happen before. And here I'm consenting to it—in cold blood."

"I wouldn't want you to consent to it any other way. I've thought about this a lot, Chris. It's been on my mind all week. But I don't want to do it in the heat of passion. I love my wife. I don't want to hurt her. Yet, I want this too. I know what I'm doing, Chris. All I want to be sure of now is that you want to do it too."

"I do, Sammy. But promise you won't hate me. Promise me that."

"I won't hate you, Chris."

We lay perfectly still for a long time. "We won't do it tonight, will we, Chris? And I'm muddy and tired. Tomorrow?"

"Uh-huh. Tomorrow," she said.

"Neither of us will resist any more?"

"No."

And last night it happened. It was wonderful.

May 4, 1944

Chris left for Finchaven today. I didn't get to see her, but Terry gave me a note from her this evening:

Dear Sam,

So sorry to leave so suddenly but know you will understand. Would have loved to have had one more evening with you—shall miss it all, even you, you know I mean it. Will drop you a line as soon as I arrive at my destination. Am not saying goodbye, but So long,

Love, Chris.[2]

May 4, 1944

Another date with Barbara. I miss Chris.

May 6, 1944

Instead of going to Oro Bay, we are going to Sydney. I don't know when however.

May 7, 1944

I took Holy Communion this morning. For over two years I have attended rather regularly Chaplain Dubra's Sunday morning services, but I had never taken Communion when he gave it. This morning, for the first time in my life I did. It made me feel strangely happy.

May 8, 1944

The thing in life which man believes will bring him true happiness is rarely gained yet the substitute which he accepts for it often becomes the real thing and the real thing only a dream.

May 9, 1944

Orders today to start loading on the *Bulch*. I found that that ship was going to Oro Bay.

"We're going to Sydney" I told them at troop movement office.

"We have no orders to that effect." We argued, then agreed to send a wire to CG USASOS [Commanding General United States Services of Supply] for some kind of decision. What a messed-up mess.

May 15, 1944

Took inventory of letters I have accumulated since overseas. There were 1,104 in all—460 from Dora and 644 from other people. I destroyed the 644 and started through Dora's destroying all but one from each month. I got as far as up to the time Ian was born. It was like living in another world reading all those letters. I had a half foot locker full of them and almost had to get rid of them. Don't know why I was saving them in the first place.

May 16, 1944

Derby arrived this evening. He was well pleased with the way things were running in general and told me to write up my recommendation for promotion. I told him I hadn't been a captain nine months yet; so he said as soon as the time is up to write up the papers. Hope he doesn't change his mind between now and the 4th of next month. He is sailing with us to Oro Bay in the morning.

May 25, 1944

Derby left for the mainland today. He is going to get Thomas up here right away and try to expedite the movement of the remaining 96th Engineers elements to this base. Then we can start reorganizing properly.

May 29, 1944

Dearest Dora,

I'm teaching some regular courses in surveying now during the mornings. It is part of our training program. It surely is hard to teach men surveying when you have to teach them basic arithmetic first. For two hours this morning I went over long division and decimals. They are eager to learn, but many of them only went to fifth or sixth grade and haven't had any use of arithmetic since they quit school. A fine war I'm fighting over here when my biggest problem is to teach some boys how to multiply and divide. That's the way it goes I guess.

I love you, Dora. Especially when I'm not particularly busy like now and when there are no other women around do I miss you. That isn't a flattering thing to say, but it's the truth. When I'm really busy or when I meet up with some nurses I don't miss you half as much. But the funny thing is that when the nurses are gone I don't miss them ever, but I always miss you.

June 1, 1944

Dearest Dora,

I got a letter from you yesterday that you wrote on May 7th. You told me that you were getting over a case of diarrhea and food poisoning. Gosh, little girl, it seems that everything is catching you. What's the matter, honey—aren't you taking care of yourself? I wish I were home.

June 2, 1944

I always thought that I had the kind of patience which would enable me to teach anybody anything, but I have changed my mind. It is truly a difficult task teaching surveying to these men.

June 4, 1944

Scott is doing a good job as chaplain. He isn't the speaker that Dubra is, but he makes the services attractive.

June 5, 1944

I feel in a better mood today than I've felt in a long time. Surveying class went off fine, and I have a strange feeling that I'm going home this year.

June 6, 1944

Thomas arrived today. We are not going to be converted into a construction battalion. That's definite—for the time being anyway. Derby gave Thomas instructions to make Knight executive officer and me operations officer and to put in my recommendation for promotion. My premonition last night was all wet. Well, I'll be happy to be wearing a gold leaf. After that I want to go home.

June 7, 1944

It is difficult to build up a good operations section. There is so much to be done. We want to let as many men as possible go on leave. We want to have an intensive training program. We have so damn much work to do! And we don't want to overwork the men during the rehabilitation program. It is an impossible thing to accomplish.

June 11, 1944

Dearest Dora,

I bet there was a lot of excitement (and to a certain extent rejoicing) back home when you all learned of the Allied landings in Europe. It is amazing how unconcerned the men over here responded to the news. Of course there is nothing that any of us here can do, but you'd think there would be some sort of excitement. But there wasn't. A letter from a man who went home on the rotation policy (a letter which proved that it *is* possible to get home from this place) caused more excitement and rejoicing among the men than did the recent landings.

June 12, 1944

Thomas told me today that as a staff officer, I stink. I laughed at his face and merely answered, "I think I'm pretty good. I like me." He bellowed back that he didn't care what I thought.

"Good staff officers are supposed to think," I said, "and relieve the C.O. of some of his burden. I believe you lose sight of that and expect me to say 'yes, sir' to all your ideas." He laughed back at me.

June 13, 1944

In addition to my duties as S-3 and teaching classes in surveying and drafting, I am teaching classes (along with Chaplain Scott) in reading and writing. And now Thomas has made me T. J. A. [trial judge advocate] on our special court. I raised hell about it and asked "Why don't you give it to some 'new' lieutenant?" Half sarcastically he told me, "This court is to be a *model* court for others to learn from and I want the best man for T. J. A. on the court."

June 14, 1944

Enjoyed an afternoon at the beach. Am getting a lot of exercise and feeling swell. I am teaching a number of men how to write their names. It isn't easy.

June 17, 1944

The parade this morning went off fine. The men are terribly restless and unhappy. Thomas is riding the company commanders too closely, trying to run their companies himself. It is an unwise policy and I fear will lead to trouble.

There was a lot of mail today. On May 15th Dora received a letter I wrote her the day after Chris and I had had our little affair. I don't know why I wrote Dora right away, but my mind was on her and I came as clean with the whole story as I possibly could without involving someone else's name. The answer that Dora wrote was— well, I'll quote several paragraphs of it which pertain to the way she felt:

> And about your going out with women—well, really at first when I heard about it it did sound "funny" to me—I can't explain how I felt—but really I can't and never could imagine you doing anything "bad." And do you think for one minute that that is what is bothering

me—about your being "unfaithful" to me as you put it? How can you know me so little, you stinker? All I ask is for you to come home to me—for you to keep loving me. All I want is a chance to see you again, to hold you close to me—to make you happy again. That seems to me to be the most important thing. And I understand, really I do—I never know quite what to say when you tell me about this woman—or that, but I do understand about them. And as far as your doing anything "bad," I don't know what you mean. What you may think is bad, I might not. And really no matter how bad you are I don't think you could do anything worse than not come out in the open with me.

You're such a child, Hymie, that I feel as though I have to mother you more than anything else. You've had it hard—all your life you've had to face things that were heartbreaking and you've been bruised up pretty well. But you aren't as hard-boiled as you think you are. Just wait until you meet your baby, until you see him smile and he puts his little arms around you and puts his little nose close to yours and says "Di deee. Di deee" You'll feel just like a human being again. You'll feel alive.

That was Dora's first reaction. At any rate that is what she wrote me. Of course I could read between the lines and see that the letter had been written by a person who had been hurt by someone she loved dearly. Poor kid didn't know what to write. She put up a wonderfully brave front.

On the evening of the 22nd of May, just one week after Dora wrote this letter, Papa sat down and wrote me a letter. It was one of those rare occasions on which he found himself alone in the house. The first type-written page of his letter was about the dogs, the boat, tobacco, different people. Then suddenly he went on like this:

Now Hymie I want to tell you something, yet I do not know how to get to it, without embarrassment. I know just how you feel, or at least I try to think I do. Being away from home, relatives and friends, your lot is not a pleasant one, and it is but natural that you must have an outlet to your feelings, and are bound to enjoy the company of women especially when for a long time you did not see the sight of any white woman. I think that you are entitled to any enjoyment you can find out there especially if same does not violate the moral laws. While I do not favor immorality in any case, yet no matter what you do that may cause jealousy I would not write to Dora about it. The reason I am writing you this is that Dora came here crying last week and showed us a letter which you wrote her, and all women more or less are jealous. Things are none too pleasant for her. Hymie, it all boils down to this: try as far as possible not to write to Dora anything that may cause her to lessen her opinion of you, and by all means try and get whatever little pleasure you can while you are out there. If you think it is none of my business, I don't blame you, but believe me I am trying to suggest that which I think is best for all concerned. Do not write Dora anything I wrote in this letter as I do not want her to think that I am interfering in your and her affairs.

The next morning (May 23rd) Dora wrote another letter. In all, it was a normal, pleasant, enjoyable letter, except for one paragraph near the end.

Well, bye for now, stinky. I don't have any news to write about. Oh, Hymie, I'm so tired of writing you. I wish you were home. What can I put down on paper that could make you understand how lonesome I am for you? Have you changed so much—have you gotten so hard that you won't even—oh, no, I won't cry all over the place, little boy, it won't do any good. It surely won't move you any. You are probably good and hardened to things like this. You've built a strong wall around your heart and your mind and I have done my best to try to find a way in. Now it seems as though you are softening, but I think it's just my imagination. Anyway I'm not going to risk getting hurt any more than I have been already.

Eleven days later she wrote another letter that had bad news in it:

And guess what happened to me yesterday? I took Ian downtown. I started to cross the street. Ian wanted me to carry him. I stooped down and started to pick him up when something popped in my back, and down I went. I must have passed out because when I came to there was a whole crowd of people around me, mostly soldiers. When the ambulance came they saw my scar from my operation and so I had to tell them about that. After about two hours they decided that nothing was wrong. But don't think that I didn't enjoy it all. It's been so long since a man has held my hand, or rubbed my head or anything.

It isn't hard to see that Dora has been under a severe strain. Having the baby while her husband was away made her somewhat of a hero, and I really feel that it did her a lot of good. Dora is still a child. Living with her mother and confiding in her has helped matters I guess; but on the other hand, her mother must think I am a scoundrel, although I have no proof of this, and must tell Dora how cruel I am to her. Ethel has hinted at this in her letters. At any rate, Mrs. Reiner, especially after Dora shows her letters in which I write that I am going out with other women, must tell her daughter some pretty awful things about me. And I imagine Dora must side with me. I can picture the arguments—unpleasant to say the least. Another thing that is hard on Dora is seeing other girls' husbands who went overseas after I did come home to their wives. Her own illness and the fact that she probably cannot have another child are tough blows too. Her faithfulness and love for me torture her too. Oh, it's a rotten set-up. I knew what I did when I did what I did with Chris. I could have done without it. I am rather cold sexually. But I wanted to—more just for the hell of it than for the desire. At the time I didn't feel that it was morally wrong, nor do I feel that way now. But how does Dora feel? She can't fool me by telling me the things she wrote in that first letter. I know her too well. Perhaps the best thing for me to have done was to tell her nothing—or better still, to have done nothing. No, that would not have been best. I enjoyed it. I'd do it again if I had the opportunity. It would have happened many times over if Chris had not gone away after the first time. I have been so restless here lately that I have even given serious thought to going down to Australia with Chris and live with her for a couple of weeks. Of course it would not have to be Chris. Myrt would be as good; so would Peggy—or even some woman I have never met. No, I don't want that either. I don't know what I want. I want to get back to Dora. But how? Men are returning so slowly from this theatre. I've tried to get on the rotation list, but the old man won't place me on it.

June 18, 1944

Dearest Dora,

Your letter wasn't a happy one. I know how it is when all the other girls you know have their husbands at home. Over here hardly anyone gets to go home. I can remember when we were first sent to New Guinea we thought that it would be for only six months.

"That's all that a man can take," we were told. But now we are in our 26th month, and there is no relief in sight for most of us. Darling, I want to go home, more than anything I can think of. But remember that nearly every man in the 96th is in the same boat. And only a few can return every month. There are hundreds who deserve going home more than I do. There are men who have lost their wives and children and suffered things that thank God I've been spared. There are men who have suffered themselves physically, who are only part of the man that went overseas. Those are the men who have to return first. I'm not trying to be heroic; and if I had the chance to go home, I'd say the hell with the rest and jump the first boat or plane going that way. But the people over me know what the score is, and they are the ones who decide who will go and who will stay. We can all present our cases. My case (yours and mine) is a weak one compared to the others. To you and me it seems like the all-important one, but, sweetheart, it is only one of many. We just have to wait.

I'm beginning to worry that you don't care what happens to you. I've seen the same thing happen to men over here. They get tired of waiting, tired of being patient, and they take an attitude of indifference. Little girl, do you realize how things would be if I took that attitude? We owe it to ourselves and each other to take care of ourselves. Oh, I know I'm just beating my gums. You can't help those things. But please be careful.

June 19, 1944

Received some pictures of Dora today. She has lost a lot of weight and doesn't look at all well. But she looked frail and beautiful, and I miss her like hell. Also got a long letter from Chris. She says she misses me and a lot of other junk. I answered her letter with a rather cold reply. I don't want to be rough on her but I don't feel like having any more to do with her.

June 24, 1944

The surveying classes are doing swell. The men really like the work.

June 26, 1944

Dearest Dora,

I have a sad-eyed letter here that you wrote on May 8th. You told me that before you were going to be operated on, you thought about writing a letter telling me to find a good mother for Ian when I remarried. Isn't it a funny thing how people want to do something like that. I remember I did the same thing once when I was sent on a mission where I might have caught mine. Before I left, I wrote a letter to you and put it in my foot-locker. Its sealed envelope is still there. That was nearly two years ago. I don't remember what I wrote, but it was something to the effect that I wanted you to remarry and so on. At the time I was very solemn and serious about the whole thing. I bet we'll laugh when we open the letter and read it after I get home.

June 29, 1944

My operations section is developing into an efficient, small, flexible team. The few men I have all seem to like the work. They are giving me their best and I think they're getting a lot out of their work.

July 13, 1944

Derby is back. He plans to have me take over H & S. Holmes says the Sixth Army squashed my promotion because of my age. I'm disappointed. I don't think Derby tried to push it hard enough. I'm tired and disgusted. Marie called and wants me to come over tomorrow night. Damn it—she is an escape from reality—wonderful while it lasts. But it isn't what I want or need.

July 14, 1944

Dearest Dora,
No joke, little girl, you have no idea how fascinating most of this work is. I would really like to command a regiment some day, but I hope I never do, because the only way that could come to pass would be if the war dragged on for another eight or nine years or there were another war. And I hope that neither one of those ever happens.

July 23, 1944

Around two o'clock in the morning last Wednesday, the Old Man had called an emergency meeting of the staff, the two battalion commanders, and the H & S Company commander. We had been alerted to move forward and were to move out within a week's time. Two Liberty ships had been allocated to the 96th for the move. One was on its way down from Finchaven, the other--well, they didn't know just where it was. I yawned, thought to myself that it was the usual army racket of "hurry up and wait." We stayed up most of the remainder of the night, getting information about our boats and so on. Before going to bed, Derby told me that in addition to all the work H & S had to do, he wanted me to prepare for him a list of the names of all the men I wanted to have transfered into my company. "I want your company ready to go into action just as soon as we land," he said.
The Old Man has put me in command of H & S because as he put

it, "After considering all the officers in the Regiment, I think that you are the best qualified."

It is a mean assignment and I told him that I thought it was pretty nasty, and that the job could be accomplished only if I received cooperation from every officer and man in the Regiment. He told me to prepare a report on what I would need in order to do the job. I did so and he approved it without exception. It required the physical transfer of 84 men into H & S. He wanted to know the names of the 84 men I wanted transferred into the company.

"I want those men transferred tomorrow," he said. "I beg your pardon, I forgot that we are already in the morning. I want them transferred today."

July 26, 1944

Latitude 1059' S, Longitude 138058' E. At dawn on the 25th we saw a large flotilla of ships lying ahead, anchored in a naturally sheltered bay. It was an impressive site. We learned, as most of us had already guessed, that it was Talmahera Bay, scene of our recent landings against the formerly held Japanese base of Hollandia. There was no evidence of any recent heavy fighting, such as one still finds at Buna. We lay at anchor in Talmahera Bay all day yesterday. In the late afternoon we formed a moderate size convoy, including three LCIs and one LST.[3] Most of the convoy consisted of liberty ships with a rather small Naval escort, especially when the type of waters we had to pass through is considered. We traveled throughout the night, and this morning found us in sight of another base. This base has no name. It is located down the coast from Sarmi, which the Japanese still hold. Just off the shore is the island of Wakde, where the Japanese built an airdrome some time ago. We have destroyed many of their planes on this strip, but the Nips retaliated recently, after our capture of the strip, and destroyed quite a number of ours. This morning we counted fifty B-24's take off the strip and head on up the coast of New Guinea. The base—or rather, our anchorage—was attacked allegedly by three submarines this morning. Whether three enemy submarines were in the area or not I do not know, but it was exciting to watch our destroyers skirting through the waters dropping depth charges. If submarines were in the area at all, they did not surface, nor did they fire any torpedoes. The shore is apparently filthy with Japs. We hold only a small beachhead and it seems that we are making no attempt to expand it. We have a strong perimeter set up around the beachhead. The Japs, cut off from outside supplies, have been trying to break through, and about half an hour ago we witnessed from the deck of our ship a hot skirmish. It was just about dusk and the sight of the flying tracers in all directions was—well, I don't know the proper word—perhaps "thrilling" is the best I can think of. Throughout the day there has been spasmotic firing on the shore. Every now and then the artillery opens up. The shore is not a welcome looking spot, not green and peaceful like Talmahera. Here the trees are stripped from exploding shells. It is believed that the enemy has more troops than we have in the area, but his are so dispersed and so inadequately supplied that they will have a most difficult time trying to take from us the beachhead which we have established. We will be going ashore as soon as there is enough ground for us to camp on. The area we hold now is too small to accommodate us. In the meantime, we will sit out on the water and watch the show.

July 28, 1944

Dear Hymie,

Hello again, honey. I am in New Orleans today. I came in by myself and I left the baby at the Point with Ethel. I got the picture you took with Marie Isaac. Honestly, little boy, you look wonderful. You don't know how happy I am seeing you laughing and having a good time like that. You just don't know. A few days ago I was at Ethel's house and she let me read a letter you wrote her about two months ago. It was so awful. You wrote about how one fellow went nutty and kept crying like a baby, and how another one killed himself by shooting himself through the heart, and you sounded so down in the dumps that I really hadn't been able to get it out of my mind—until now. I know you could come home if you developed a case of nerves, but for heavens sake, sweetheart, I don't want you home like that. I'd rather have you out in New Guinea laughing and cutting up and being nicknamed Euphoria than have you home a nervous wreck today. And I like this nurse you have out there. She really looks cute and all you say she is. Tell her I love her because she keeps you so cheerful.

August 2, 1944

Dear Hymie,

Herman just asked me to ask you if it was all right with you if he and Ethel adopted Ian. Ethel really is crazy about him. We are watching his growth by the number of little pompons that are off the curtains. As he gets taller there is one less pompon. When you look at him and say, "Oh, look what you're doing to Nonnee's curtains," he just says real quick, "I fikth it," and he pulls another one off. If he does anything destructive at all he right away says, "I fikth it." And sometimes he does. Ethel always corrects him by saying, "No, Yonnee, we don't do that, or the other." You should hear her saying, "No, Yonnee, we don't pull the puppy by the tail." Or "No, Yonnee, we don't carry the puppy by the neck." And he sings, "Wock a bye baybee on dee dtee dtop, wan dee wa-bllothes dee baybee wi-wock. Wan dee bow blakthes de kwadle wi-fall and down witom babee kwadle and alllll." And he goes around all day singing, "Tiddell tidoll tumplind," and anything else that comes to his little mind. He also shuts off the icebox and defrosts it and lets all the water run in the meat. And he also takes a rag and wipes the woodwork with it. He is very mess conscious. If one speck of food drops on the table he says, "Mess, oooh, mess. I fikth it," and he picks it up or wipes it up. Isn't he wonderful?

August 2, 1944, Sarmi, New Guinea

Our ship, the *Wallace* is nearly unloaded. So is the *Hough*. Two other liberties carrying additional supplies for the Regiment have arrived but as yet have not been discharged. There are no docks at this place and all unloading has to be done by barges. LCT's are proving very valuable in this work. LCH's are too small for most of our equipment but are satisfactory for jeeps, command cars, small trailers, etc. Ducks are the best bet for crates that have not been mobile loaded.[4] The almost unavoidable confusion on land has been present, but the general mix-up aboard the vessels among the Army, Navy, and Merchant Marines has been irritating. Original enthusiasm has died down because of the delays in unloading, and a feeling of indifference is prevalent throughout the command. H & S will be off the *Wallace* completely by tonight. There are detachments with other companies and other ships and to be truthful I have lost control of the men.

There is quite a bit of action on shore. Artillery, mortar, machine gun and rifle fire is heard all day long. Company A has dug in to protect its camp site. H & S is camped near the beach; and although the confusion is nerve racking, we do not have to defend our area. Allie James was drowned and sergeant Scott broke his nose and arm while landing. Within a week we will be moving up to the top of the Vogelkop to land between the two Japanese strongholds of Sorong and Maniquasi. It advances us two hundred miles nearer Lohis. The real rat race is about to begin.

Dora, Ian, and Floozie, New Orleans, 1943.

August 9, 1944, aboard the Wallace *en route between Oro Bay and Sansapor, Dutch New Guinea*

Dearest Dora,

You're still talking about my coming home. Dora, I can't. There seems less chance now than ever before. But, honey, that's the best way when you look at the whole picture. It's the only way to hurry up and win the war. I have about 300 men in my company now, and they all want to go home as much as I do. One brings me a letter that his mother has lost her mind and is crying for him and that he wants to go home. Another comes in and tells me that his two children have died, that his wife is all alone. Every one of the 300 has many reasons why he should go home. They ask me why after having spent 27 continuous months in New Guinea they should be shoved right into the spearhead again. Honey, you have no idea how hard it is to explain to them *why*. To tell the truth, I can't explain, because I don't know why myself. The only thing I can do is tell them that they're fighting to preserve all the things we used to enjoy. I keep telling them that it won't be much longer. The men really like me. I know it. I can get them to do anything. They know that I won't leave them. You see, Dora, I could get a soft job in Australia or a rear base now. Colonel Thomas is leaving us, and that means there are only five of the officers of the 96th who came overseas with us who remain with the organization: Al Mouron, Jimmy King, Joe Stine, Jim Humphries, and I. I told Colonel Derby that if he wouldn't send me home on rotation or give me a leave back to the 'States (and he said that he couldn't) I wanted to stick with the 96th. Although I'm not a patriotic fanatic, I don't believe in wasting my services when I can put them to use. And they are best used in the 96th. The men know the score. They like me for it, and things are coming along fine. I have never seen them work harder than they did on this last move. When we staggered aboard yesterday we flopped as a company—and slept. It was good to walk around the deck this morning and chat with them all about the job that lies ahead. Dora, I wish you could see it all; you'd realize how important they are—every one with his own problems. I might write again tomorrow. It will be my last chance for some time.

August 19, 1944, Sansapor

Sansapor is a strip of land at the top of the Vogelkop. Some maps I have seen show it north of the Equator, whereas others show it south.

Hymie aboard *The Wallace* en route
from Milne Bay to Sansapore,
August 1944.

At any rate it is less than half a degree from the line which divides the
earth into a Northern and Southern hemisphere. Our occupation of
the place has neutralized the Japanese bases of Monokwasi on our
east and Sorong on our west and places the Allies 200 miles closer to
the Phillipines than they were three weeks ago. The place was taken
without enemy opposition. The few Japs who were here either
surrendered or fled. Those who fled probably died in the jungle.

The area is enchanting with its huge trees and strange insect life.
Some ants are nearly an inch long. It is the most inhospitable spot of
New Guinea I have seen so far. The typhus mite is everywhere; and in
spite of precautionary measures, troops are going down with the
deadly disease at the astounding rate of from thirty to sixty every day.
So far the 96th has had no cases, but we have been here only eight
days or so. I cannot describe the turmoil that we have gone through
since debarking from the *Wallace*. The Japs did not leave Sarmi the
way they pulled out of here. Almost every night they tried to pene-
trate our perimeter, mostly around the Quartermaster dump to secure
food. We were camped about three hundred yards from the dump,
and every night there would be constant rifle fire and intermittent
machine gun chatter, and occasional artillery roaring. We just kept
unloading, assorting supplies, assembling equipment. It was hell to
arrange supplies, heavy equipment, and vehicles for a forward move
on a beach as small, muddy, and confused as that little strip of land

we held at Sarmi. Originally we were scheduled to move forward on D + 10 on five LST's, but only four arrived for loading on the D + 10 echelon. About 400 tons of bulk cargo, mostly petroleum, had to be loaded onto each LST, and then every square foot of space had to be utilized in order to get all our equipment aboard as scheduled. Again there was friction between the Army and the Navy. Part of my men had gone ahead on another LST as an advanced party, and I placed four more H & S detachments aboard these four LST's. I was a happy man when they were completely loaded and pulled out into the ocean. I was exhausted but managed to get four hours' sleep before the rat race began again loading another LST the following morning with the remainder of H & S personnel and equipment. Fortunately, the captain of our LST was a reasonable sort of bloke—not like most Naval officers. The loading went along rather smoothly. Ours was the second of the nine LSTs to finish loading although much of our plant was "dead" stuff which they couldn't get aboard the first four. Ours was the flagship of the LST convoy and General Murray traveled with us. I couldn't get all our supplies aboard our LST but managed to get additional space on another LST for nine major items. I had to send a detachment to Wake Island to work with C Company. It meant that H & S had been split into eight groups. It had been split into four on the move from Oro Bay to Sarmi, and keeping track of nearly three hundred men was quite a job: almost as big a job as keeping track of my equipment, consisting of approximately 125 vehicles and 100 pieces of major engineering items. We did not lose a single piece of engineering equipment and are short only one truck on the entire move and we are not sure that we ever drew it at Oro Bay.

The trip from Sarmi to Sansapor was uneventful. Our escort for the voyage was small, an indication of the relative safety in these waters and the marvelous job our Navy has done in clearing them of the Japs. The week we have been at Sansapor has been a continuous grind. I was greeted with the disturbing news that because of Lt. Black's being put out of action during the loading operations (a tractor fell on his leg and smashed it), Lt. Moore, my truck motor officer had to be transferred from H & S to Company D. Joe Stine, my motor officer for the heavy equipment motor pool, broke his ankle and had to be evacuated. Derby, Knight, Mouron and Thomas wanted more and more equipment. Things were in an utter state of confusion. Partly because of luck, partly because of my organizing ability, but mostly because the men like me (most of them do in spite of my cold-hearted ways) and their willingness to work sixteen straight hours if the job requires it, we started repairing broken down equipment.

We actually repaired it faster than they were tearing it down on the job. The first night I reported nine tractors down, the next night, six; and the third night only three. Everyone threw bouquets at me, especially Colonel Derby and Major Knight.

THIRTEEN

Coming Home

August 19, 1944–January 19, 1945

August 19, 1944, Sansapor, Dutch New Guinea

I received a blow that I still haven't been able to realize, something which makes me walk around more dead than alive. It was a wire from Papa. It read: "Dora seriously ill. Make every effort obtain leave at once. Come fastest way."

I thought I was dreaming when I read it. I stuck the wire in my pocket and went about my work. I pulled it out and read it again. "Seriously ill." Good God, what did he mean by that? I didn't want to let my imagination run away with me. I hoped that Papa only sent the wire to make me hurry home. Dora was probably seriously ill—say pneumonia—and he thought it would be an opportunity to get me home. I think that they believe I can come home any time I want to just by asking for it. But Papa wouldn't send me a wire like that unless—oh, no, God, she can't be going to die soon. They didn't mention that she was going to be operated on for a tumor several months ago as anything other than an ordinary occurrence. If anybody other than Papa had sent the wire, I wouldn't worry so much. But Papa sent it and I'm afraid—afraid to face the truth. If Dora has a cancer and is going to die—I can't even picture it. I've seen men torn to shreds, friends killed. That's fast. But my Dora—Oh, I wish I could pray. I wish—no I don't. I'll face the facts. I'm a man and I'm hard and I'll make the most of the situation regardless of what it is. The Red Cross is sending home to find out just what the score is. It only takes one day to wire from Australia to the States and back but it will take nearly a week to get the message from here to the mainland. So it means that I won't know for another couple weeks.

I hope I get a reply "your wife is in good health." Will I bawl out

Papa and Dora and everybody! I'll—oh, God, please make it that way. I don't know what I'll do if anything happens to Dora. Our house, all our plans—our baby! I don't want him without his mother. What am I saying? What am I worrying about? I must work hard, harder than ever before. I mustn't think of Dora. I must concentrate on my company. Everything will be all right.

August 20, 1944

Everything is going along smoothly. Great progress is being made on the bomber strip. The fighter strip is in operation already. All tractors but two are running. All shovels are going. Things are perking up.

August 21, 1944

With the let up in work, I feel tired. I don't know whether I'm sick or not: just a dullness all over. I just stumble along. Plenty mail from Dora. Gosh, they were wonderful letters. She seemed so natural.

August 23, 1944

More mail. Good mail. I wish I'd hear about Dora's condition. I'm keeping up with my work, doing a good job the Colonel tells me, but I don't seem to care.

August 29, 1944

Still no word about Dora from the Red Cross. I noticed myself in the mirror today. I look like hell. I must quit worrying.

August 30, 1944

Playing chess in my spare time. Reading some too. But I'm spending most of my spare time thinking about Dora. Oh, God, don't let it be what I know it is. Please don't.

August 31, 1944

Feel in better spirits today than I have in a long time—a silly buoyant feeling. Feel as if I'll hear some good news about Dora—or perhaps the Germans will surrender—or perhaps I'm going home. I think I've just about worried myself silly.

September 1, 1944

Received notice from the Red Cross that Dora has a cancer: "INFORM CAPT HYMAN SAMUELSON WIFE CRITICALLY ILL INOPERABLE MALIGNANCY DOCTOR ROBBINS RECOMMENDS OFFICERS PRESENCE CONDITION INCURABLE."

Wrote a letter to C.O., U.S. Troops, APO 159, thru C.O. 96th Engrs., requesting transfer to a post near New Orleans or that I be granted a leave to visit New Orleans. The letter has to go all the way to USAFE [United States Army Far East Air Force] headquarters in Sydney to be approved. I feel no pain now. I have no feelings. Right now life has very little meaning at all.

September 1, 1944

Col. George T. Derby, Commanding Officer, 96th Engineers to Commanding Officer, United States Forces: "This officer has rendered outstanding services in this regiment for over two years of active tropical duty. He has fully demonstrated his qualification to perform the duties of the next higher grade. He has retained his energy and enthusiasm thereby setting an example to others who have become discouraged by long periods of field service. He is therefore considered worthy of every possible consideration. He is of course one of our most eligible officers for rotation and would have been placed on quota heretofore had there been any knowledge of his wife's ill health."

September 2, 1944

Dearest Dora,

Hello, little girl. Don't think that I don't have the happy eyes. Guess what! I've been placed on the October quota to go home. And then too I got a letter from you saying that you were much better. Don't think that I wasn't worried for a while though. But don't think that I worried too much. Gosh, sweetheart, do you know what that means? Another two months and we'll be together again. Actually some of the men who were placed on the June quota are still here, but I understand that they are speeding up sending the fellows home, and the October group ought to be home by the end of November or early part of December. I won't be home for Ian's birthday, but I'm sure I'll be home for our third wedding anniversary. Do you realize that it will be the first one that we'll be together on? I can hardly think straight since I've heard the news.

There's just one thing that's worrying me. Do you mind if I bring my son Oscar home with me? You see, on this last move, we landed in a place where we couldn't have pets. I'll tell you why we couldn't have them when I get home, but anyway we had to get rid of all cats and dogs. And so for awhile I had to do away with my cats and was all alone. Then one day I met Oscar, and I adopted him. Oscar is a lizard, just as tame as any cat or dog you have ever seen. He looks just about the same as any lizard back home; the only thing is that he is about 18 inches long. (Some lizards over here grow up to six feet in length, no joke.) Well, I found Oscar under my bed one evening as I was sitting at this table. He looked like any other pest, so I grabbed my jungle knife which was lying on the tale and prepared to throw it at him. I aimed, but he just kept looking at me, cocking his head from one side to the other. For some reason I couldn't throw the knife at him while he was standing still. So I kicked a little dirt at him so that he would run, but he wouldn't run either. Just then a fly buzzed around me; so I killed the fly instead. Then I tossed the fly to the lizard. Well, that was the start of our friendship. Oscar has been hanging around ever since. He isn't under the bed this evening for some reason, but he'll be back later on. I hope you don't mind if I take him home with me. You can have Ian to play with, and I'll have Oscar. We can swap around every now and then too to break the monotony.

It's sort of late. I heard the good news yesterday about being placed on the October quota, but I've been too busy to write. To tell the truth, we're all busy as the dickens. I'll write you a long letter tomorrow and we'll make plans about what we're going to do together when I get home. You see, little stinker, I told you to have faith, that I'd be home this year. Take care of yourself and the baby, sweetheart. I'm glad you don't have to go to the doctor's for shots any more and I hope that Ian's Indian Fire has all cleared up. Write me a long letter. Just think, in another two months we won't have to be writing each other letters any more and instead of writing it, I'll be able to *tell* you that I love you.

September 2, 1944

Dear Papa,

I received word yesterday from the American Red Cross telling me of Dora's condition; and although I feared that her condition was what it is ever since I got your wire telling me that she was seriously ill, I kept hoping that I was letting my imagination run away with me. I'm sending this letter to the store because I want you to see it first. I know that my letters are distributed around home to anyone who wants to read them, and there may be a few things in here that you might not want to show Dora or Jenny or anyone else.

Col. Derby recommended that I be placed on duty at a post near New Orleans rather than going home on leave. The whole damn trouble is that the only headquarters which can grant the leave is located down in Sydney, Australia, and it will be weeks before the orders are published. I asked for air transportation, told them that I'd carry no more than my toilet articles if necessary; but I don't know whether it will be any good. I feel sure that they will transfer me back to the states or at least give me a leave, but it will still take time. You see, we are way up the line now and communications between here and any of the rear bases is terribly slow. The wire from the Red Cross telling me about Dora took over a month to get here!

I don't know whether Dora knows how sick she is. If she doesn't, for God's sake don't let her know. And don't let anyone else tell her. I don't know how much time is left, but I want to make whatever time remains as pleasant for her as possible. All of you at home are going to have to help. You went through the same ordeal with Mama, and I only pray that I am the man you are to go through with my job. But please don't let any tear-infested females mess up the works. I am going to have to act as if I know nothing. That's the way I want it to be. When I get home, I want everyone to act as natural as he can; and I'll fuss at Dora in my usual way for looking so thin. I only hope that she still will be well enough to get around for some time.

I guess I sound pretty cold-hearted. I guess I should be writing things like "Can't they do something? Can't they operate? Isn't there a way out?" But I think I know what the score is, and I've got to be inhuman and play the part of an actor; otherwise I would make her miserable too. Don't worry about me. I'm all right, and I'll be home as soon as possible. I'm afraid that it will be from six weeks to two months though. I hope the rest of you are well. Please see that everybody at home acts *natural* towards Dora. I'll try writing often.

September 3, 1944

I'm gradually slipping. I must get hold of myself. I must look good when I go home. I'll quit smoking cigarettes starting tomorrow. I must eat and exercise and rest. I must put on weight. At 135, I look like hell. I can't look this way when I get home. I've got to stop worrying. I mustn't work so hard. I got to get Dora off my mind.

September 5, 1944

News from Papa that the doctors operated on Dora. She is feeling fine and knows nothing about her critical condition; but the doctors all agree that there is no hope for her. I am thankful that she doesn't know how sick she is.

September 7, 1944

Played chess with Colonel Derby all evening. Waiting for orders from USAFE is hell.

September 8, 1944

Courts-martial cases tonight. Damn it—I'm getting weak. I don't know what's wrong.

September 9, 1944

After our regular daily meeting Derby told me that 6th Army had turned down my request to go home. He said he was going to wire back to them. Apparently Derby knew how I felt and asked me to play chess with him after supper. After winning three games from him, I stood up and told him that I had to go to 6th Army Hq. personally. He must have thought I was losing my mind, but he said he would help. I told him I wanted to go see the Chief of Staff *tonight*. He agreed to go down to Task Force Headquarters with me. They said they would put out orders the first thing in the morning for me to go to Hollandia for spare parts. When I got back to camp I told Colonel Derby that I wouldn't return from Hollandia. He put his arm around me and said that he knew. He wished me luck. I have just finished packing, enough to last me until I get home.

September 10, 1944

Flew to Hollandia, some 600 miles. The pilot was going to Nadjab but I talked him into dropping me off at Hollandia.

"What do you think this is, a streetcar?" he said. I didn't answer. I must have looked pretty sad, because with a moment's hesitation, he added, "Hop in Cap'n. I'll take you."

Tomorrow morning I'm going to Sixth Army Headquarters. I understand it is about thirty miles from here. I'll make them change their minds. *I'll make them.* Just how I don't know, but I will. I don't know who I'll have to see, but I'll see them all if necessary. They can't stop me from going home.

September 11, 1944, Hollandia, Dutch New Guinea

When I went into Army Hq. this morning I shook like a leaf expecting a big battle on my hands. Already they had changed their minds, had sent a wire to USAFE recommending that I be sent home by air on the September quota. I feel pretty happy this evening.

September 12, 1944

Dearest Dora,

I've been traveling around a bit lately. The Old Man got mad at me for bothering him so much and sent me down the line on special duty. "I'll never send you home again." he said "You act like a little kid." Don't think that I don't feel like a little kid too. I think I've lost five years in the past two weeks. If I continue losing five years every two weeks, in another month I'll look as old as my years. I understand that they are going to put out orders on men going home in October right around the first of the month. If they do and I can get a boat out by the middle of October, I ought to get home by the middle of November. That's a full month sooner than I expected at first. Boy, oh boy, and the Colonel doesn't want me to act like a little kid. After nearly 2½ years in New Guinea, I at last know I'll be home in another two months! How can I act? Well, Derby sent me down here to do some work. "I'll work you right up to the last minute," he said. So I don't have much time to write you long love letters. In another two months, little girl, I'm going to give you more loving than you'll be able to handle. So take care of yourself. You'd better toughen up the baby a little too, 'cause I'm going to put him through an infiltration course as soon as I lay hands on him too. You'd better not write any more, because I know I'll be gone by the time your letters get here. I love you.

September 14, 1944

I'm making a pest of myself at the Adjutant General's office, but it is the only way I stand a chance of getting back home. I'm reading a lot. That helps pass time but doesn't help enough. If I could just get my mind off Dora and home.

September 15, 1944

If I don't hear from USAFE soon, I'm afraid I'll lose my mind. Never before have days seemed so long. These past three days are like an eternity. I'm half tempted to go back to Sansapor to get my mail.

September 17, 1944

A wire from USAFE at last. They are sending orders to Lae. The orders (according to the wire) authorize air transportation to the States for assignment. Sixth Army Hq. gave me orders today to go to Lae. I hope I can catch a plane out in the morning. I wonder whether I'll ever get home.

September 19, 1944, Lae, Papua New Guinea

I am now at Lae, caught a plane ride from Hollandia to Nadjab the first thing yesterday morning. I was the only passenger on the plane and the co-pilot let me sit in the pilot's seat while he caught some sleep. I enjoyed the ride very much.

September 20, 1944

My orders from USAFE came in today. They call for air transportation on class 3 priority. That is indeed high priority. However before I can leave I must obtain several personnel records that are still at Sansapor. They will get off a wire for these tonight. Graham should get the papers together and down to the strip at Sansapor tomorrow. If they leave Sansapor the next morning, I should get them by Saturday. I'll go out to Nadjab Sunday, have my physical examination, line up a ride; and if there is a plane leaving Monday, I ought to be on it. Next Wednesday—just a week from today—I may be in the United States. Gosh, I'll probably be home for Ian's second birthday after all.

September 22, 1944

How well I know now that there are 1440 minutes in a day. And how well do I know that each minute contains sixty definite intervals.

September 23, 1944

The papers didn't come in today the way I had expected. Well, after over two and a half years, what is one day more or less? I went to shoul this morning. It was the first time in over three years. In a way I enjoyed it. I was surprised that I could still read—with difficulty of course—Hebrew. I'd like to study Hebrew when I get home. I'm going to do a lot of reading and studying. It will be a temporary escape from the reality I shall have to face and eventually will lead to my understanding why people are subjected to such realities.

September 27, 1944

I didn't write my diary last night because I was keeping Yom Kippur as I have never kept it before. Not only did I fast, as I have done many times before, but I didn't write or lift a finger to work. I spent last evening and all day today in the chapel. I read Hebrew with its English translation hour after hour. I followed the services closely. I tried and tried to pray—to get some divine soothing inspiration. I should have prayed for Dora's life, but I knew that that was of no avail, and nothing else seemed worthy of prayer. I was afraid that He would disappoint me (even if I temporarily felt that He would save her for me), and I didn't want God to disappoint me anymore. I didn't pray for anything in particular; yet I prayed. I wanted to feel near to God. I didn't succeed. I just wanted to feel near Him, to tell him that I understood what He was doing and that I'd make the most of life regardless of what happened. Sometimes I felt that He heard me, but then I knew that He didn't hear—or else, He wasn't interested. My comfort lay in the people I know—in Papa, Dotsy, Beryl, Ethel, other friends and relatives. More comfort in them than in God.

September 28, 1944

I picked up *A Tree Grows in Brooklyn* by Betty Smith this morning and didn't put it down until a few minutes ago when I had finished the last page. It is a beautiful novel and I enjoyed it very much. There is still no word from Sansapor. I am half-tempted to try to go home without my papers. I think I could get away with it. But I'll wait a few more days. I am learning to be patient and get a certain amount of pleasure out of the people of this place.

Christmas Day, 1944, Ft. Belvoir, Virginia

This is my first attempt to write anything in the form of a diary since I left New Guinea, nearly three months ago. The flight from Nadjab, New Guinea to San Francisco was long and uneventful. We landed on Guadalcanal; and then after two hours from the island, one engine conked out; so we had to return. But there was only a short delay and we took off again for Canton Island. Here we refueled, bought some cigars. It was the first opportunity for some of us to buy anything with American money in over two and a half years. We landed in Hawaii on the morning of October 3rd. Here we had to go through the censors and customs, and I had to forfeit my diaries. I believe I could have smuggled them through, for the examination was carried out in a half-hearted manner, but I was afraid to take a chance and consequently bundled all my papers and photographs and turned them in. If the diaries had contained nothing of military importance, I would have tried to get them through, but there was a certain amount of objectionable material in them; and if I had been caught trying to sneak them into the States, it might have been embarrassing.[1] I took a hot shower in a tile bathroom. Although it was in an army building and was anything but a private bathroom, the shower and shave were a treat. Civilization was rushing at me.

The hop from Hawaii to 'Frisco was twelve hours long. Two ferry pilots and I sat on the floor of the large C-54 and played fan-tan to help pass the time. We played for nine straight hours, and I won $7.95. But then the anxiety of nearing home was too much for me, and I could play no more. All of us—all except the ferry pilots— pressed our faces against the small windows of the airplane peering out into the darkness ahead, looking for a light, a light coming from the United States. Time seemed to stand still. The inside of our plane was dark. We had turned out the lights so that we could see farther ahead. There was Major Smith, a flight surgeon, coming home on emergency leave because his wife was dying of a cancer. And there was a little Frenchman, Captain R——, who sat next to me looking, looking for America. He was 36 years old. In the past two months he had lost two younger brothers in Normandy and was returning because his folks had become deathly ill over hearing the unfortunate news of the loss of their two sons. It seemed that all of us were coming home because of some misfortune; yet we were returning to America, and that made us happy.

We had long ago crossed into the Western Hemisphere and were north of the Equator. And just ahead, maybe but a half hour's time ahead, was the United States. My hands were wet with perspiration as I strained and pressed my cheek against the window. Suddenly someone saw a light blinking in the distance. If I had been blind all my life and if that had been the first light that I had ever seen, it could not have been more welcome. We cheered and whooped like a bunch of lunatics. As we passed over the United States for the first time I wanted to pray that I'd never leave my country again, but I didn't. A man should never pray for such a thing. But I wanted to get down and hug the ground. Then the plane started down. We were settling down on the United States! I can't explain the feeling. We cheered when we hit the ground, and we stumbled out the plane like madmen. Oh, it felt so good. It was around 3 A.M., October 4th, exactly thirty-one months to the day since I had sailed out of New York. There were a few questionnaires to be filled out, a "mock" medical examination, and then we went up to the officer barracks.

The corporal on duty was very apologetic. "I'm sorry," he said, "but we cannot accommodate you." A hell of a note, we thought. We come back from New Guinea and we can't even find a place to sleep. "Mind if we catch a little sleep on these sofas?" One of the officers in our group asked the corporal. "Of course not, sir; but if you're that sleepy, sir, we have some beds, but they don't have sheets on them," the corporal said. "Who in the hell needs sheets!" the officer asked. "Yeah, I'd like one too," said another. The corporal looked surprised. "We have plenty of beds. They just don't have sheets on them. Here are some clean sheets. If you want to put your own sheets on, you can all have beds." Gosh, a bed with a spring and a mattress! We knew this was really civilization.

Although I had hardly slept a wink since leaving New Guinea, I couldn't sleep when I got in bed. My mind was on Dora and Ian—on so many things. How was Dora? I hadn't heard in over a month. The last news I had received before leaving Sansapor was that she had been operated on again and that she didn't have much longer to live. Was she still alive? I'll wait until around 6 o'clock and then call up. It will be 8 o'clock in New Orleans then and she should be up. When the operator called Chestnut 2127 and I could hear the phone ring, my heart skipped a beat. I heard Dora say "hello." A lump the size of a grapefruit swelled in my throat. Before the operator could finish asking her "Is this Mrs. Samuelson," I was sobbing, "Dora, Dora, how are you, little girl?" We didn't have much to say. I cried, and she was too surprised to cry.

I had a delicious breakfast; never knew that fresh milk could taste so good. There was still a certain amount of red tape to go through before I could leave for home. Orders had to be indorsed, travel priorities established, and so on. I should have bought some clothes. The suit of khakis that I had been wearing since before leaving New Guinea were rather offensive. But I compromised and bought a khaki tie so that I wouldn't look like a tramp even though I didn't look the part of an officer. I caught a commercial plane to Los Angeles that evening. The airport in L.A. was crowded. I was conscious of my untidiness. I had on a suit of dirty khaki and an old field jacket that hadn't been cleaned in nearly three years. Most of my belongings I had left in New Guinea, but I had to take this field jacket with me because it was warm, the only warm thing I had. There were grease spots and dried blood stains on the jacket. I knew I should check into a hotel, take a bath, and get some sleep. But sleep would be impossible. I wanted to get home.

At a few minutes past midnight (October 5th now) I got on a plane out of Los Angeles. For an hour or more I remained awake although I felt exhausted, but finally in my comfortable chair and with the drone of the airplane engines humming in my ears, I fell asleep. It was a jerky sleep, but it was refreshing. I cat-napped half way across the country, all the way to Dallas. At Dallas I had to get out and they told me there that I couldn't get a plane to New Orleans until the next day. I was so keyed up by this time that I told the ticket girl that I *had* to get to New Orleans today. She said that I could sell my ticket and she could sell me another ticket to Jackson, Mississippi. I might be able to catch a plane in Jackson that was going from Chicago to New Orleans. Well, Jackson was a lot closer to New Orleans than Dallas. Gosh, if necessary I could hitch-hike from Jackson to New Orleans. The way I was feeling, I could run that last two hundred miles or so. While I sat in the airport waiting for the plane that was to take me to Jackson, a woman asked me whether I would keep my eye on her baby for a few minutes. Naturally I was only too glad to do that. She thanked me. I watched her as she played with the baby.

"I got a baby too," I said. I don't know why I blurted out with that remark.

"You have. That's nice," she said.

"How old is your baby?" I asked.

"He's eight months," she said rather coldly, I thought.

"Mine's going to be two years old the day after tomorrow."

"That's nice," she said. I could see that she didn't want to talk with me, so I said no more. But I felt proud that I had a two-year-old boy, even if I had never seen him.

There was a short wait in Jackson, and then I got on the plane that would take me on the last lap of my 8,000 mile exodus—8,000 miles in three and a half days! Louisiana looked beautiful when we flew over it. When we landed at the New Orleans Airport I was so happy that I couldn't keep the tears out of my eyes. I trembled like a leaf while I rode from the airport into town. Then I caught a cab home. Dora had moved since I was away. I climbed out the cab in front of what I thought was the new house. My knees turned to water as I stumbled up the stairs. I met Mrs. Reiner at the door, kissed her but asked, "Where's Dora? Where's Dora?" and when she said in the back, I pushed her aside. And there she was—my Dora. I grabbed her around tightly. She seemed to have melted in my arms. I was weak and I leaned against the wall and held her close and cried and cried. I had imagined many times how I would do it. I would pick her up and kiss her and tell her how much I loved her. And I imagined that she would be the one who would cry and that I would only laugh and tell her that we'll never be apart again and that she will never cry again. But instead, I was so weak that not only could I not pick her up but I needed the wall to support myself. And she didn't cry. I cried. I cried like a baby. And she was the one who kept saying, "My darling. My darling little boy. You're home. You're home." She said it softly and she kissed me. She looked so beautiful. There was so much love and happiness in her eyes. In the meantime Mrs. Reiner called up Papa and Ethel. When Papa, Aunt Shanie, and Dotsy arrived I cried again. I didn't want to cry, but I was so happy that I didn't give a damn. When Ethel, Herman, and Gwendy arrived, there were more tears.

We stayed up so late that first night, talking and laughing. I held Dora on my lap and she seemed to notice no one but me. She was staring at my face and my hands, touching me, kissing me. She didn't seem to notice that anyone else was in the parlor. "When did you get this scar," she asked. She knows more about the little scar on my hands and arms and legs than I do. Ian was asleep; so we didn't wake him. He looked beautiful in his little bed and I was content with just kissing him. He and I would have a good man-to-man talk in the morning. That night in bed with Dora was filled with so much happiness and bliss that it would put heaven to shame. Next morning I was awakened by Ian. Dora was still asleep. He started to cry, "Mommy, Mommy."

Dora woke up and said, "Are you still here sweeheart? It still seems like a dream."

"Yes, darling I'm still here," I said and I kissed her. Ian stood in his crib and shouted, "Mommy, Mommy don't! Don't Mommy!"

"He's jealous," Dora said.

"Let him yell," I said. And I took her in my arms and kissed her. "He's got to learn who's boss around here and there's no time like the present for him to learn."

After awhile I took him out of the crib and put him in bed with Dora and me. He pushed away from me.

"Who's this man, honey?" Dora asked him. He wouldn't answer. I looked at him and smiled. I tried to look pleasant so that he would like me.

"Who's this man, Ian?" Dora asked again, and she kissed me.

"No, Mommy, don't!" he said, and he climbed between us and tried to pull us apart. Dora and I just lay there kissing and his little hands trying to pull our faces apart felt wonderful.

"Don't you know who this man is?" Dora asked him. He grinned. He knew, but he wouldn't tell. Do you want to give Mommy a kiss, honey?" she asked the baby. The little monkey threw his arms around her and kissed her. Then Dora kissed me. "And now, do you want to give the man a kiss too?" Dora asked him.

"Nope," he said.

"Um-mm Mommy likes to kiss the pretty man," she said and she kissed me. I kept my eye on Ian.

"No, Mommy. Mommy, no" he said, and he was half choked with tears.

"Mommy loves this pretty man. Umm it's so good to kiss him. Don't you want to kiss him too, huh baby?" Ian was almost crying, but he leaned over carefully and kissed me lightly on the cheek. Then he laughed. I didn't bite, he must have thought to himself. I picked him up while laying on my back and held him high. He laughed and I let him down with his little belly on my face and I kissed his belly and bit it and rolled him over and kissed him all over.

"You stupid little bastard," I said, "I'm your daddy. Don't you know me? I'm your old man!" Then he started jabbering like a little monkey. "Mommy, Daddy, Mommy, Daddy." He jumped out of our bed and went to the dresser and picked up my picture.

"Daddy! Daddy!" he shouted. And then he looked at me and laughed and kept saying "Daddy." He really seemed to be happy about finding his Daddy. And it wasn't long before he didn't even object to his Mommy kissing his Daddy.

On the second day, October 7th, I went downtown with Dora to get some clothes for me to wear. Every place we went people offered me a drink. I killed about a quart of bourbon. Well, in my already somewhat rundown condition, this was all I needed to knock me for a loop. But I didn't give a damn. I insisted on going to Canal Street. I bought three pairs of trousers and three shirts and two black ties. I didn't know that the army was wearing khaki ties with winter uniforms. Then I bought a diamond wrist watch for Dora. I paid $250 for it, but apparently it is worth a lot more. I was still drunk when I got home, and we celebrated Ian's second birthday with some other children from the neighborhood. And I was stinking drunk. But I was happy. So happy. Nobody mattered. If the whole world had stopped then and there, it would have been all right with me.

The next day was a Sunday, and Papa gave a big party at the house in celebration of my return. It was wonderful, but I was dazed by seeing so many people. And then the thing happened that I always feared would happen. I forgot peoples' names. It was horrible, but the names of relatives, of people I have known all my life, became hopelessly mixed up. It was strange but I could remember names of people I hardly knew, but those whom I have known a long time I forgot. This has bothered me ever since I came home.

Then Dora had to return to the hospital. I don't remember the exact date, but it was a very unhappy date for me. I went to see Dr. Tyson about Dora's condition and he explained to me why she had to return to the hospital. It was to take some shots. They would produce high fever, perhaps, and make her uncomfortable, and it would be best that she be in a hospital.

"Will they do her any good?" I asked him rather abruptly.

He hesitated, then answered simply, "No."

"Then why do you want to give her these shots?" I asked.

"They *may* help her. Some success has been achieved with these shots. And as long as there is any hope at all, we must keep trying."

So Dora went into Touro Infirmery. The first day they gave her no shots. The next day they gave a shot and there was no reaction. The third day they gave her another shot, but the reaction was very mild. In another day my leave would be over. Dora was restless, wanted to know why she must take these shots. The room cost $10 a day. I saw Dr. Tyson again and he admitted that he had little faith in the shots, that it was practically experimental. I saw Dr. Mattas and Dr. Roberts. They told me that there was no use. Yet none of them would say that the shots should be discontinued. Then the intern told me that Dora could go home. But she couldn't check out the hospital.

"She will have to keep her room and come in every third day for her shots."

"Hey, this room costs ten bucks a day, and with the blood tests and all, it'll run around four hundred a month. Is it necessary to reserve this room continuously? Can't I get a room just on those days when my wife needs the shots?" I asked him.

"We can't do that. You're lucky you can get a room at all. If you give up your room for even a day, you'll lose it. There's a long waiting list to get into this hospital. You're lucky to have a room," he said.

"You mean that there are people waiting to get in this hospital and I'm able to keep an empty room by just paying for it?" I growled. "Why in the hell don't you let them in and treat them? You don't know what a crowded hospital is! No, you'd rather wait 'til you can do them no good. It's rotten—your whole medical set-up. You'd rather fumble around with a patient that you know you can't do any good for as long as he pays you than to treat someone that you can help if that person doesn't pay you as much." I was tempted to give him some real hell, but then I realized that he was only an intern and that it wasn't his fault. He was just becoming a victim of a filthy system.

But I took Dora out the hospital. We came back for shots whenever it was necessary for her to have them. Poor kid is still taking them, remaining in bed at home, and they are not doing her any good. I tried to forget that Dora was so ill. I tried to imagine that she was as well as ever. And we had a wonderful time. Everyone was so good to us. We were invited to go everywhere, but we turned down most of the invitations and spent our days in the park with Ian. During the entire 28 days I was home it didn't rain even once. The park was beautiful. We walked and talked, we listened to records and read to each other. Everyone was good to us. There was a big affair at the Jung Hotel that the Shriners gave which we enjoyed very much. In all, we crowded so much happiness into those four weeks that our life made heaven look like a dungeon.

But my orders read that I would report to Camp Shelby on November 1st; so the morning of that day I took the train to Hattiesburg, Mississippi. Here I learned that I had another two weeks vacation coming to me in Miami, Florida. And Dora could go with me. I caught a ride back to New Orleans. Before leaving for Miami, Dora had some shopping to do so I spent another day at home. We left for Jacksonville by plane on the afternoon of the 3rd. It was the first time Dora had flown, and she enjoyed the ride very much. I thought that it was the best plane ride I had ever been on too. It felt good to fly over familiar country. But what really made the trip so wonderful for me was the fact that I was with Dora.

Our train to Miami was four hours late. The train ride was a rough one. Dora was uncomfortable but I tried to make her as comfortable

Hymie and Dora, New Orleans, fall 1944.

as possible. She was sleepy and cranky, just like a little girl, but it felt good to have her squirm in my arms trying to get comfortable so that she could sleep. Toward dawn, the porter came to our rescue and gave us a couple of seats so that we didn't have to try to sleep on that little bench. We fell asleep in our new seats and slept all the way to Miami. And in Miami I spent the happiest two weeks of my life. I knew that it would be the last bit of heaven that Dora and I could grab together. We went swimming, fishing, sight-seeing. We made love night and day: on the beach, in our luxurious hotel room, everywhere! The Shebourne Hotel, where we stayed, was filled with officer returnees, most of them with their wives, a couple hundred people in all enjoying perfect bliss after many months of loneliness.

But all too soon it was over. I received orders assigning me to the Engineer Pool at Fort Belvoir, but Dora didn't come with me. I left her in Jacksonville on November 18th. On the 23rd of November I started a field officers course and have been attending it ever since. It has been rather interesting and I have studied hard and have tried to get a lot out of it. But I shall be glad when January 3rd rolls around and we grad-uate. I still don't know where I shall go after I finish the course. Dora is now too ill to come up here, and I have had no promises about being assigned near New Orleans. In fact I have had no indication of being assigned anywhere. They may even try to ship me out again.

December 13, 1944, Ft. Belvoir, Virginia

Dearest Dora,

I miss you, sweetheart. I miss something. I'm not sure what it is, but I've felt so empty these past three days. I feel more homesick than I did when I was in New Guinea. I used to say if I ever got back in the States, I'd always feel at home, even if I were in Maine or Washington. But here I am in the States, and I *am* homesick. And I'm not homesick for New Orleans. I'm homesick for a home—a little house with a yard I did when I was in New Guinea. I used to say if I ever got back in the States, I'd always feel at home, even if I were in Maine or Washington. But here I am in the States, and I *am* homesick. And I'm not homesick for New Orleans. I'm homesick for a home—a little house with a yard and sunshine, and you and Ian. I want my own bedroom, a dresser: some place to put my clothes. I want to have my own—our own—icebox. I want to have you cook for me: just you, Ian, and I eating in our own house. I want to tell you "so long" when I go off to work and I want to love you when I come home each evening. I want us to have our week-ends together.

I want us to be the way we always planned to be. I'm tired of this not knowing where we shall be a month from now. I guess it's all these things that make me homesick. Homesick isn't the correct word: not in the usual sense, anyway. I'm homesick for a home I've never had but which I want very much. The main reason I want that home so much, honey, is that you and Ian will be so much a part of it.

I love you, sweetheart. I love you and I miss you. I'll be home in January or at any rate we'll know where I shall be assigned, and we can be together again. Give Ian a kiss for me. I love you.

December 24, 1944, New Orleans

Dearest Sweetheart,

Today is Christmas Eve. It's awful knowing that you are spending it way up in Virginia and I am spending it here. And it is only four days until our third anniversary and we'll be so far apart then, too. Don't think I don't have the sad eyes. I tried calling you today. I should have known you wouldn't be in today. You said you wouldn't be. But I tried anyway.

The doctor came to see me today. He said that I have a lot of fluid in my abdomen from all the shots and I think they will have to take it out; pump it out, I think. I am going to see Dr. Matas Tuesday and I'll know for sure then. I don't know any more than that. All I know is I can't wait until they relieve me of all the gas that I have in me.

I am going to close now, darling. I am too tired. I can't sit up long, and I'm just worn out lugging my belly around. Good night. I love you so much and I miss you. And I can hardly believe that in less than two weeks I'll be in your arms again. Yours, Dora.[2]

December 27, 1944

I just finished talking with Dora. I call her at least twice a week. She told me that her stomach has become so swollen and painful that for the last two nights she has had to take a sedative to sleep and she is going into the hospital this evening. They intend to draw some of the fluid out of her abdomen. My poor little darling. Thank God you don't know. Or do you? You're such a wonderful little actress! Sometimes I think you *do* know, but you're too game a little gal to let anyone else know that you do know. If there were only something that I—no, I mustn't go into that. I know there isn't, and I mustn't make believe.

December 27, 1944

Dearest Dora,

Gee, honey, you don't know how bad it makes me feel to know that you're sick again. It is awful, isn't it, little girl? But I'm sure Dr. Tyson knows what he is doing; so have faith in him and do what he tells you and I know you will be all right again soon. I'm glad I called up when I did; otherwise you might have gone to the hospital without our even talking to each other.

Tomorrow makes three years that we are married. We surely find good ways to celebrate our anniversaries, don't we? But maybe, sweetheart, by starting off like this, we will have many, many happy anniversaries together later on. We have each other and the most wonderful baby in the world, and we really love each other. Do you realize how few married couples have all that?

We leave tomorrow morning at 5 A.M. It's sleeting and raining and freezing and getting slushy like the very dickens outside. Something tells me that these next four days in the field are going to be anything but comfortable. I told you that Colonel Derby called me up last night. He wanted to know why I hadn't got in touch with him. He asked whether I had got an assignment yet; and when I told him that I hadn't, he said he might be able to help me. He invited me over for dinner New Year's Day. I think I'll enjoy talking with the old man again. It will be good to meet his wife and children too.

I miss you, Dora. I feel so empty here lately, much worse than I did when I was in New Guinea. Days seem longer and longer, and the day when I'll be able to go home to you never seems to come around. But I know everything will work out all right. So have faith, darling. Everything has always turned out all right for us so far, and I know that it will again. I love you, my darling. I love you so much, little girl. Please do what the doctor tells you to do and take care of my beautiful little wife.[3]

December 27, 1944

Colonel Derby called me up last night. It was a pleasant surprise.

"How are you, Sammy?" he asked several times as if I was a long-lost son. Then he wanted to know, "Why didn't you try to get in touch with me? I've been trying to get hold of you. Have you got an assignment yet?"

"No, sir, I haven't" I said.

"Well, perhaps I can help you with that," he said.

"Thank you, sir. I thought of going to see you about an assignment, but you know how it is. I—"

"Yes, I know, but I want to help you. You deserve it. And how's Mrs. Sammy?"

"She's not so well, sir. She's at home."

"I'm sorry. . . . Look, can you come over for dinner Sunday?"

"Sunday? No sir, I can't. We leave for A. P. Hill Thursday morning and don't get back until Sunday evening."

"What about New Year's Day?" he asked. I told him it would be a pleasure. I am really looking forward to seeing the old man again. Actually I have met so many old friends up here, and they have all been after me to go out with them; and although I know I should, I just feel too empty to try it.

January 19, 1945, New Orleans

Dora died on December 30, 1944. On the evening of the 29th an officer from Company N came out into the field and told me that my wife was sick and that I should return to camp. We had been working out field problems around Cold Harbor and had just moved to A.P. Hill Reservation, about eighty miles south of Belvoir. It had been snowing and sleeting and it felt good to get out the cold weather. I had spoken to Dora just two days before on the phone and she seemed happy because she was going to the hospital to get some of the liquid drained out of her stomach. Perhaps the operation hadn't gone very well.

I knew Dora didn't have long to live. All the doctors had told me that, but it couldn't be this soon. I tried calling Papa, but he wasn't home; so I rang Ethel.

"No, it isn't a matter of hours," she assured me, "Nor is it a matter of days. But I don't think she will last more than a couple of weeks." I asked Ethel to send Dora some flowers for me and then hung up. For a while I thought I'd return to A. P. Hill and finish my course. We were graduating on January 3rd. I'd get a leave at the end of the course. Then I said to hell with the course, I'd leave as soon as I could get away. It was already rather late. I'd get a train out of Washington in the morning. Then I got a long distance call from Moose Plummer. He wanted to come down to see me. He is now in Philadelphia. I told him that I was leaving for New Orleans in the morning and had to tell him why. He seemed more upset about the news than I did. He went to work trying to get me an airplane ride, but because of the bad weather most of the planes were grounded and he had no luck. Next morning (Dora was dead by now but I didn't know) I cleared the post, turning in equipment, paying mess bills, getting my orders, and so on. I dropped in to see Colonel Derby to break my appointment with him for supper and told him that I was returning to New Orleans. He expressed his sympathy over the matter and said that he could help me by getting me a position at Belvoir. I thanked him but told him I wasn't interested.

"Nobody can make me leave the country while my wife is still alive," I told him, "and after she is dead, it doesn't make too much difference where I go." He made no comment, merely wished me luck in his usual awkward manner.

I left Washington at 1:00 P.M. on the 30th and arrived in Atlanta at 7:00 A.M. the next morning. The train was packed solid. I stood up most of the way, didn't get any sleep. I caught another train out of Atlanta at 9:30 A.M. and got a whole seat to myself. I curled up like a kitten and slept most of the way to New Orleans. It was New Year's Eve. There was much drinking and celebrating on the train. Although I did no drinking, I did join in conversation with them all and enjoyed the laughter and jokes.

I hadn't expected anyone to meet me at the station; so I was helping an old woman by carrying her suitcase to the bus. Then I saw Ethel—and Papa, and Jenny—and—and then Ethel came up to me. Her eyes were full of tears and when she threw her arms around me and kissed me, she said, "You're too late, honey." She quickly told me the details. All that seemed to matter was that she hadn't suffered.

"She loved the flowers. She kept saying, 'Oh look what my darling sent me!' And she left a note for you."[4]

Finally someone asked me where I wanted to go.

"Where's Dora now?" I asked. Then Jenny started to cry.

"We couldn't wait any longer. She was buried this afternoon."[5]

I still maintained my composure. "Then I'd like to go see the baby."

"He'll be sleeping," they told me. So they drove me home. I wanted to cry but tears wouldn't come.

Papa, Jenny, Ethel, Herman, Uncle Mitchell, Uncle Israel and Dotsy were home with me. I must have looked pale. I felt that way. Papa offered me a drink. I gulped it down, took another and another. The whistles and bells rang in the New Year and I toasted a Happy New Year to them all. I stumbled into the bedroom and flopped across the bed. Ethel came in and took me in her arms and I cried myself to sleep. I must have got it all out of my system, for I haven't cried since.

Hymie and Ian after Dora's death.

Editor's Epilogue

Throughout Dora's funeral, her mother wailed that it was *Hymie* who went to war, and *he* was the one who should have died, and Dora died in his place. But a lot of Hymie died, too, although he was never listed as a casualty of World War II. He gave up his profession and never worked as a civil engineer again. No more sand and gravel, no more roads, no more bridges, no more causeways, no more docks, no more dromes, no more dams, no more reservoirs, no more maps, no more hydrographic surveys. He never became a college professor, or a professional writer, or a regimental commander. He quickly remarried and started a new family. On Christmas Day 1946 Ian was killed in a tragic, bizarre accident.

Reverting to his family traditions, he established a small but successful retail business in Austin, Texas, in partnership with his younger cousin Daniel Samuelson, a returning Air Force veteran who had survived thirty-five missions over Europe. Danny has retired, but Hymie continues to work and to write in his diaries every day.

On October 16, 1942, Hymie wrote in his dairy, "If a man dies knowing that he has accomplished something which will benefit others, either his children, or their children, or people five centuries after his death, he dies happy."

If our little world on earth lasts for another 450 years, historians will play a very different role than they do now. They will become the makers of true myths: stories about the past that teach humans how to control their destructive impulses. They will teach about the barbaric twentieth century, when the world was divided into primitive groupings called "nations," "races," and "classes" that sought to dominate and exploit others. Their pagan gods were "wealth" and "progress," which meant ever-increasing productivity by dominating and destroying nature as well as humanity, grinding most of the world's population into the dust. In those primitive times, society forced people to hate, fear, despise, and exploit those who were different from themselves.

Dissenters were persecuted brutally. The result was a terrible war called World War II that tore up the earth. Tens of millions of people were senselessly killed or wounded. Many more were maimed emotionally.

But during this terrible war, some people began to understand what was really important. For example, there was a very young American officer who served with the U.S. Army Corps of Engineers in New Guinea. He loved music, literature, nature, and animals, and he enjoyed building things. He learned from his experience there that despite what he had been taught, all human beings are one. We know about him because he left his diaries. But there had to be others like him, because otherwise the world would never have survived.

Notes

Editor's Preface

1. Ulysses Lee, *United States Army in World War II: The Employment of Negro Troops* (Washington, D.C.: Office of the Chief of Military History, United States Army, 1966), 601, 607.

2. Samuel Milner, *United States Army in World War II: The War in the Pacific: Victory in Papua* (Washington, D.C.: Office of the Chief of Military History, United States Army, 1957), 3–27.

3. John Miller, Jr., *The War in the Pacific: Cartwheel: The Reduction of Rabaul* (Washington, D.C.: Center for Military History, United States Army, 1984), 1–8.

4. Milner, *United States Army in World War II: The War in the Pacific: Victory in Papua*, 45, 46, 56–100.

5. Ibid., xiv, xv, 75, 76. Captain Samuelson reported that an advertisement for Caterpillar equipment showed false photographs of white soldiers building the Tatana Island causeway.

6. Lee, *United States Army in World War II*, 606–8.

7. Ibid.

8. In the diaries and letters, the word *Negro* was uncapitalized and, for the sake of authenticity, this aspect of the text has not been altered. Before the beginnings of the civil rights movement during the 1950s, whites normally did not capitalize the word.

9. Lee, *United States Army in World War II*, 28, 225, 429–32, 435–36.

10. Ibid., 180, 182, 185–87, 191, 234.

11. ROTC recruits and trains university students during their undergraduate years and gives them officers' commissions upon graduation.

12. Steven Ambrose to author, November 9, 1992.

Chapter 1: Leaving Home: September 17, 1941–March 5, 1942

1. Henderson's Point, Mississippi, is on the coast of the Gulf of Mexico, where his parents as well as his other sister, Ethel Samuelson Midlo, had vacation homes.

2. A critique is an open, collective evaluation of any military operation among officers and enlisted men.

3. Evidently Samuelson was not aware that a serious riot took place among African-American troops aboard a bus at Fayetteville and Fort Bragg two months earlier on August 5–6, 1941 and resulted in the death of one white military policeman, the wounding of two others, the death of one African-American soldier, and the wounding of three others. See Lee, *United States Army in World War II*, 351.

4. The Headquarters and Service Company was responsible for administration and supplies and attached to all army battalions.

Chapter 2: The Voyage to Australia: March 10-April 21, 1942

1. Lake Ponchartrain has a concrete wall to protect New Orleans from flooding. The steps leading down into the lake are a favorite spot for young lovers.

2. The reference is to the Big Dipper and Little Dipper.

3. Although reference to the position of the stars was censored in one of Captain Samuelson's shipboard letters, evidently the reference here was not caught.

Chapter 3: Port Moresby, Papua New Guinea: April 23-June 17, 1942

1. Kittyhawk P-40s were the best U.S. fighter planes at that time. The Zero, Japan's best fighter plane, was inferior.

2. According to the official history of the New Guinea campaign, "Boston" was the code name for the Abau-Mullins harbor area, which was abandoned in favor of Milne Bay, whose code name was "Fall River." Milne Bay, at the extreme southeast tip of the Papua Peninsula, was less visible, more defensible, and allowed airplane attack of Japanese positions without crossing the Owen Stanley Mountains. See Milner, *United States Army in World War II: The War in the Pacific: Victory in Papua*, 40–41.

Chapter 4: Establishing an Air Base, Milne Bay: June 18-July 15, 1942

1. Lacking pile drivers, the Papuans placed straight logs in the water and attached guy lines to hold them vertically. Climbing on top of the logs to give added weight, they shook them back and forth to drive them into the soil.

2. This is a clear example of the denigration of white officers serving in "colored" military units. See Lee, *United States Army in World War II*, 185.

Chapter 6: Outlanking the Japanese: September 18-October 26, 1942

1. For a discussion of the Abau track strategy from official military records, see Milner, *United States Army in World War II: The War in the Pacific: Victory in Papua*, 94.

2. The official history reported that only a handful of prisoners were taken and that six hundred Japanese soldiers were killed at Milne Bay. Most of the Japanese invaders, 1,300 of the 1,900 troops landed, were reportedly evacuated to Rabaul, nearly all of them suffering from "trench foot, jungle rot, tropical ulcers, and other tropical diseases." In the entire New Guinea campagin, the Allies buried 7,000 Japanese and took 350 prisoners. Ibid., 87, 373, 374.

3. The correspondent was Vern Haugland of the Associated Press, who on his flight from Australia to Port Moresby had to bail out with the rest of the crew because Port Moresby was closed in. He did not recall being brought to Abau, having become delirious in the jungles. See his *Letter from New Guinea* (New York: Farrar and Rinehart, 1943).

4. In the Hiri Motu language spoken throughout the Papuan region, *mero* means *child* or *boy*; *ilapa* means *bush knife* or *machete*. So *mero ilapa* means *bush knife boys*, or a team of men who used machetes to cut the bush and do other types of labor. Letter from Professor Nicholas Farraclas, Department of Languages and Literature, University of Papua New Guinea, November 3, 1994.

5. Ramus are belts from which clothing hung.

Chapter 8: Colonel Derby Takes Command: December 2, 1942-March 16, 1943

1. For a discussion of gays in the military during World War II, see Allan Bérubé, *Coming Out under Fire: The History of Gay Men and Women in World War Two* (New York: Free Press, 1990). Captain Samuelson's copies of the documents of Company A contain a psychiatric report about a gay soldier serving in the 96th Batallion.

2. For combat psychoneuroses, see James A. Stouffer, *The American Soldier*, vol. 2 (Princeton: Princeton University Press, 1949).

3. Captain Samuelson organized informal classes to teach enlisted men various subjects.

4. Sanananda was between Gona and Buna, Japanese beachheads on the northern coast of Papua.

5. Wau was occupied by Allied troops on January 29, 1943. Salamau, located on the coast of northeast New Guinea, was captured by Allied troops on June 30, 1943.

6. African-American troops were not allowed to go to Australia on leave.

Chapter 9: The Hood Point Airdrome, March 17-April 22, 1943

1. From the foregoing passage, it is clear why the military did not allow servicemen to keep diaries overseas.

2. A lister bag is a canvass bag in which water is cooled through evaporation.

Chapter 10: Malaria: April 24-May 21, 1943

1. Oro Bay is located a few miles south of Buna on the Solomon Sea side of Papua.

2. New Britain is a large island in the Bismarck Archipelago located off the coast of northeast New Guinea. Rabaul, the most important Japanese base, is on New Britain.

3. Merauke is on the south coast of Dutch New Guinea near the border with Papua.

4. Attu Island is the western most island in the Aleutians; Kiska Island is slightly east of Attu.

5. A "fogey" was a salary increase based on length of service.

Chapter 11: Taking Command of Company A: May 22-December 5, 1943

1. Compare official histories with Lee, *United States Army in World War II*. He probably is citing this diary.

2. Three men known only to Samuelson and not known to one another who reported rumors and actions that might be considered subversive. The information they supplied was passed on to an intelligence officer whose identity Samuelson did not reveal to anyone else.

3. For Bishop Gregg's account of his experiences during World War II, see John Gregg, *Of Men and of Arms* (Nashville: A.M.E. Sunday School Union Press, 1945).

4. Casuals, unassigned soldiers, drifted from one unit to another.

5. Woodlark is an island located southwest of the Trobriand Islands. Allied troops captured both islands on June 30, 1943.

6. A "charge of quarters" was an enlisted man stationed in the orderly room.

7. A *dead man* is a term for an anchor locked into the ground.

8. This diary is extant but too detailed to be included in this book.

9. Lae, located on the coast of northeast New Guinea, was captured by Allied troops on September 4, 1943.

Chapter 12: Moving Forward: December 14, 1943-August 19, 1944

1. Finschhafen, located on the coast of northeast New Guinea, was occupied by Allied troops on September 22, 1943.

2. The original letter is in the collection.

3. An LCI (landing craft for infantry) was considerably smaller than the LST, which carried equipment as well as troops.

4. LCHs and Ducks were vehicles used for landing cargo.

Chapter 13: Coming Home: August 19, 1944-January 19, 1945

1. The diaries were condemned for the duration of the war and returned after the war ended. John D. Knappenberger, Lt. Col., Infantry, chief censor for Central Pacific Base Command, to Capt. Hyman Samuelson, January 16, 1945.

2. This is Dora's last letter.

3. This letter was mailed on December 28, 1944, their third wedding anniversary. Dora died on December 30. She never received the letter, which remained sealed until I opened it in May 1992.

4. This note has not been found.

5. Under Jewish law, burial takes place one day after death.

Index

GWENDOLYN MIDLO HALL is a historian whose most recent book, *Africans in Colonial Louisiana: The Development of Afro-Creole Culture in the Eighteenth Century*, won nine prizes during 1993, including the John Hope Franklin Publication Prize of the American Studies Association, the Elliott Rudwick Prize of the Organization of American Historians, the Louisiana Literary Award of the Louisiana Library Association, and the Willie Lee Rose Prize of the Southern Association of Women Historians. She is also the author of *Social Control in Slave Plantation Societies: A Comparison of St. Dominque and Cuba*, as well as articles, chapters in books, essays, and a screen play. She is professor of history at Rutgers University and consulting research professor of history at the University of New Orleans.